D1071606

SOUTHERN LITERARY STUDIES

Southern Literary Studies
Louis D. Rubin, Jr., EDITOR

Literature AND *Society*
IN EARLY VIRGINIA, 1608–1840

Literature

AND

Society

IN EARLY VIRGINIA

1608–1840

Richard Beale Davis

LOUISIANA STATE UNIVERSITY PRESS
Baton Rouge

ISBN 0-8071-0215-6
Library of Congress Catalog Card Number 72-89896
Copyright © 1973 by Louisiana State University Press
Manufactured in the United States of America
Printed by Kingsport Press, Kingsport, Tennessee
Designed by Dwight Agner

For
NATHALIA WRIGHT
Friend and Colleague

Contents

Acknowledgments

I wish to thank all those persons who have read and criticized previous versions of several of these essays. For permission to use the essays, now in somewhat altered form, I am grateful to the following persons, organizations, and journals: for Chapter I, Thad W. Tate, the *William and Mary Quarterly*, and the Institute of Early American History and Culture; for Chapters II, V, VIII, IX, XI, and XV, director John M. Jennings and editor William M. E. Rachal of the Virginia Historical Society; for IV, the American Philosophical Society through its executive officer, Dr. George W. Corner; for III, the University of Tennessee Press through its director Louis Iglehart; for VI, the University of Wisconsin Press; for X, Fredson Bowers and the Bibliographical Society of the University of Virginia; for XII, President Ronald E. Carrier of Madison College, where this essay was presented as a Founder's Day Lecture; and for XIV, librarian Robert O. Dougan and the Henry E. Huntington Library.

Introduction

Law and politics, said Henry Adams almost a century ago, are the only distinguishing and distinguished qualities of the Virginia mind. Later he added a third quality, an understanding of agriculture. But Adams and others have denied in the colonial and early national Old Dominion mind any significant literary creativity, any profound moral and religious introspection, or any other sustained form of cerebration which has lived on into recent generations. A decade ago, in *Intellectual Life in Jefferson's Virginia, 1790–1830,* I attempted to show how mistaken such critics were about the oldest commonwealth during the first national period. In the years before and since that publication, I have picked up here and there evidences of a many-sided colonial Virginia mind, with traits which persisted through the lifetime of a nineteenth-century adopted Virginian, Edgar Allan Poe. The essays in this present gathering represent various aspects of the colonial mind—from the first real poetry composed in the South to the extension of that mind's social and political ideas into other regions during the age of Jefferson.

The seventeenth-century Chesapeake world was primarily agrarian, military, and religious; above all, it was transplanted Renaissance English. The fertile, mild-climated region represented a potential paradise which might in time be termed an Arcadia. Despite the red man's sporadic resistance to encroachment and the hardships of planting and clearing, Virginia was never the howling wilderness of the Puritans' northern rock-bound coast. For many reasons, Virginia required a military structure, and quite early each county was organized into militia units. Each unit was commanded by a colonel and a lieutenant-colonel, titles which remain characteristic for certain southern gentlemen to the present. The military organization guarded against Spanish, Dutch, or French attacks; in Nathaniel Bacon's time, especially, it carried on an aggressive war against the Indians, and later it was to give training for formal and informal warfare to such illustrious soldiers as George Washington and Harry Lee. Most middle or upper class men—planters, lawyers, physicians, interpreters—held military titles, and it was a group of colonels (Richard Bland, Landon Carter, Thomas Jefferson, and others) who were the active literary pamphleteers prior to the Revolution. Years earlier, another colonel, William Byrd II, had been the colony's leading man of letters, and before him Colonels Philip Ludwell, William Fitzhugh, and the elder William Byrd were the late seventeenth century's most articulate epistolarians.

Virginia remained Anglican in religion throughout its colonial period, little disturbed by a few forays of Quaker missionaries in the later seventeenth century, or by the Presbyterians at the beginning of the eighteenth century. The Anglicans were as pious, if not quite as superstitious, as their New England brethren. Fond of reading the Bible and sermons, they never carried superstition as far as the Massachusetts Bay men; and they were only mildly interested in the theological controversy *per se*, even after the Great Awakening of the mid-eighteenth century. They tried to Christianize the Indians in various ways, primarily through teaching them to read and use the Bible. They made similar efforts with the relatively small number of blacks they were beginning to acquire, though slaves were not a really appreciable problem until the next century. One earnest missionary did write a tract urging education and conversion of Indians and blacks. The clergy in the seventeenth century preached, taught, wrote, established libraries—and too frequently died, as did their fellow colonists, from diseases against which they had no immunity.

Above all, seventeenth-century Virginians were Renaissance Englishmen. They brought with them an eager curiosity about the strange and marvelous, a respect for learning, an aggressive spirit which would push aside all obstacles. "We hope to plant a nation where none before hath stood" was part of the spirit of their age as well as a line in one of their first verses. To build that nation, they established endowments and fellowships for an Indian-white university and a secondary school for each race and for *all* classes of each. The 1622 massacre destroyed the first university as it was a-building; despite efforts in 1660 and later, it was not until the 1690s that the Royal College of William and Mary opened its doors. The endowed schools became permanent earlier, and the oldest in America is now a unit of the public school system of a Tidewater Virginia city. Better be never born than ill bred, said William Fitzhugh, and he spoke for yeoman and new and old aristocrat alike. On the isolated estates, there was by mid-century familial education by parents and tutors, which blossomed just before the Revolution into the superior plantation tutorial schools of Fithian, Harrower, and Boucher. And in the later seventeenth century were laid the foundations for the great libraries of the age of William Byrd II, Sir John and Peyton Randolph, and Thomas Jefferson.

"Books are the choicest company" in a new and thinly populated land, a John Pory in 1620 or a William Fitzhugh in 1685 might have testified.

True sons of the Renaissance, the early Virginians read the classics for pleasure and to understand the past and present. The classics formed a large segment of any fair-sized library. William Byrd II composed in Greek and Latin and read in the two languages almost daily. The first belletristic product of British America was George Sandys' translation of Ovid's *Metamorphoses*. In later generations, the Virginia founding fathers of the republic read and studied Latin and Greek. In the Virginia Historical Society library, John Randolph's Elzevir editions—dozens of little Greek and Latin volumes with innumerable marginal annotations made by their owner —bear irrefutable testimony that Virginians, even as late as the nineteenth century, were knowledgeable heirs to the Athenian and Roman tradition, not mere textbook-quoters of a few tag phrases.

In the eighteenth century, there were one, two, or three golden ages, depending on whether one considers a great cluster of plantations and their aggressive, self-made owners— men like William Byrd I, Robert Beverley I, Richard Lee I and II, William Fitzhugh, and others—as forming a great age. They were the begetters, these hard-driving men who made great fortunes in land and/or trade and educated their children abroad. Most historians consider the next age as *the* great one—that in which the little capital of Williamsburg became a cultural and political center which controlled a large part of British America, possessed a theatre and a good acting company, a village whose citizens wrote much and published little, gave their own concerts, and developed a three-sided struggle among planters, governors, and clergy.

This was the era of William Byrd II, of Robert Beverley the historian, of the Carters, the Burwells, the Robinsons and others. They were usually British-educated, collectors of at least fair-sized libraries, and builders of handsome houses adapted from the pattern-books of Palladio and Vitruvius. They laid out beautiful gardens and designed their houses with the same care and intellectual exercise that their New England contemporaries employed in sermons or tracts on complex theological disputes. These men clearly prepared the way for the third age or generation, that of the Revolution, when Montesquieu, Locke, *Cato's Letters,* and the *Independent Whig* had been absorbed and employed for continuing and new purposes. Scores of social, economic, and political tracts and essays began to be printed by Virginians in Williamsburg, London, or Edinburgh. These colonists defied viceregal, royal, and parliamentary edicts, governors and clergy; they embarked pen in hand upon the Parsons' Cause, the Pistole Fee Dispute, and the Stamp Act Debate. The result was a body of distinguished polemical writing in the style of Cicero, Quintilian, and the scholastics, but also reflecting current English political and satiric writing and the colonists' own experience in legislative argument. Richard Bland, James Maury, Landon Carter, Peyton Randolph, Edmund Pendleton, and Thomas Jefferson, all native-born, were more than equal in penmanship, politics, and cerebration to their ablest loyalist British-born opponents, such as John Camm and Jonathan Boucher. Colonial thinking found expression in prose and poetic satire, in invective, in cogently reasoned essays in the *Virginia Gazette*—either as separately printed pamphlets, English editions, or manuscripts. Conservative or liberal, depending upon one's definition and the age in which he writes, these writers were concerned for their property but just as clearly for the cherished rights of Englishmen. They were Whiggish, but whether they really were representative of any British form of Whiggism is perhaps doubtful.

These writers were the leaders, springing from among the men who had themselves or through their parents risen to the top in a still fluid society. This third or Revolutionary group came largely from established wealthy landowning families, but they included the orphaned Edmund Pendleton and the scantily educated Patrick Henry. What they wrote or spoke was comprehensible, one must surmise, to their constituencies of small farmers, merchants, sailors, town artisans, and perhaps even still indentured persons who would soon join the freeholders. All classes read the Bible, the Catechism, the Prayer Book, *The Whole Duty of Man,* and something of law, medicine, and the classics. Most, free and indentured, had studied Lily's famous Renaissance grammar which had been adapted and revised for each generation. Presumably, most readers knew something of Cicero and perhaps of Horace and Virgil, for surviving speeches and tracts appear to take this for granted. Whether the average pew-holder in the Puritan congregation actually knew what Cotton Mather, John Cotton, or Jonathan Edwards was talking about is still a moot question; but there is strong written evidence in the newspapers that the white-man-in-the-furrow in Virginia understood his representatives' arguments, even when the arguments were buttressed by literary and classical allusions.

An element considered in the following essays, from William Fitzhugh to William Byrd II to James Reid, is the indentured servant. It has been said, surely with truth, that any Virginian whose ancestry goes back to colonial times has one or more "indented" servants in his family tree. And surely an appreciable percentage of those who shaped early Virginia were at some early stage of their lives bound to serve a master for a few years in a trade or profession. Undoubtedly some indentured servants, especially early ones, were convicts (perhaps political), as the protests from the 1620s on through the first century indicate. But many more, almost all of whom eventually became farmers, professional men, or artisans, came under indenture as a means of paying their way to new opportunities. Certainly the Christ's Hospital graduate whom William Fitzhugh thus obtained to act as his bookkeeper (and there were many of these from this same school) was an educated youth who would probably quickly assume a respectable place in the community. And there was Fitzhugh's own "cousin," to whom the lawyer-planter in his will gave the remaining years of his term. John Harrower was an educated indentured tutor in a prominent Virginia family on the Rappahannock, and the poet-essayist James Reid, who had attended the University of Edinburgh, was probably under bond. The great Edmund Pendleton, son of a poor Virginia farmer, learned his profession under apprenticeship or indenture to a county clerk of the court. The Chesapeake country was full of all sorts of apprentices and bonded servants, whom one can hardly designate as lower class. Actually, even if they did not rise to the upper levels of society, as did Adam Thoroughgood who became the wealthiest man in Princess Anne County, they usually came to form a sort of middle class of substantial citizens engaged in a variety of occupations. Many were writers, such as George Alsop in Maryland and James Reid in Virginia; all had by law a chance to learn to read. Virginia colonial newspapers directed much of their material to these men and women.

Despite its array of presidents of the United States, a distinguished chief justice, and other national leaders, Virginia discernibly declined in prestige and power after the adoption of the Constitution. The black problem, which had concerned

Virginia too little in earlier years, became a major and crucial matter which colonization societies came nowhere near solving. The northwest territories were ceded irrevocably, the tobacco lands were worn out, many of the once wealthy had exhausted their resources, and ambitious young Virginians were moving west or south, as James Madison had advised them to do. Yet the Virginians of 1790–1840 were able and educated men who in individual cases remained or became American leaders. But fearful of losing their all by abolition and conscious of their decline in wealth and power, they became increasingly conservative economically and sometimes politically. After 1800 they turned more and more away from agriculture and toward the profession of law as a means of attaining eminence, perhaps one reason for Henry Adams' generalization. The gradually increasing Scotch, Scotch-Irish, German, and other national or ethnic elements in the population brought changes. But in most respects the Anglo-Celtic stock of the first two centuries assimilated and molded the newcomers. Whatever his European origin or social station, the white Virginian showed generally good taste in gardening, landscaping, and building. He liked to write seriously or lightly when moved by a lady or an economic or social problem. Even if he were a Presbyterian, he was likely to take his religion (including the mild Calvinism which was also the heritage of his low church Anglican neighbor), in stride, as part of but not the whole of life. Despite his conservatism in many areas, he was likely to be tolerant of the foibles of those not so fortunate as he, or simply different from himself. He appreciated the natural beauties of his native clime from the blue Chesapeake to the equally blue mountain ranges of the western boundaries, for he half realized that physically, at least, his Virginia had become Arcadia. He believed in the middle way, the Horatian-Aristotelian mean—a philosophy which, compared with that of his fellow Americans, seems to be a distinctive quality which endures.

But to turn to the particular essays included here: law and politics are indeed present, from the second through the last essay. But in most instances they are discussed in their relation to matters which may be considered more purely artistic or intellectual. William Fitzhugh, William Byrd II, George Tucker, Thomas Jefferson, William Munford, and Francis Walker Gilmer, all lawyers by training and usually by practice, are shown to be men who could compose verse or witty letters or satiric character portraits. George Sandys translated Ovid's *Metamorphoses* into heroic couplets while he was director of industry and treasurer at Jamestown, and two centuries later William Munford rendered Homer's *Iliad* in blank verse while he was clerk of the Supreme Court of Appeals in Richmond. Presbyterian Samuel Davies also translated from the classics, composed hymns and elegies. James Reid satirized the arrogant planter in a prose treatise, celebrated the birth of Christ in a meditative ode, and wrote witty or tender occasional pieces.

It is quite clear that from the first generation in Virginia to the death of Jefferson, roughly the period represented in these essays, there were men with the potential ability but little time to create in art or in science. Most of them seem to have assumed that the active everyday life must come first—the duties of governmental office, the building of a fortune for family security, the attainment of a university professorship, or even the spread of the gospel. Francis Gilmer, in his correspondence with George Ticknor of Boston and Hugh Swinton Legaré of Charleston, gives the key to the situation of the early gifted Virginian. He yearned to write, to make a name for himself as a man of letters, but he knew that the time and place were not yet ready for him to do so. Therefore, more or less philosophically, he accepted his lot and channeled his ambition into more "practical" areas.

Many of these first Virginians, who lived their lives on plantations remote from those with whom they wished to communicate, were inveterate and gifted letter writers. George Sandys' trenchant, whimsical, sometimes bitter epistles addressed to friends in England, and the individual expressions of the expatriates in Georgia, Florida, Mississippi, Louisiana, Illinois, or Ohio who wrote back to intimates and relatives in Virginia, indicate their many-faceted interest in books, art, architecture, landscape gardening, religion, morality, education, and philosophy. In their first century in America they seem, more than their New England contemporaries, "compleat" men of the Renaissance. In the eighteenth and early nineteenth centuries, their rich and varied interests mark them as true sons of the Enlightenment.

Even in the seventeenth century when New England was hanging its witches, Virginians were common-sense rationalists who refrained from executing anyone for the alleged practice of the black arts, though their laws and the ignorance and bigotry of certain colonists caused them to bring a few persons to trial. From Sandys to Gilmer, they were consistently self-critical—personally, socially, politically and religiously—up to a certain point and on things which they considered important. Yet a certain tolerance remains evident in witchcraft judges and juries, in the Calvinist Presbyterianism of Samuel Davies, in the regional prejudices of William Byrd, although the tolerance may have been accompanied by sharp-tongued or tart criticism.

Books and reading were an omnipresent element of the lives of all the individuals here considered. Men like Byrd, Fitzhugh, Davies, and Jefferson gathered great libraries. Jefferson's library contained perhaps the most significant materials in an American book collection before 1840. Interestingly enough, the 1626 verse of George Sandys appeared on the shelves of Byrd and Jefferson in the eighteenth century; and Gilmer, in the early nineteenth century, was primarily responsible for the first American edition of the works of Virginia's first major writer, Captain John Smith.

Arthur Blackamore, Samuel Davies, and James Reid were critical of the established church, from within and without. In their quite different ways, and using different modes of literary expression, they prepared for Jefferson's later Statute for Religious Freedom.

All these Virginians, whether native-born or not, appear to have had in common an affection or fascination for this land. In his relatively quiet old age in England, Sandys wrote of Virginia and served on the Council for the Plantations, in some respects becoming Great Britain's first colonial civil servant, or expert on colonial affairs. Fifteen years after his return home he was appointed agent for the colony. Arthur Blackamore, also back in England, felt compelled to write two novels on Virginia themes dedicated to Virginians, and he left his imprint on education in the colony. Davies died as president of Princeton, but he is remembered as the Presbyterian "Apostle of Virginia." Those who viewed and wrote of the scenic Valley of Virginia documented their love of the physical features of the commonwealth. Jefferson's avid search for Virginiana was but the bibliophilic side of his profound attachment to his "native country," the Old Dominion.

The last essay here included is concerned with the individual Jeffersonian Virginians who carried beyond the state's borders not only her law and politics, but her manners, her codes of morality and conduct, and her scientific and religious attitudes. The essay is primarily meant to suggest further investigations of the effect of the early Virginia mind and character on the rest of America.

The men and the literature here presented by no means form a complete picture of the early Virginia intellect. They fail to show the repeated bitter struggle to establish an adequate system of education, and the striking documentary evidence of the continuous interest in education from the beginnings of the colony. They do not consider the Virginians' ambivalent attitudes toward both the red and the black races. But this collection is not meant to be a complete delineation. It came into being over a period of a quarter of a century, as this or that aspect of early intellectual Virginia came to my attention. It does have, however, a common thesis and purpose: to illustrate that the early Virginia mind, and through it the early southern mind, was dynamic in other areas than politics and law. It was a lively, creative, critical intellect encompassing a dozen kinds of cerebration. As surely as those of the Puritan mind, its qualities helped form this nation's art and artistry, its scientific curiosity and achievement, its eagerness to learn and to know, its common-sense rationale of the middle way, as well as its law, politics, and agriculture.

Literature AND *Society*
IN EARLY VIRGINIA, 1608–1840

America in George Sandys' Ovid

[This essay grew out of a combination of circumstances, including a Guggenheim Fellowship which enabled me to complete the gathering of material for a critical biography of George Sandys, and the appearance of the first version of Howard Mumford Jones's monograph, here referred to as a point of departure. Sandys' "Ovid" represents many qualities of American literature and life, particularly in relation to European parallels. Thus the article still seems highly pertinent.

The tendency of American writers to adapt Old World material to New World settings, to see Old World myth and fable in a New World frame, has continued into our own time. Poets have translated Homer, Dante, and Goethe, and adapted the Arthurian romance or Chinese philosophical literature for our own readers, as many major poets are now devoting great effort to translating and adapting contemporary Spanish, Italian, and Portuguese writers. Dozens have done this—from James Logan of Philadelphia through William Munford of Richmond on through Bayard Taylor, Longfellow, and Edward Arlington Robinson to Ezra Pound.

The attraction of the Greek and Roman classics, especially the latter, for the southern colonies was pointed out long ago by Louis B. Wright and others. The southern colonial saw many political and moral correspondences between the New

World and the European tradition. From George Sandys to William Alexander Percy, with William Byrd II and Thomas Jefferson and dozens of others between, is a long period, but their writings represent an obviously continuing interest.

Sandys' work offered precedents for later southern intellectual habits. Gathering material about all America—North, South, and Central—was a primary interest, as can be seen from the inventories of the dozens of major southern libraries from the mid-seventeenth century to the Revolution. Later southerners knew as Sandys did that all parts of the western hemisphere had much in common, and that to understand one part of it was often to understand all of it. Tremendous curiosity about the world of fauna and flora, about the red aborigine, about geological and geographical matters, though not scientific interest *per se,* is obvious in this translation. In another great work, a popular travel book of Mediterranean lands, the translator has shown how wide-ranging and accurate his observations of men and things could be. In the notes to his "Ovid" and in a few letters, he leaves us his only hints of an early observant and sophisticated attitude toward the Virginia natural world.]

I

THE TRANSLATION of the fifteen books of Ovid's *Metamorphoses* by George Sandys has been called "the first utterance of the conscious literary spirit articulated in America."[1] The circumstances of its production provide the basis for this assertion. Sandys, treasurer and director of industry at Jamestown from 1621 until late in 1625,[2] probably brought his

1. Moses Coit Tyler, *History of American Literature during the Colonial Time* (2 vols.; New York, 1897), I, 54.
2. For details of Sandys' activities and time spent in the colony, see Susan Myra Kingsbury (ed.), *Records of the Virginia Company of London* (4 vols.; Washington, D.C., 1906–1936), and H. R. McIlwaine (ed.), *Minutes of the Council and General Court of Colonial Virginia, 1622–1632, 1670–1676* . . . (Richmond, 1924).

translation of five books of the *Metamorphoses* with him to Virginia and translated the remaining ten during his hours of recreation on the voyage and in the colony.[3] At any rate, in 1626, a few months after his return to England, the first edition[4] appeared.

Though America has been proud to claim a share in this work, the exact extent and nature of the share have been subject to question. In the first edition of an interesting and valuable monograph on "The Literature of Virginia in the Seventeenth Century,"[5] Professor Howard Mumford Jones

3. See Drayton's well-known lines, in which he urges Sandys to continue as he had begun in the first five books in J. W. Hebel (ed.), *The Works of Michael Drayton* (Oxford, 1931–41), III, 206–207, ll. 37 ff. For Sandys' statement that he translated two books on the voyage see his letter to Samuel Wrote in Kingsbury (ed.), *Records*, IV, 64–68. Also see R. B. Davis, "The Early Editions of George Sandys's Ovid: The Circumstances of Production," *Papers in the Bibliographical Society of America,* XXXV (1941), 258 ff. Here the matter of the Ovid's "firstness" is discussed. Sandys spells Ovid's title *Metamorphosis.*

4. See R. B. Davis, "Early Editions," 268–70. The title page reads: OVID'S / METAMORPHOSIS / Englished / by / G. S. / [*ornament*] / Imprinted at / LONDON / MDCXXVI / Cum Privilegio / . This is a small folio.

5. H. M. Jones, "The Literature of Virginia in the Seventeenth Century," in *Memoirs of the American Academy of Arts and Science* (Boston, 1946), XIX, Pt. 2, p. 3, *n.* In a second book edition of this work with the same title (Charlottesville, 1968, p. 3, *n.*). Professor Jones has altered considerably his charge of the un-Americanness of Sandys' translation. But he still finds its American qualities incidental, though he admits its American interest. He argues against this essay and its thesis that Sandys' work is in many respects as American as Bradstreet's or Smith's, partly by pointing out the new evidence since this essay was written that the first five books were translated and published in 1621 before Sandys came to America. Besides the evidence here presented, in R. B. Davis, *George Sandys, Poet-Adventurer* (London and New York, 1955), I have shown that the phrasing and style of even the first five books of 1626 and 1632 are very different from those of the 1621 pre-American translation. Our amicable exchange on this matter is also represented in my review of Jones's second edition in the *Virginia Magazine of History and Biography,* LXXVII (1969), 116–18). That Jones's conception of what constitutes early American literature seems hazy is indicated by his reference to John Ferrar's "characteristic American brag," when the fact is that Ferrar never set foot on American soil but merely "promoted" from the eastern side of the Atlantic.

gives reasons for denying it a place in genuine American literature:

> The first five books of Ovid Sandys seems to have translated before he came to Virginia, but an indefinite amount of the rest of the work was done in Jamestown. However, *neither the life nor the landscape of North America seems to have left any trace on the poem, which does not properly belong to American literature.* Almost the sole evidence of Sandys' Jamestown experiences (and he survived the massacre of 1622!) lurks in the dedication to Charles I, wherein the author apologizes for a poem "bred in the New-World, of the rudenesse whereof it cannot but participate, especially having Warres and Tumults to bring it to light in stead of the Muses."[6]

The matter of definition as to what constitutes colonial American literature is, of course, involved in this statement. Surely, one might argue on the contrary, the Ovid is as much American, from the mere fact that most of it was done in Virginia, as the majority of the poetry of the seventeenth-century

6. Jones, "The Literature of Virginia." Italics added. In reference to Jones's statement that Sandys did an indefinite amount of the translation in Jamestown, see note 3 above. Professor Jones's quotation from the Dedication given below shows, of course, that the poet claimed his work as a product of America. In the earlier part of the Dedication not quoted by Professor Jones, we have even more evidence of this: ". . . Your Gracious acceptance of the first fruites of my Trauels [*i.e.*, George Sandys, *A Relation of a Journey Begun . . . A.D.* 1610 (London, 1615)], when You were our Hope, as now our Happinesse; hath actuated both Will and Power to the finishing of this Peece; being limn'd by that unperfect light which was snatcht from the houres of night and repose. For the day was not mine, but dedicated to the service of your Great Father, and your Selfe: which, had it proved as fortunate as faithful, in me, and others more worthy; we had hoped, ere many yeares had turned about, to haue presented you with a rich and wel-peopled Kingdome, from whence now, with myselfe, I onely bring this Composure:
Inter victrices Hederam tibi serpere Laurus.
It needeth more then a single denization, being a double Stranger. Sprung from the Stocke of the ancient Romanes; but bred in the New-World, of the rudenesse whereof it cannot but participate. . . ." George Sandys, *Ovid's Metamorphosis Englished, Mythologized, and Represented in Figures . . . By G. S.* (London, 1640).

colonies. Its verse forms are no more un-American than those of Edward Taylor or Ann Bradstreet. Nor is its subject matter less our own than that of the translations of Longfellow, Bryant, or Bayard Taylor. Ovid needs no more naturalization than Dante, Homer, or Goethe.

Actually there is more of American life and landscape in Sandys' work than Professor Jones's summary indicates. It does not appear in the 1626 edition[7] to which he refers, but in the large "complete edition" of 1632. Sandys said in his "Address to the Reader," written for the earlier edition (p. [327]), that he had intended to polish his verse and include commentaries or explanations of each book, but that an unexpected want of leisure[8] prevented his doing so. In 1632, while he was a member of King Charles's special commission for Virginia,[9] he published a new edition, a beautiful large folio with elaborate engravings for each book and the frontispiece, and detailed commentaries occupying as much page space as the Ovid text itself. These commentaries or explanations, based on Sandys'

7. Although Sandys seems to have had his voyage to America in mind in at least one translation, namely when he describes the storm at sea in *ibid.*, Book XI, ll. 483 ff. See R. B. Davis, "Early Editions," 374.

8. Sandys' lack of leisure was most probably occasioned by Virginia business. He was reappointed a member of the Virginia governing council while he was in England, in 1626 and 1628. See W. Noel Sainsbury (ed.), *Calendar of State Papers, Colonial Series, 1514–1660* (London, 1860), 77; and "The Randolph Manuscripts," *Virginia Magazine of History and Biography*, XVI (1908), 125. During this period Sandys remained actively interested in the colony, corresponded with persons there, and for a time at least evidently intended to return.

9. He was appointed to the commission on June 17, 1631, along with Sir Francis Wyatt, Governor of Virginia, 1621–1625. See Kingsbury, (ed.), *Records*, I, iii, note d. He remained a member of the King's subcommittee on colonial affairs through the rest of the decade. See W. L. Grant and James Munro (eds.), *Acts of the Privy Council of England, Colonial Series* (Hereford, 1907), I, 263–64; and "Virginia in 1638–1639," *Virginia Magazine of History and Biography*, XI (1904), 46–47; and "Virginia in 1639–40," *Virginia Magazine of History and Biography*, XIII (1905–1906), 375.

enormous reading[10] and personal experiences, made the 1632 edition and its reprint in 1640[11] one of the well-known and influential[12] books of the century. And in these explanations are found frequent reminders that the work and its translator were intimately connected with the New World. These references are of two kinds: those to Florida, Mexico, and the West Indies were the product of his reading; those to Virginia stem directly from his personal experiences.[13]

II

Sandys had evidently read several of the Latin and perhaps other commentaries[14] on the West Indies, Mexico and Flor-

10. This edition of Sandys' Ovid has been called "the greatest repository of allegorized myth in English" by Douglas Bush, *Mythology and the Renaissance Tradition in English Poetry* (Minneapolis, 1932), 243.

11. Sandys, *Ovid.* This 1640 edition used the same engraved plates, text, and large folio sheet, but was printed in double instead of single columns. Smaller editions usually direct the reader to this one. The edition of 1640 is used in all textual references in this paper.

12. It was this 1640 version which Milton used. See Davis Harding, *Milton and the Renaissance Ovid* (Urbana, Ill., 1946), 59, 62, 63, and 73. Professor Harding also quotes from a schoolmaster of the 1630s, who said that Sandys' Ovid was one of five books which should be deposited in all school libraries to be used in the proper (moralized) teaching of mythology (p. 31). Keats used it, too. See Claude L. Finney, *The Evolution of Keats' Poetry* (Cambridge, 1936).

13. There are also several references to the Indians of South America, particularly of Peru (Sandys, *Ovid,* Book IX, 175, 182; Book XI, 212). Sandys quotes "Acosta" as the source for some of these Indian references. He evidently refers to José de Acosta, who first published two books of his *Natural History of the Indies* in 1588. Sandys may have used this version; the Spanish version, *Historia Natural y Moral de las Indias* (Seville, 1590); or one of the French versions (Paris, 1598, 1600, 1616, 16⸱ ⸱). He also had access to Edward Grimston's English translation (1604). It is most probable that Sandys followed his usual practice of using the Latin version even when English editions were available. All references to Acosta in this paper, however, are to Grimston's 1604 translation, edited by Clements G. Markham (London, 1880), under the title *The Natural and Moral History of the Indies, by Father Joseph de Acosta,* hereinafter cited as Grimston, *Acosta.*

14. Sandys himself mentions only "Linscot" (Book VII, 144 [134]) and "Acosta" (Book IX, 182; Book XI, 212); but his habit had always been to use more sources than he cited. See Esmond S. de Beer, "George

ida. His first mention of tropical America occurs in Book IV,[15] where he has been explaining Ovid's story of Hermaphroditus: "There are many [hermaphrodites] this day in Aegypt, but most frequent in Florida; who are so hated by the rest of the Indians, that they use them as beasts to carry their burdens: to suck their wounds, and to attend on the diseased."[16] In Book VI[17] he compares the offering of human sacrifice in classical mythology and in ancient Israel with the practice among "the salvages of Florida." Then, in Book VII,[18] in commenting on Medea's potions to make the old young, he mentions with scorn a now famous American myth: "I have read in the histories of the West Indies of a ridiculous *Spaniard*,[19]

Sandys's Account of Campania," *The Library*, XVII (1937), 458–65. Linscot, *John Huighen Van Linschoten, his discours of Voyages into the Easte and West Indies.* . . . (London, [1598] and earlier European versions), contained only a brief and general account of parts of America.

15. Sandys, *Ovid*, Book IV, 79.

16. Hermaphrodites are mentioned in René Laudonnière, *L'Histoire Notable de la Florida* . . . (Paris, 1596); in the English edition, R. Hakluyt, *The Principal Navigations, Voyages* . . . (reprinted in Hakluyt Society, Extra Series, VIII [1904] 453, and IX, 16). The best known reference, which Sandys surely knew, is Plate XVII and the accompanying legend in Theodore de Bry's *Brevis Narratio Eorum Quae in Florida Provincia Gallis* . . . (Frankfort, 1591). This engraving of "Hermaphroditum officia" shows the Indians at their labor of carrying the wounded or slain. It is a combination of Laudonnière's text and Le Moyne's drawing. A modern reprint appears in Stefan Lorant, *The New World* (New York, 1946), 69. Sandys' references may have been based in part, of course, on the tales carried by English and Spanish sailors.

17. Sandys, *Ovid*, Book VI, 118. He later returns to his topic, and again mentions "these bloudy Ceremonies among the salvage Americans" (Book X ˙96), though he may be thinking of Virginia Indians here. Almost all commentators spend some detail on Indian sacrifices. See note 26 below.

18. *Ibid.*, 146 [actually 136].

19. Ponce de Leon. The ultimate source was probably Peter Martyr D'Anghera, whose *De Orbe Novo* had appeared in 1516. There were many Latin versions and the English translation of Richard Eden (1577, 1612, or 1625) available to Sandys. I have used the translation by Francis Augustus MacNutt, under the title, *The Eight Decades* . . . (2 vols.; New York, 1912). The fountain of youth is referred to in the Second Decade, I, 274, with Martyr taking Sandys' attitude towards it. There are of course other versions of the tale. Antonio de Herrara, *Historia de los Hechos de los Castellanor en las islas y tierra firma* . . ., Madrid, 1601–

who with much cost and labour, travelled in quest of a foun-
taine, famous for rendring youth unto age; which is rightly
ranked among incurable Diseases." In Book XI,[20] in pointing
out the lesson to be derived from the story of King Midas,
Sandys says: "Covetousness is Idolatry; and of this divine
verity the barbarous *Indians* had a naturall notion; who
imagined that gold was the God of the Spaniards, in that they
hunted after it so greedily." Even in a discussion[21] of the
centaurs the poet finds an American example, for he points
out how the Mexicans thought the men and horses "to be
but one creature"[22] when Hernando Cortez invaded their empire. And in a story of mortals who deserve deification, Sandys
thinks[23] of one of those who have made the New World
known: "Columbus by his glorious discoveries more justly
deserved a place for his ships among the Southerne Constel-
lations, then ever the *Argonautes* did for their so celebrated
Argo."

In Book XIV the West Indies was evidently on the poet's
mind, for he makes three references to happenings there.[24] In
the first[25] he is commenting on the Cyclops and cannibalism:

1615, gives a detailed account. See John Stevens (trans.), *The General
History of the Vast Continent and Island of America* . . . London, (6
vols.; 1725–26), II, 37.

20. Sandys, *Ovid,* Book XI, 213. See Grimston, *Acosta,* I, 190–93 or
almost any other book on Spanish America for evidence of Spanish greed.
The Renaissance Englishman naturally always made all he could of this.

21. Sandys, *Ovid,* Book XII, 231.

22. MacNutt (trans.), *The Eight Decades,* II, 34, the Fourth Decade.
Sandys' words are a close paraphrase of Martyr's Latin.

23. Sandys, *Ovid,* Book XIII, 252. Sandys mentions Columbus in one
other place (Book VII, 144 [134]), telling the story of the use of knowledge of an eclipse to overawe the Indians (his source was probably Herrara, *General History,* I, 294).

24. The terms *West Indies, Florida,* and *Peru* were used by the Renaissance European to refer to much larger regions than they now do. Sometimes *West Indies* appears to refer to Spanish America generally. Sandys
uses all three terms, however, and seemingly distinctly.

25. Sandys, *Ovid,* Book XIV, 263. See Grimston, *Acosta,* II, 320, 346–
50 for the first part of this account. Much of it is also in the first three

For injustice, armed with power, is most outragious and bloudy. Such *Polyphemus,* who feasts himselfe with the flesh of his guests; more salvage then are the *West-Indians* at this day, who onely eat their enemies, whom they have taken in the warres; whose slighting of death and patient sufferance is remarkable; receiving the deadly blow, without distemper, or appearance of sorrow; their fellowes looking on, and heartily feeding on the meate which is given them; yet know how they are to supply the shambles perhaps the day following. The heads of men they account among their delicates, which are onely to be eaten by the great ones, boyling oft times not so few as a dousen together, as hath beene seene by some of our Country-men.

Then, in discussing[26] the magic properties of a certain herb, Sandys draws from one of the floating oral tales of the strange new world:

And I knew a fellow, who sixe or seven yeares had beene a slave to the *Spaniard* in the *West-Indies,* who with desperate oathes would averre, how such an hearb was common in those countries; insomuch as the shackles would often unbolt, and fall from the feet of the horses, as they fed in the pastures; and how himself therewith had often opened a passage in the stuffing of his emptie belly. Whether true or no, no doubt but he believed himselfe in telling it so often. . . .

Even in the suckling of Romulus and Remus by a wolf, Sandys is reminded[27] of an American incident: "But why not might a Wolfe give them suck, as a Bitch gave suck unto *Cyrus;* being both one creature, & differing in nothing but the tamenesse of the one & wildnes of the other? For those fierce

---

decades of Peter Martyr's *De Orbe Novo,* but an exact source for the details of the last two sentences has not been located. Sandys may be suggesting that the story came to him orally. Probably the most detailed account of cannibalism and human sacrifice occurs in . . . Samuel Argall, *Hakluytus Posthumous or Purchas his Pilgrimes* (4 vols.; London, 1625). See the reprint edition (Hakluyt Society, Extra Series, XVI [1906], 431–40), from "A Treatise on Brazil, written by a Portugall which had lived there. . . ."

26. Sandys, *Ovid,* Book XIV, 266.   27. *Ibid.,* 269.

Mastives carried by the *Spaniard* into the West-Indies, to hunt and worry the Natives: turning after wild, became Wolves, and preyed upon the Cattle of their rejected masters."[28]

III

The majority of Sandys' references to Spanish North America are products of his reading, but in speaking of Virginia he gives some insight into his personal interests and experiences while he lived on the banks of the James. His first reference shows that he had learned something of the Indians' religion and superstition. He has been commenting on Ovid's account of Deucalion's flood:[29] "There is no nation so barbarous, no not the salvage *Virginians*, but have some notion of so great a ruine. . . ." In his next two comments the fauna of the country concern him. In telling of the base yokels metamorphosed into frogs, he says[30] of the latter:

These depopulated a City in *France*, and now not a little infest *Virginia* in Summer: called Pohatans hounds by the *English*, of their continuall yelping. And as they croake and ride one upon another in shallow plashes: so Pesants baule and gamball at their meetings; soused in liquor, as frogs in the water. It is worth the observation, that a frog, though she have her heart and liver puld out, will skip up and down notwithstanding.

Then, in speaking of weasels (Galanthis was turned into one), Sandys is reminded[31] of Virginia animals: "I have seene a Beast, which the *Indians* call a *Possoun,* that hath two flaps beneath her belly, which she can shut and open at pleasure:

28. See Grimston, *Acosta,* I, 272. Sandys follows the source closely, apparently.

29. Sandys, *Ovid,* Book I, 18. Sandys may also have learned that the West Indies had stories of a similar deluge. See Grimston, *Acosta,* I, 70.

30. Sandys, *Ovid,* Book VI, 117.   31. *Ibid.,* Book IX, 179.

within which, when affrighted, she receives her broode, and runnes away with them: whereupon, by a like mistake, it was supposed at first by some of the *English* that they reenter'd her belly." Finally, in the margin of the text in Book XV,[32] the poet indicates the way his thoughts are running:

VVhere once was solid land, Seas have I seene
And solid land, where once deepe Seas have beene. ᵍ Such have
ᵍ Shels, far from Seas, like quarries in the ground; I seene in
And anchors have on mountaine tops beene found. *America.*

Even in his hurried first edition of this work sprung from the stock of the ancient Romans, the poet has claimed its breeding in the New World. In his definitive edition of 1632, in commentaries and notes based on his reading and personal experience, American life and landscape appear several times. Whether the *Metamorphoses* is colonial American literature must remain a matter of definition, but no reader can peruse its pages without being frequently reminded of its American associations. Strange men, fantastic creatures, marvelous lands, these were stimuli which quite clearly had urged Sandys to the translation of Ovid. And strange men, fantastic creatures, and marvelous new lands he and his fellows had found in America. His stay in Virginia had enabled him to translate the fantasies of an old world while he was sur-rounded by the marvels of a new, and in the act of translation he brought to a creative focus the parallel interests of litera-ture and colonization. These comments scattered through the work are but graphic indications of his consciousness of the America which he had known. If American literature is a fusion of European intellect and American environment, Sandys' Ovid may well be included in it.

32. *Ibid.,* Book XV, 273. The 1632 form (see R. B. Davis, "Early Editions," 272–73) differs only in position on the page and the number-ing of the footnote, from this 1640 form.

⤙ II ⤚

The Devil in Virginia
in the Seventeenth Century

[The first Virginia colonists, like their neighbors to the North-east, seemed to take for granted the existence of black magic or of the devil as a factor in aboriginal religion.* The bluff realist Captain John Smith and the idealistic learned scholar the Reverend Alexander Whitaker were equally confident that the Indians were worshippers of Satan. Smith's observations are relatively detached, good examples of Renaissance curiosity. Whitaker's are more concerned, for as a missionary one of his principal duties was to wean the Indians away from the evil idol-god Okee to the saving spirit of Christ. Although southern lay observers and clerics alike, from the age of Powhatan to that of the last eastern Cherokees, accepted Indian devil-worship as a fact admitted by the red men themselves, after the first few decades it was not a major anxiety of the settlers. They made sporadic efforts to christianize the Indians, and they were occasionally successful. But there was never a crusade against the Indian devil, north or south.

The devil among white settlers was another matter, and the records of his presence among Virginians and other southern-ers make a very different story from that of his Satanic Majesty in New England. To be sure, some persons believed he actually existed, and those who did not dared not aver their

* The material for this essay was gathered while the author was a Fellow of the Folger Shakespeare Library.

convictions at public gatherings, civil or ecclesiastical. An educated planter-lawyer like William Fitzhugh in Virginia believed witchcraft, or the practice of it, to be one of the most heinous of sins. So did the sophisticated and learned chief justice Nicholas Trott of South Carolina, who in a charge to a grand jury gave a classic early eighteenth-century statement of belief in black magic and of its legal reality; and many clergy believed in the devil as a palpable presence.

Yet the present essay suggests, as do investigations into the records of other colonies from Maryland through South Carolina, that there was almost no capital punishment for witchcraft in any southern colony. There are records of many trials, of examinations for witches' marks on the body, and of duckings as punishment or to determine guilt. But there are nearly as many records of warnings and even heavy fines for those who accused without accepted proof. Justice Trott, in the very speech in which he declared that witches existed gave a rational as well as legal warning as to what constituted proof of black magic, implying that reliable evidence rarely existed. Thus there is no black page of witch-hanging hysteria in southern colonial history. Regarding legal evidence, the southerner was wholesomely skeptical.]

IN ITALY IN 1611, George Sandys informed a rustic that "in England we were at defiance with the devill, and that he would do nothing for us." Sandys was evading an appeal that he use the black arts, reputed by Italians to be at the disposal of all Britons, to assist in locating a hidden treasure.[1] Ten years later in the New World as Virginia treasurer, Sandys was surrounded by aborigines reputed by every European nation to be in league with "the Black Man." To the earlier

1. George Sandys, *A Relation of a Journey Begun* . . . *A.D.* 1610 (London, 1615), 250.

seventeenth-century man, Evil was still incarnate. Particularly was it present in remote and primitive places. King James himself had written in his *Dæmonologie* in 1597 that the Devil was present "where [he] finds greatest ignorance and barbaritie," and that the abuses of witchcraft, derived directly from Satan, were "most comon in . . . [the] wild partes of the world."[2] At the same time the King was pointing out that certain of his own subjects might be witches or wizards themselves, and that if they were they should be rooted out. Evidently the devil was doing something for Britons.

Through the settlement at Jamestown in 1607, James became sovereign over the barbaric as well as the civilized. Both he and his English subjects were much interested in the manner and result of the presence of "the Black Man" among the Indian and white Virginians. Much has been written about the presence of the devil in England and New England in the seventeenth century, but most of us remain in ignorance of the frequency and form of his Satanic Majesty's personal appearance in the Virginia of the period.

Actually the literature of early exploration and settlement is full of allusions to and exemplifications of the Indians as followers of Satan in a quite literal sense. And the court records give us interesting indications of the colonists' attitudes toward the presence of the Evil One in witchcraft and other sorts of crime among themselves. As the century goes on, there are fewer references to the Indians as the chief servants of Satan, and more to the evil practices of transplanted Englishmen. Yet even though the belief in black magic apparently persists among some of the educated into the eighteenth century, there never was in Virginia a "darkest page"[3] of history such as the witch persecution in New Eng-

2. King James, *Dæmonologie* (1597), 69.
3. G. L. Kittredge, *Witchcraft in Old and New England* (Cambridge, Mass., 1929), 329.

land. A brief look at Virginians' attitudes toward the *idea* of black magic through the seventeenth century does afford us an interesting and perhaps unusual approach to the southern colonial mind.

I

The Mediaeval and Renaissance European believed that all infidels or pagans were really direct worshippers of Evil as opposed to Good, or of Satan as opposed to God. As we have noted, Evil was incarnate, and the personalized devil was an acknowledged deity in heathen lands. The early Spanish historians of America were careful to point out that the natives of the New World worshipped Satan as sovereign. Englishmen accepted this idea without hesitation. Master George Percy, who stopped in the West Indies on the first voyage to Jamestown, describes the Caribbean "Canibals . . . [who] worship the Devill for their God, and have no other beliefe."[4] Six years later, in dedicating Alexander Whitaker's *Good Newes from Virginia* to a noble lord, good Master William Crashaw assures the reading public that the plantation has been made "to resolve the works of the Divell," for "Satan visibly and palpably raignes there, more then in any other known place of the world."[5] Thus early Virginia was claimed

4. George Percy, "Observations," in Lyon Gardiner Tyler (ed.), *Narratives of Early Virginia, 1606–1625* (New York, 1907), 6. See also Alexander Roberts, *A Treatise on Witchcraft* (London, 1616), 33, who assures us that the "devil in man's form" inhabits the West Indies; and Joseph Glanvill, *Essays on Several Important Subjects in Philosophy and Religion* . . . (London, 1675[6]), 54–56.

5. William Crashaw, dedication to Alexander Whitaker's, *Good Newes from Virginia* (London, 1613), C2r. See also Ralph Hamor, *A True Discourse on the Present State of Virginia* (London, 1615), 48, *passim* (photostat of the original in the Folger Shakespeare Library, Washington, D.C.); and *A True Declaration of the estate of the Colonie in Virginia* . . . , *London 1610*, in Peter Force, *Tracts and Other Papers Relating Principally to the Origin, Settlement and Progress of the Colonies in North America, From the Discovery of the Country to the Year 1776* (reprinted New York, 1947), III, i, 26 (or see original in Folger Library), which

as the favorite dwelling place of Evil, and as a battle ground for the forces of Light and Darkness.

That the Virginia red men were really devils—in their chiefs, their priests, their idols, and their ceremonies—is stated again and again in the literature of the entire century. Even in their fairly ordinary appearance the savages reminded the nervous Englishmen of the dark deity. Percy observed of the first landing at Kecoughtan that the natives were like "so many Wolves or Devils."[6] Captain John Smith alludes to the Indians again and again as devils, and he was certainly thinking as much of their appearance as of their diabolic ways. When he was captured, "They entertained him with most strange and fearful Coniurations; As if neare led to hell,/Amongst the Devills to dwell" Then, "round about him these fiends danced a pretty while, and then came in three as ugly as the rest, with red eyes, and white stroakes over their black faces." Even Powhatan was "more like a devill then a man, with some two hundred more as black as himself."[7]

The religion itself, however, was what interested most observers, including Smith. "In this lamentable ignorance doe these poore soules sacrifice themselves to the Divell, not knowing their Creator."[8] The Indians' chief idol is usually described—from Smith to Robert Beverley almost a century later—as being the inanimate representation of the devil. Smith mentions "their *Okee* (which was an Idoll made of skinnes, stuffed with mosse, all painted and hung with chaines and copper) borne before them," and that that Okee is the devil-witch.[9] In 1612 William Strachey stated flatly that

exhorts, "cast down the altars of Divels, that you may raise up the altar of Christ."

6. Percy, "Observations," 12.

7. Edward Arber and A. G. Bradley (eds.), *Travels and Works of Captain John Smith* (2 vols.; Edinburgh, 1910), II, 398–99, 400–401.

8. *Ibid.*, II, 393.   9. *Ibid.*

the chief god they worship "is no better then the divell, whom they make presentements of and shadow under the forme of an Idoll which they entitle *Okeus* and whom they worship as the Romaynes did their hurtfull god Veiouis."[10]

Okee's nature may have changed slightly in the second half of the seventeenth century, for later accounts differ in describing his attributes. Actually most later historians mix Smith's descriptions with their own observations or with simple hearsay. In 1670 the Reverend Samuel Clarke gave an account ultimately based on Smith and other early recorders: "But their chief God is the Devil whom they call *Oke*, and serve him more for fear than love. In their Temples they have his image in an ilfavoured shape, and adorned with Chains, Copper, and Beads, and covered with a skin."[11]

In 1672 John Lederer observed that their god was called *Okaee*, or Mannith, but that he was a creator who committed the government of mankind to the "lesser deities, as Quiacosough and Tagkanysough, that is, good and evil spirits."[12] In 1705 Robert Beverley quotes from Smith the conception of Okee as a devil who sucks under the left breast in the best witchcraft tradition, but he gives the "Religious Romance" a more rational explanation.[13] Beverley, an acute observer of Indian customs, distinctly represents a new era. Okee is now a mere thing of sticks and stones, and the devilish sacrifices

10. L. B. Wright and Virginia Freund (eds.), *The Historie of Travell into Virginia Britania* (1612) (London, 1953), 88.

11. Samuel Clarke, *A True, and Faithful Account of the Four Chiefest Plantations of the English in America. To Wit, of Virginia, New-England, Bermudus, Barbadoes* . . . (London, 1670), 10.

12. Sir William Talbot, Bart., (ed.), *The Discoveries of John Lederer, In Three Several Marches from Virginia* . . . (London, 1672); reprinted in C. W. Alvord and Lee Bidgood (eds.), *The First Explorations of the Trans-Allegheny Regions by the Virginians, 1650–1674* (Cleveland, 1912), 143.

13. L. B. Wright (ed.), *The History and Present State of Virginia* (Chapel Hill, 1947), 198, 206, 208.

are merely means by which the priests gather worldly goods unto themselves. Yet the Swiss traveler Francis Louis Michel reported in 1701–1702 that "Regarding their religion I heard from reliable people, who have much intercourse with them that they fear Satan, who torments them frequently."[14]

The early narrators relate with some relish stories of diabolic religious sacrificial ceremonies. Smith and Strachey give accounts of the child sacrifice of the Indians. Referring to these practices in a sermon before the Virginia Company of London, the Reverend Patrick Copland declared that Opachankano had confessed "that God loved us more then them; and that he thought the cause of his anger against them, was their custome of making their children Black-boyes, or consecrating them to Satan."[15]

Even less bloody ceremonies reminded the colonist of the devil. Whitaker earnestly inquired of Master Crashaw in England what he should make of certain things he had seen, and then concluded by giving his own opinion.

In a march upp Nansemund river as our men passed by one of their Townes, there yssued out on the shoare a mad crewe dauncinge like Anticks, or our Morris dancers before whom there were Quiockosite (or theire Priest) tossed smoke and flame out of a thinge like a censer. An Indian (by name Memchumps) amongst our men seeing this dance tould us that there would be very much raine presently and indeed there was forthwith exceedinge thunder and lighteninge and much raine within 5. miles and so further of, but not so much there as made their pouder dancke.

---

14. This is a modern translation from the German. William J. Hinke, (ed. and trans.), "Report of the Journey of Francis Louis Michel from Berne . . . to Virginia," *Virginia Magazine of History and Biography,* XXIV (1916), 131.

15. Patrick Copland, *Virginia's God be Thanked, or, a Sermon of Thanksgiving for the Happie successe of the affayres in Virginia this last yeare . . .* (London, 1622), 29.

. . . All which things make me think that there be great witches amongst them and they very familiar with the divill.[16]

A year later Whitaker informed his friend that he was now sure that "Their priests . . . are no other but such as our English Witches are."[17] Whitaker was a Puritan clergyman, and his comment reminds us that the theology of the period, especially as interpreted by the Puritans, more than accepted a belief in witchcraft. A recent historian of the colonial Church has pointed out that in the early days the Virginia clergy generally were inclined toward Puritanism, as was the Virginia Company of London, and that the "temper of the government in the colony"[18] was quite puritan. A few years later under Laud, when Virginia had become a royal colony, the situation changed. Fundamentally the Virginia Church never returned to the attitude of these early years, even during the commonwealth. And here may be the explanation as to why there were no Salem Village witch executions in the Chesapeake region.

II

Throughout the seventeenth century devil-worshipping neighbors such as those described by Master Whitaker were for New Englanders "a constant reminder of the possibility of danger from witchcraft."[19] Yet in Virginia, one who follows the record must believe that the trials for witchcraft or dealing in black magic had little connection with any white man's consciousness that the Indians were practicing devilish arts.

16. Alexander Whitaker to William Crashaw, August 9, 1611, in Alexander Brown, *Genesis of the United States* (Boston, 1897), I, 498–99.
17. Whitaker to Crashaw, July 28, 1612, in Whitaker, *Good Newes from Virginia,* 24.
18. George M. Brydon, *Virginia's Mother Church and the Political Conditions under Which It Grew* (Richmond, 1947), I, 25.
19. Kittredge, *Witchcraft,* 363.

Witchcraft was a subject for discussion in the Virginia county and general courts from 1626 through 1706, but in no instance is it ostensibly related by any colonist to the demonism of the aborigines.[20] It is rather the natural outgrowth of folk and theological beliefs about themselves which the settlers brought from Britain with them, beliefs some of them might buttress, if they wished, by reading certain of the books which had accompanied or followed them to the New World. These beliefs had more to do with folklore than theology,[21] and there was no black page of real torture or persecution—apparently because the Anglican clergy rarely took part in or supported such beliefs, and the juries of laymen were rational men who shunned hysteria and superstitious credulity.

That there should be investigations of alleged witchcraft was inevitable in any seventeenth-century European society. As a legacy from the Middle Ages, the belief in the existence of witches was widespread and through the sixteenth century almost universal. In Great Britain it was true that as early as 1584 Reginald Scot's *The Discoverie of Witchcraft* had warned men that they should proceed with caution before they persecuted or prosecuted for alleged black magic, and that so-called witches were really "melancholick doting" old women. But James VI of Scotland, soon to be king of England also, had answered Scot's rational arguments in his *Dæmonologie* in 1597, a treatise which seemed to his contemporaries a powerful reassertion of the necessity for faith in the existence of Satan's arts. And soon after James's accession to the English throne a new "Act against conjuration, witchcraft and dealing with evil spirits" superseded the act of the

20. Unless one considers the below-mentioned case of the recovered-from-the-dead Indian boy such an instance.

21. Thomas Jefferson Wertenbaker, *The First Americans* (New York, 1927), 147.

fifth year of Elizabeth's reign, the new law being much more severe in its punishment of practitioners of black magic. By 1610 the great Puritan preacher William Perkins had written his "Discourse of the Damned Art of Witchcraft," a sermon-essay included in all later editions of his popular *Works*[22] and more than reinforcing James's *Dæmonologie*. During the rest of the century there were dozens of other writers on the subject. A few, like John Cotta in 1616 and John Webster in 1677, warned against prejudiced persecution or suggested that individual cases be examined rationally, like other objects of investigation.[23] But even in the latter half of the century such men as the pious and productive Joseph Glanvill more nearly represented majority opinion. In "Against Modern Sadducism in the Matter of Witches and Apparitions"[24] and *Saducismus Triumphatus; or, a Full and Plain Evidence concerning Witches and Apparitions*[25] Glanvill reasserted full belief in witchcraft for a multiplicity of reasons, among them "because it suggests palpable and current evidence of our Immortality."[26]

The unlearned in the colony did not need the king or Glanvill to support a belief in witchcraft. They had brought a deeply grounded conviction of its truth with the rest of their folklore when they came to America. The more literate, before they came to the colony or during visiting periods of

22. William Perkins, *The Workes of That Famous and Worthy Minister of Christ in the University of Cambridge, Mr. William Perkins* (3 vols.; London, 1612–13). The "Discourse" first appeared separately at Cambridge in 1610.

23. John Cotta, *The Triall of Witchcraft, Shewing the True and Right Method of Discovery: With a Confutation of Erroneous Wayes* (London, 1616); John Webster, *The Displaying of Supposed Witchcraft . . .* (London, 1677). It is significant that both these authors were physicians.

24. Glanvill, *Essays*, 54–56.

25. Published 1681. This is an enlargement of his 1666 *Philosophical Considerations Concerning Witchcraft*.

26. Glanvill, *Essays*, 60.

education in England, had opportunities to read the treatises which might confirm or controvert their natural skepticism. But there is evidence that many of the most renowned of the polemical books or pamphlets were to be found in Virginia. By 1621–1622 there had been sent to the colony a set of "Master *Perkins* his works,"[27] a three-volume edition which included in the last the "Discourse" noted above. Private Virginia libraries well into the eighteenth century included either Perkins' *Works* as a whole or the "Art of Witchcraft."[28] When Ralph Wormeley died in 1701 he owned Webster's *The Displaying of Supposed Witchcraft,* a reasoned anti-persecution argument.[29] Later William Byrd II had Glanvill "on Witchcraft" as well as Perkins;[30] Thomas Thompson in Westmoreland County in 1716 numbered "Glanceck [*sic*] of Witches Observances"[31] among his possessions. Since our record of these books usually comes from the inventories accompanying probated wills, we may be fairly sure that many or most of these volumes were in the colony long before 1700. Many of Byrd's books, for example, had belonged to his father William Byrd I. Since early Virginia court records are frag-

27. Susan Myra Kingsbury (ed.), *Records of the Virginia Company of London* (4 vols.; Washington, D.C., 1906–1936), III, 576; also W. S. Powell, "Books in the Virginia Colony before 1624," *William and Mary Quarterly,* Ser. 3, V (April, 1948), 177–84.

28. Captain Charles Colston in 1724 had "Pirkins Works the last vollume" in his library ("Libraries in Colonial Virginia," *William and Mary Quarterly* Ser. 1, III [1894], 132); Colonel William Byrd II owned "Perkins Art of Witchcraft" in 1744; see J. S. Bassett (ed.), *The Writings of 'Colonel William Byrd of Westover in Virginia Esqr'* (New York, 1901).

29. "Libraries in Colonial Virginia," *William and Mary Quarterly,* Ser. 1, II (1894), 171. Inventory of Will. Dr. L. B. Wright points out that Wormeley's friend William Fitzhugh asserted his own personal belief in the damnable sin. L. B. Wright, *The First Gentlemen of Virginia* (San Marino, Calif., 1940), 181, 204.

30. Bassett (ed.), *Writings of Byrd,* 420, 439.

31. "Books in Colonial Virginia," *Virginia Magazine of History and Biography,* X (1903), 399. This is probably a misspelling of Glanvill.

mentary, it seems safe to assume that many other similar printed materials on the subject were present in the colony. Thus the Virginia gentlemen had almost as much opportunity as the New England theocrat to know the learned arguments on the subject and be influenced by them.

The Massacre of 1622 had set back the infant colony in almost every respect. Virginia's "second start," including a steady and uninterrupted growth in population, came in the years immediately after 1622. It was in these years of increase that the "great witches" ceased to be exclusively Indian.[32] There were enough colonists now to represent all forms of sin. The suspicious and the unfortunate might hope to find among the whites black magicians on whom to blame all sorts of major and minor calamities.

Most or all witchcraft cases originated as hearings before county courts or grand juries and were sent on, if considered serious, to the general court at Jamestown. In some instances there were actual trials of accused persons; in many more, civil suits were brought by individuals defamed as witches against those who spread the scandal. From either situation, the modern reader can learn a good deal about the temper of plaintiff, defendant, jury, and judge.

The first case of which we have a record came up in September, 1626.[33] The rather detailed extant evidence is perhaps fragmentary, though the records of this particular period are fairly complete. This evidence consists of a series of depositions attempting to prove Goodwife Joan Wright guilty of

32. Philip A. Bruce, *Institutional History of Virginia in the Seventeenth Century* (New York, 1910), I, 278.

33. All known Virginia witchcraft records of any apparent significance are noted in the textual discussion above. It is possible that in some county court records there may be a few other cases entered. Virginia county archives have been so thoroughly examined, however, that this seems unlikely.

practicing witchcraft. Mrs. Wright lived across the river from Jamestown in Surry County and had formerly lived at Kecoughtan in Elizabeth City County. The investigation may have originated in a Surry court. At any rate, the evidence we have came before the general court, acting perhaps as grand jury, of September 11, 1626, at Jamestown, with Sir George Yeardley, the governor, presiding. Trivial and even absurd as this evidence may seem today, it was certainly weighed seriously, though there is no existing record of actual trial or presentation for trial. Since the outcome remains in doubt, we see in this case only what certain laymen thought, and not what the judges decided. The evidence is both first and second hand. The first witness, presumably a county militia lieutenant and therefore possibly an educated man, appears as credulous and superstitious as the humbler folk who follow him.

Liv^t *Gieles Allingtone* sworne and examined sayeth, That he harde Sargeant *Booth* saye that he was croste by a woman and for twelve months space he havinge very fayre game to shute at, yett he could never kill any thinge but this deponent cannot say that was good wiefe *Wright*. Fourther this deponent sayeth, that he had spoken to good wiefe *Wrighte* for to bring his wiefe to bed, but the saide goodwief beinge left handed, his wiefe desired him to gett Mrs *Graue* to be her midwiefe, which this deponent did, and sayeth that the next daye after his wiefe was delivered, the saide goodwiefe *Wright* went awaye from his house very much discontented, in regarde the other midwiefe had brought his wiefe to bedd, shortlie after this, this deponents wiefes brest grew dangerouslie sore of an Imposture and was a moneth or 5 weeks before she was recovered, Att which tyme This deponent him selfe fell sick and contynued the space of three weeks, And further sayeth that his childe after it was borne fell sick and soe contynued the space of two moneths, and afterwards recovered, And so did Contynue well for the space of a moneth, And afterwards fell into extreeme payne the space of five weeks and so departed.[34]

Rebecca Graye testified that Goodwife Wright prophesied correctly that she, a Mr. Felgate, and Thomas Harris should soon bury their spouses, and that another woman who complained of "a cross man to my husband" was assured that she should bury him shortly, "(wch cam so to pass)."[35] The other witnesses continued in the same vein: *"Daniell Watkins* sworne and examined sayeth that about *february* last past, this deponent beinge at Mr. *Perryes* Plantatione Ther was *Robert Thresher* who had a cowple of henns pourposinge to send them over to *Elizabeth Arundle* And good wiefe *Wright* beinge there in place, saide to *Robert Thresher, why do you keepe these henns heere tyed upp, The maide you meane to send them to will be dead before the henns come to her"*[36] Even a plantation owner's wife, Mrs. Isabell Perry, told how Goody Wright threatened to use occult powers to compel a suspected thief to make restitution:

. . . vppon the losinge of a logg of light wood owt of the fforte, good wiefe *Wrighte* rayled vppon a girle of good wiefe *gates* for stealinge of the same, wherevppon good wiefe *gates* Charged the said good wiefe *Wright* with witchcrafte, And said that she had done many bad things at *Kickotan,* wherevppon this Examinate

34. H. R. McIlwaine (ed.), *Minutes of the Council and General Court of Colonial Virginia, 1622–1632, 1670–1676* . . . (Richmond, 1924), 111. Alexander Brown *Genesis of the United States* (Boston, 1897), II, 813 discusses a "Giles Allington, gent.," a member of the Virginia Company and grandson of the first Earl of Exeter. He mentions as another person the man who patented lands in Virginia in 1624, though the two were probably close relatives. The ownership of several tracts of land and a military commission indicate the present witness' social position in the colony. For other evidence of Lieutenant Allington as a man of affairs, see McIlwaine, *Minutes,* 53, 147, 157, 197.

35. McIlwaine, *Minutes,* 111.   36. *Ibid.,* 112.

Chid the saide Good wiefe *Wright,* And said vnto her, *yf thow knowest thyselfe Cleare of what she Charged thee, why dost thow not complaine And cleare thyselfe of the same,* To whom good wiefe *Wright* replied, *god forgive them,* and so made light of it, And the said good wiefe *Wright* Threatened good wiefe *Gates* girle and told her, that yf she did nott bringe the light wood againe she would make her daunce starke naked and the next morninge the lightwood was founde in the forte.[37]

Mrs. Perry also quoted Dorethie Behethlem as repeating to her the gossip that Joan Wright was a witch in Kecoughtan before she came to Surry. Mrs. Perry went on to connect the accused's practices with her former life in England, though to what purpose is not exactly clear.

And fourther this deponent [sayeth] that good wiefe did tell her that when she lived at *hull,* beinge one day Chirninge of butter there cam a woman to the howse who was accompted for a witch, wherevppon she by directions from her dame Clapt the Chirne staffe to the bottom of the Chirne and clapt her handes across vppon the top of it by which means the witch was not able to stire owt of the place where she was for the space of six howers after which time good wiefe *Wright* desired her dame to aske the woman why she did not gett her gone, wherevppon the witche fell downe on her knees and asked her forgivenes and saide her hande was in the Chirne, and could not stire before her maide lifted vpp the staffe of the Chirne, which the saide good wiefe *Wright* did, and the witch went awaye, but to her ⊕severance [perception] the witch had both her handes at libertie, and this good wiefe *Wright* affirmeth to be trewe. Fourther Mrs *Pery* sayeth that good wiefe *Wright* told her, that she was at *Hull* her dame beinge sick suspected her selfe to be bewiched, and told good wiefe *Wright* of it, wherevppon by directione from her dame, That at the cominge of a woman, which was suspected, to take a horshwe and flinge it into the oven and when it was red hott, To fflinge it into her dames urine, and so long as the horshwe was hott, the witch was sick at the harte, And when the

37. *Ibid.*

Irone was colde she was well againe, And this good wiefe *Wright* affirmeth to be trwe alsoe.[38]

A brief testimony from Alice Baylie that Goodwife Wright confessed that she could prophesy death concluded this day's testimony. A week later two people whose testimony had been given second hand appeared in person. Robert Thresher deposed the story of his hens and the prognostication of Elizabeth Arundle's approaching demise. Elizabeth Gates now testified personally regarding Goody Wright's putting spells on chickens in "Kickotan" and further that "goodwiefe *Wright* Threatened her maide she said she would make her dance naked and stand before the Tree"![39]

Poor Goodman Robert Wright, probably in real perplexity, was able amid all this only to swear that "he hath been married to his wiefe sixteene yeers, but knoweth nothinge by her touching the Crime she is accused of."[40] Since he arrived in the *Swan* in 1608,[41] it is clear that they were married in Virginia.

Evidently the case against Joan Wright was not considered a strong one. As we have noted, there is no record of a presentation for trial. The pattern of evidence, however, is similar to that appearing in the later records of the colony. There are here none of the melodramatic events testified to by children and adults in Salem Village in the 1690s, nor even the accusation of depraved and vicious living on the part of the accused and those associated with her. Here is a series of charges growing out of the griefs and resentments accompanying untimely deaths and perhaps partially from the ill

38. *Ibid.*   39. *Ibid.*, 114.   40. *Ibid.*, 112.
41. J. C. Hotten (ed.), *The Original Lists of Persons of Quality . . . Who Went from Great Britain to the American Plantations, 1600–1700 . . .* (New York, 1931), 261. The couple had two children who were living in 1624/5.

temper of Goody Wright, who may have herself more than half believed that she held the powers her detractors claimed for her. Whenever she lost her temper, it is probable that she at least pretended to possess these powers.

There is extant no known record of another case until 1641, when the period of the commonwealth had actually begun. Perhaps the several Virginia cases of the next twenty years after this date are more the result of increase in population than of Puritan influence. There is no slightest hint of any ecclesiastical influence save in one of them. And this is the only case for which the extant record indicates severe punishment of the accused. In November, 1656, in Northumberland County a minister, David Lindsaye, brought accusations against William Harding of "witchcraft sorcery etc.": "And an able jury of Twenty-four men were empanelled to try the matter by verdict of which jury they found part of the Articles proved by several deposicons. The Court doth therefore order that the said Wm. Harding shall forthwith receave ten stripes upon his bare back and forever to be Banished this County and that hee depart within the space of two moneths And also to pay all the charges of Court."[42]

One is tempted to suspect Puritan leanings in the Reverend David Lindsaye, a Scot of excellent family.[43] More strongly one may suspect that it was the voice of ecclesiastical authority which resulted in the conviction. In Scotland, in New England, and in the Puritan parishes of old England the clergy thundered if any person charged with witchcraft

42. Lyon G. Tyler (ed.), "Early Presidents of William and Mary," *William and Mary Quarterly*, Ser. 1, I (1893), 69.
43. David Lindsey, Lindsy, Lindsay, or Lindsaye (1603–1667), minister of Yeocomico Parish, was "the first and lawful sonne of the Rt Honorable Sir Hierome Lindsay, K^{nt} of the Mount, Lord-Lyon-King-at-Arms," and a Doctor of Divinity. He left children in Virginia. "Rev. David Lindsy," *ibid.*, XVI (1908), 136–38.

was not prosecuted to the limit.[44] But before we return to 1641 and the more characteristic Virginia investigations, we should perhaps mention the one situation in which an execution for witchcraft is recorded in Virginia.

The reader will observe that I do not say record of an execution which *took place* in Virginia. Conway Robinson summarizes the matter laconically in the only surviving evidence: "Captᵃ Bennett had to appear at the admiralty court to answer the putting to death of *Kath Grady* as a witch at sea."[45] Thus Virginia in 1654 called immediately to account a sea captain who had probably been pressured into executing a poor old woman during a storm or period of sickness in the long voyage. And the court did so despite the fact that witches' malignancy at sea was a common superstition. More than ten years later the English State Papers were to include an official letter solemnly describing the anticipated loss of a British ship with all on board, because two witches sat in the maintop and could not be dislodged.[46] Virginia can hardly be held responsible for this death, which came within its jurisdiction only because Jamestown was the ship captain's next port of call.

In April of 1641, the wife of George Barker was accused of being a witch by Jane Rookens. The depositions before the general court, however, are directed against Jane Rookens as a scandalmonger, not against the alleged witch. "The said Rookens" claimed that she did not remember what she had said but was sorry anyway. The court ordered that William

44. Wertenbaker, *The First Americans*, 147.

45. McIlwaine, *Minutes*, 504. The actual records for this period are missing. We have only the summarizing notes of Conway Robinson as evidence.

46. Captain Silas Taylor to Sir Joseph Williamson, November 2, 1662, Harwich, in Mary A. E. Green (ed.), *Calendar of State Papers, Domestic, Charles II, November 1662–September 1668* (London, 1893), 4.

Rookens, Jane's husband, pay the Barkers' expenses and the charges of court.[47] This was the first clearcut triumph for sweet reason in the handling of the subject.

On December 1, 1657, Barbara Wingborough was arraigned as a witch before the general court but acquitted—no further record exists.[48] But we do have a few entries for the period from county court books of other cases and enactments concerning them. Lower Norfolk jurors, especially, had become incensed at the increase in gossip and accusation regarding witchcraft. They resolved to take severe measures against the principal culprits. On May 23, 1655, at a private court held "at the house of Mr. Edward Hall in Linhaven" they ordered:

Whereas div[rs] dangerous & scandalous speeches have beene raised by some psons concerning sev[r]all women in this Countie termeing them to be Witches, whereby their reputacons have beene much impaired, and theire lives brought in question (ffor avoydeing the like offence) It is by this Co[rt] ordered that what pson soer shall hereafter raise any such like scandall concerninge any partie whatsoev[r] and shall not be able to pve the same, both upon oath, and by sufficient witnes, such pson soe offending shall in the first place paie A thousand pounds of tob: and likewyse be lyeable to further Censure of the Co[rt].[49]

Four and a half years later, in December, 1659, the court showed that it meant business. Ann Godby was arraigned for "Slanders & scandalls Cast upon Women under the notion of Witches," especially for taking and abusing the good name of Mistress Robinson in this respect. After receiving several depositions attesting the scandalmongering, the court decided: "It is therefore ord[d] that the s[d] Tho: Godby [her husband] shall pay three hundred pounds of tob[o] & Caske fine for

47. McIlwaine, *Minutes,* 476.   48. *Ibid.,* 504.
49. E. D. Neill (ed.), "Witchcraft in Virginia," *William and Mary Quarterly,* Ser. 1, II (July, 1893), 58; also in *Lower Norfolk County Virginia Antiquary,* III (1899–1901), 152.

her Contempt of the menconed order, (being the first time) & also pay & defray the Cost of sute together with the Witnesses Charges at twenty pounds tob° p day als exec."[50]

Perhaps Thomas Godby and other husbands like him touched in that tender part, the purse, complained to their legislative representatives. Whether instigated by the burgesses from Lower Norfolk or not, the general assembly in 1662 passed "An Act for Punishment of Scandalous Persons" which gave the innocent husbands of such persons some protection.

Whereas many babling women slander and scandalize theire neighbours for which theire poore husbands are often involved in chargeable and vexatious suits, and cast in great damnages. Be it therefore enacted by the authorities aforesaid that in actions of slander occasioned by the wife after judgment passed for the damnages, the woman shall be punished by ducking and if the slander be soe enormous as to be adjudged at greater damnages then five hundred pounds of tob° then the woman to suffer a ducking for each five hundred pounds of tob° adjudged against the husband if he refuse to pay the tobacco.[51]

Thus during a period when the greatest English witch hunter, Matthew Hopkins, was at work,[52] Virginia colonists were becoming more and more skeptical regarding allegations of witchcraft—if we are to believe their treatment of such matters. And after the Restoration this skeptical treatment in general continued, as the 1662 enactment indicated that it might.

50. Neill (ed.), "Witchcraft in Virginia," *William and Mary Quarterly*, Ser. 1, II, 59; also in *Lower Norfolk County Virginia Antiquary*, IV (1902), 36.
51. "Acts of Grand Assemblie holden at James Cittie," (MS in Jefferson Collection, Library of Congress); also in William W. Hening, *The Statutes at Large; Being a Collection of All the Laws of Virginia from the First Session of the Legislature in the Year 1619* (13 vols.; New York, 1823; reprint facsimile, Charlottesville, Va. 1969), II, 166–67; and G. L. Chumbley, *Colonial Justice in Virginia* (Richmond, 1938), 129–30.
52. Kittredge, *Witchcraft*, 331–33.

In November, 1668, a judgment was secured before the general court for calling a woman and her children witches. Pardon was craved, though we do not know what the penalty was.[53] In 1671 in Northumberland County the local court or jury heard depositions accusing a prominent woman, wife of Captain Christopher Neal, of praying that evil befall certain persons. The first deposition was apparently that of a man (Edward Le Breton) who testified that he had heard Master Edward Cole defame Mrs. Neal in that way (he had already reported Cole's gossip of her putting death spells on people and cattle): "And further depose that now that his wife was sick he did accuse Mrs. Neal of it alsoe. But a certyne time he sent for Mrs. Neal to come to see his wife, and she did come and after that he saw her come over the threshhold where there is an horshoe nailed and that when she was by his wife shee prayed heartily for her he was then psuaded to the contrary again. And this I heard him relate of all that is above not 10 days since at the house of John Cockrell"[54] Others attest to Cole's defamation of the woman, and the record concludes with Cole's own acknowledgment of the truth of the depositions "as [to his] tending to defame her with the aspersion of being a witch." He admits that the words "were passionately spoken," and obligates himself to pay all costs of the suit. The whole case affords evidence that all the babblers were not women.[55]

Lower Norfolk County, which had indicated its exasperation with witch-accusers and scandalmongers, was still hav-

53. Another Robinson notation in McIlwaine, *Minutes*, 513. This may be the same woman mentioned in an entry of October 16, 1668: "Alice Stephens accused as a witch, but not cleared."
54. "The Good Luck Horseshoe," *William and Mary Quarterly*, Ser. 1, XVII (1909), 247–48.
55. Northumberland County, Record Book, 1666–72, pp. 179–81, 186–87. A number of depositions not printed in the *William and Mary Quarterly* (cf. note 56) appear in the original records; only a part of the apology was printed in *ibid*.

ing trouble after the Stuarts returned to the throne. Certain women continued to act in suspicious ways, and now even people of position in the county were accusing them. On June 15, 1675, the Lower Norfolk jury considered the charges of a justice of the peace and quondam member of the house of burgesses, Captain William Carver, against Joan or Jane, the wife of Lazarus Jenkins, "concerning her being familiar with evill spiritts and useing witchcraft &c."[56] Carver was a quarrelsome man, and there was already ill feeling between him and the Jenkinses recorded in a property suit. But the jury ordered a special investigative committee of men and women to "Repayre to the house of the said Lauzarus Jenkings upon the 17th of this Instant June and there to make diligent search concerning the same according to the 118 chapter of doulton."[57] If anything was found, she was to be dealt with after the report was returned to the jury. Presumably the women of this panel made the personal "investigation."

The order was of course that they search the body of the accused for secret witch's marks and probably her house for images. The most prominent of the marks, and the most usual, was the teat by which the devil was said to suck his victims and collaborators. It might be found in the privy parts or even behind the ear,[58] but it was most commonly dis-

56. *Ibid.*, III (January, 1895), 163–66. Carver was to end his life as one of the principal followers of Nathaniel Bacon in the rebellion.

57. Michael Dalton, *The Country Justice* (London, 1618). This manual prescribes tests for the detection of witches, including a discussion of the location of the teat or teats mentioned below.

58. See, for example, the testimony of John Bridgeman, Bishop of Chester, May 11, 1635 (*Pryings among Private Papers, Chiefly of the Seventeenth and Eighteenth Centuries. By the Author of "A Life of Sir Kenelm Digby,"* London, 1905). In Exeter in 1682, old women who were convinced that they were witches described "the sucking devils with saucer eyes so naturally that the Jury could not chose but believe them" (Lord Chief Justice North to Secretary of State Jenkins, August 19, 1682, in F. H. B. Daniell [ed.], *Calendar of State Papers, Domestic, Charles II* [London, 1932], 347).

covered beneath the left breast. Evidently the committee found nothing, for Jane Jenkins was not brought to trial.

The Lower Norfolk grand juries were not done with such searching, however. On January 15, 1678/9, John Salmon brought complaint that Mrs. Alice Cartwrite had bewitched his child and thus caused its death. This time the sheriff was ordered to summons for the next day "an able Jury of women" to "Serch the said Alice according to the direction of the Court." Their report was terse:

In the diff betweane Jno Salmon plaintiff agt Alice the wife of Thomas Cartwrite defendt a Jury of women (Mrs. Mary Chichester forewoman) being Impaneled did in open Court upon their oathes declare that they haveing delegently Searched the body of the said Alice & Cann find noe Suspitious marks whereby they Can Judg her to be a witch; butt onely what may and Is usuall on other women. It is therefore the Judgm^t of the Court and ordered that Shee bee acquitted & her husbands bond given for her appearance to bee given up.[59]

On July 8, 1698, John and Ann Byrd filed suit in the Princess Anne (formerly Lower Norfolk—the name was changed in 1691) court in two separate bills against Charles Kinsey and John Potts, who "falsely and Scandalously Defamed them." The accused men had said, among other things, that Ann had ridden Kinsey from his house to Elizabeth Russell's and had "rid [Potts] along the seaside & home to his own house, by which kind of Discourse they were Reported & rendered as if they were witches, or in league with the Devill."[60] Both defendants acknowledged that they had made such accusations, though one admitted that he might

59. Lyon G. Tyler (ed.), "Early Presidents of William and Mary," *William and Mary Quarterly*, Ser. 1, I (1893), 70; also in *Lower Norfolk County Virginia Antiquary*, I, (1895–96), 56–57.
60. "Riding" their victims was a favorite sport with witches, according to English folklore.

have dreamed of the ride. Evidently the jury had some doubts about the whole matter, or at least some prejudice against the plaintiffs as troublemakers, for both verdicts were rendered in favor of the defendants.[61]

The most famous Princess Anne County trial was that of Grace Sherwood in 1705/6, a date lying outside the period covered in other portions of this essay. Since origins of the case lie in the seventeenth century, however, it should be considered briefly. As early as February 4, 1697/8, and September 10, 1698, James and Grace Sherwood had sued Richard Capps, John and Jane Gisburne, and Anthony and Elizabeth Barnes for defamation or slander. The Gisburnes had said that Grace "was a witch and bewitched their piggs to death and bewitched their Cotton." Elizabeth Barnes avowed that "the said Grace came to her one night and rid her and went out of the key hole or crack of the door like a black Catt." As in the case of the Byrds at about the same time, the verdicts were rendered in favor of the defendants.[62]

By early 1706, Princess Anne County had obviously grown tired of Mrs. Sherwood as a general nuisance. Following a long series of investigations during the spring of 1705/6 inspired by the charges of Luke Hill and his wife, the case went to the general court (the governor and council) and the attorney general. The latter considered the charges too general and sent them back to the county. He suggested that a jury of women search Grace's house for suspicious images. This jury was summoned but refused to appear. A second

61. E. D. Neill (ed.), "Witchcraft in Virginia," *William and Mary Quarterly*, Ser. 1, II (1893), 59–60; also in *Lower Norfolk County Virginia Antiquary*, I (1895), 20–21.

62. "Record of Grace Sherwood's Trial for Witchcraft, in 1705, in Princess Anne County, Virginia," *Collections of the Virginia Historical and Philosophical Society*, I (Richmond, 1833), 69–78; Edward W. James, "Grace Sherwood, the Virginia Witch," *William and Mary Quarterly*, Ser. 1, III (1894–95), 99–100, 190–92, 242–45.

female panel was summoned to search her body as well as the house. They likewise declined to appear. On July 5, 1706, a county jury of justices of the peace, despairing of the feminine jury and wishing to settle the long-drawn-out affair, ordered Grace Sherwood "by her own Consent to be tried in the water by Ducking." Since the weather was rainy, the ordeal was postponed until the following Wednesday. On July 10 the said Grace was taken to John Harper's plantation and put into the water ". . . above mans Debth to try her how She Swims Therein, alwayes having Care of her life to preserve her from Drowning, and as Soon as she Comes Out that [the sheriff] request as many Ansient and Knowing women as possible he Cann to Serch her Carefully For all teats spotts and marks about her body not usual on Others . . . and further it is ord' that Som women be requested to Shift and Serch her before She goe into the water, that She Carry nothing about her to cause any Further Suspicion."[63]

The poor woman floated even though bound, and moreover was discovered afterwards (evidently the spectacle had attracted some women who were willing to search) to have on her private parts "two things like titts . . . of a Black Coller." According to Michael Dalton and other authorities, this evidence was sufficient to convict her as a witch. She was ordered to be committed to the "Common Gaol" and to be

63. For the best collection of the records of this case see George Lincoln Burr (ed.), *Narratives of the Witchcraft Cases, 1648–1706* (New York, 1914), 435–42. Mr. Burr examined the records personally, though many of them had been published earlier in the *William and Mary Quarterly* and the *Lower Norfolk County Virginia Antiquary*. For a description of a ducking platform and stool, see Susie M. Ames, *Studies of the Virginia Eastern Shore in the Seventeenth Century* (Richmond, 1940), 190; or E. M. Earle, *Curious Punishments of the Bygone Days* (New York, 1896), 18–20. The reader will recall from the Virginia Act of 1662 that ducking might be a punishment as well as a trial. Grace Sherwood may have accepted it in part as such.

secured in irons. But here the record ends. There is no indication of her appearing later before the general court. Almost
surely she survived further ordeal, for there is record of a
Grace Sherwood's will dated August 20, 1733, and probated
in 1740,[64] and all details indicate that the woman who was
ducked and the will-maker were one and the same. That the
name Witchduck, given the site of the ordeal on an inlet of
Lynnhaven Bay, still exists, is itself good evidence that such
methods of trial were extremely rare in Virginia.

But if we are to believe the detractors, all Satan's alleged
minions had not concentrated themselves in Princess Anne
County in the late seventeenth century. On November 1,
1694, in Westmoreland County, William Earle accused Phyl-
lis Money of casting a spell over Henry Dunkin's horse, of
teaching her daughter, Dunkin's wife, to be a witch, and of
having taught Dunkin himself to be a wizard. Though Phyl-
lis sued for damages, she received none. A year later Henry
Dunkin himself accused John Dunkin and his wife Elizabeth
of witchcraft and stated that Elizabeth boasted that she was
regularly sucked by the devil. Had this charge been proved,
she was liable to have been burnt at the stake. Instead, she
sued for forty thousand pounds of tobacco as damages; she
was awarded only forty.[65]

In King and Queen County in 1695 William Morris sued
a Mrs. Ball for accusing his wife Eleanor of sorcery. Just the
year before Mrs. Ball had been sure that Nell Cane had ridden her twice. Now the jury found Mrs. Ball guilty of defamation, five hundred pounds of tobacco being assessed in
favor of the plaintiff.[66]

64. Burr (ed.), *Narratives*, 442. See also James, "Grace Sherwood,"
William and Mary Quarterly, Ser. 1, IV (1895), 19–20. The will was
presented to the court October 1, 1740.
65. Bruce, *Institutional History*, I, 284.
66. Essex County, Orders, etc., 1692–95, *ibid.*, 285–86.

In most of these cases, had there been a strong belief in witchcraft on the part of the jury, the person accused would probably have been arrested and prosecuted on the original criminal charge. Instead, the person or persons originally accused were themselves the plaintiffs in civil suits. That they received small or no damages, or even dismissal, was probably because of the jury's belief that the actual harm to personal reputation was small. In other instances, especially when the originally accused was involved more than once in suits, the jury may have considered that the plaintiff, though wrongfully accused, was actually a nuisance to the community who had brought the scandal upon herself by boasting of supernatural powers, and that it would not encourage such a nuisance by awarding damages.

That his Satanic Majesty continued to exist as the great enemy of mankind was kept continually before later seventeenth-century Virginians by means other than the witchcraft cases. The stock phraseology in court records for many crimes, from petty thievery to child murder, was that the accused or convicted was "lead and instigated by the divell."[67] The devil's presence was felt too in trial by touch, when the suspected murderer was made to touch or stroke the body of his alleged victim. In Accomack County, for example, when Paul Carter touched the corpse the change in its appearance was proof that he was guilty.[68] Then too it must have been the devil who in 1676 bewitched the Indian boy, the son of Doegs. The apparently dead child recovered when he was

67. E.g., "Ordeal by Touch in Virginia," *Virginia Magazine of History and Biography*, IV (1896), 189, 192, 194. See also county records of Accomack and Northampton.

68. Accomack Wills, Deeds, & Orders, 1678–82, 159–60, in Bruce, *Institutional History*. See Ames, *Studies*, 175–76; "Ordeal by Touch in Virginia," *Virginia Magazine of History and Biography*, IV (1896), 159–60.

baptized.[69] This, incidentally, is the only extant end-of-the-century record even suggesting an active contemporary Indian connection with witchcraft.

Thus Satan seemed to at least a few to continue to honor Virginia with his presence. But the average Virginian of 1700 was apparently not at all convinced that Evil was incarnate, that it employed supernatural means through chosen human beings to tempt mankind. A few individuals, usually simple and superstitious country folk resentful of personal loss in family or property, looked around for a cause or outlet for their emotions. A busybody neighbor who might seriously or playfully pretend to occult powers was a natural candidate for suspicion. But for decades the Virginia justices and juries had critically weighed the charges of intercourse with Satan.[70] There is no evidence that any person was ever driven to confession. Indeed there is no evidence, even in the earlier part of the century, of self-confession—springing from personal hallucination—as had happened so often in other places. When formal or informal charges were made, the result in almost every instance, instead of being to bring the accused eventually to rope or fagot,[71] was that the accused brought suit for damages. The one severe punishment—exile and

69. Thomas Mathews, "The Beginning, Progress and Conclusion of Bacon's Rebellion," in *Narrations of the Insurrections, 1675–1690,* ed. Charles M. Andrews (New York, 1915), 18.

70. Perhaps it should be noted that as late as 1736 Virginia justices were warned that witchcraft was still a legal crime though its existence was the subject of controversy among learned men; that weak evidence should never be accepted but that most evidence would be circumstantial; and that conviction of first offense was punishable by one year in prison and quarterly pillory and confession, and conviction of second offense was a "Felony, without Clergy." See George Webb, *The Office and Authority of a Justice of the Peace* (Williamsburg, 1736), 361–62.

71. Despite the fact that the New England witches of the 1690s were hanged, there are many records of burnings in British history, especially in Scottish documents.

whipping—came only when a Scottish-born clergyman of the commonwealth period was the plaintiff or prosecutor. Usually the disposition made of the devil's alleged disciples remained in Virginia a secular and legal matter. That his Satanic Majesty made appearances in human form never got much acknowledgment from any Virginia lawyer or jury.

⌐⟨III⟩⌐

The Gentlest Art
in Seventeenth-Century Virginia

[The materials for this essay were gathered while I was a Fellow of the Folger Shakespeare Library. On this subject I originally planned a monograph five times the length of the present essay. I still have the rough draft of the longer work, which contains more generous excerpts from more epistolarians than are here included. A stout volume of highly interesting letters from seventeenth-century Virginia might be gathered. It would afford one of our best evidences that the early colonial could express himself, and in doing so would convey the spirit and fact of the times as does no other form of literature, including the promotion tract.

The agrarian South, including Virginia, was a natural nursery for the letter writer. The planters, living separated from one another and from friends and relatives across the Atlantic, expressed on paper their intellectual, spiritual, and business needs. Often they took real artistic pride in composing their epistolary essays. During Bacon's Rebellion they frequently wrote on politics, anticipating by almost a century the polemical tracts in letter form which marked the Parsons' Cause, the Pistole Fee Dispute, or the Stamp Act Crisis. In the hands of William Byrd II, as we shall see in a later essay, the letter was a character sketch, a gossip column, or a scientific treatise. The sons and grandsons of the seventeenth-century writers, as Richard Bland, Edmund Pendleton, Landon Carter, James Madison, and Thomas Jefferson were to fashion this artistic device into a weapon, and without sacrificing its grace and dignity of form, express in distinguished prose the spirit and reasoning of the American Whig. For the early Virginians, at least through the times of Francis Gilmer and John Randolph of Roanoke, the letter was a means of expressing all things to all men.]

THE VIRGINIA colonists of the seventeenth century survive most clearly today in their letters. The destruction of many official early records during the burning of Richmond in 1865, previous misplacement or destruction of similar records by the British during the Revolution, and the lack of a printing press as a formal outlet for written expression are among the reasons why manuscript epistolary communications afford the most abundant evidence of what the first Virginians thought and did. What they did is more frequently evident, perhaps, than what they thought. But there are several interesting testimonials to the fact that at least some of them were as genuinely pious and introspective as any of their kinsmen and neighbors to the north. And a study of a large body of these letters reveals a steadily evolving Virginia character, even though the author of a particular letter may have spent only a few years in the colony.

Subject and style vary according to the education of the writer, his reason for writing, and the portion of the century in which he lived. In external form, the letters range from rather stiff dedicatory epistles intended to introduce printed discourses, through official and semi-official correspondence of colonial administrators with the home government, to purely personal and relatively informal communications. Within any of these forms an account may be given of the voyage to the New World or the appearance of the country.

Letters which are almost promotional tracts are frequent: they may be official or personal. And an individual may criticize the government in the colony or at home in an official, a semi-official, or a personal communication. Financial and legal matters also are discussed at any level or in any form. Exhortations to build God's kingdom among the heathen, or expressions of satisfaction that the construction is well along, appear in printed dedications, in official correspondence, and in familiar letters. Introductions of individuals are usually personal but not necessarily so. Scientific data may be communicated in a business letter, a family letter, or an almost formal epistle intended for publication in the *Transactions* of the Royal Society.

Most of the letters, even to the end of the century, are written by men and women born in Great Britain and sometimes returning to the mother country before they die. As the century goes on, however, many of the most interesting and significant letters come from native-born Virginians like Francis Yeardley. Most letters are directed from Jamestown or some nearby plantation to England, but again the situation alters toward the end of the century, when Virginians are frequently communicating with Virginians, or much more rarely with New Yorkers or Pennsylvanians.

The earliest of even the purely personal epistles were quite clearly composed under a strong consciousness of rhetorical rules. Though the last letters of the period reflect the greater freedom of Dryden's prose and the fact that Addison and Defoe are just around the corner, the rhetorical tradition is still alive in many of them. Anyone who reads a considerable body of these letters and is already somewhat familiar with English literature of the century is immediately reminded of the popular English manuals for epistolarians which began to appear in the sixteenth century. These little volumes are really a part of the courtesy-book tradition and the rhetoric-text tradition. The rules and models presented in the more original and immediately practical of them would indicate that they may have been most useful to the colonial letter writer, for what he composed echoes them in many ways.

Inventories of several colonial libraries indicate that, toward the end of the century at least, the Virginia gentleman or business man felt that he should own one or more of these handbooks. Between 1688 and 1713, for example, the libraries bequeathed to their survivors by Arthur Spicer, Thomas Cocke, Thomas Walke, and Christopher Cocke contain such useful manuals as *The English Secretarie* (orig. ed. 1586), *The Young Secretary's Guide* (orig. ed. 1687?), and *The Young Clerk's Guide* (later version of *The Young Secretary's Guide*), often two of them in one library.[1] Since inventories of earlier libraries are exceedingly fragmentary or nonexistent for some periods and counties, it is entirely possible that the popular manuals were used by Virginians from the beginning of the colony. As indicated above, Virginia phrase and style often remind the reader of the model letters included in the manuals. And in subject and organization a colonial letter was most frequently a good example of a type represented in these same handbooks.

Editions of the manuals appeared again and again in the seventeenth century. Toward the end of the period new, more frankly utilitarian handbooks like J. Hill's *The Young Secre-*

1. "Libraries in Colonial Virginia," *William and Mary Quarterly*, Ser. 1, II (1894), 172–73; III (1894), 43 ff., 134; IV (1895), 15; (1895), 94. Later Virginians owned many others. For descriptions of these books see Katherine Lee Hornbeak, *The Complete Letter-Writer in English, 1568–1800*, Smith College Studies in Modern Languages, XV, Nos. 3–4 (April–July, 1934); and Jean Robertson, *The Art of Letter Writing: An Essay on the Handbooks Published in England during the Sixteenth and Seventeenth Centuries* (London, 1943). Also see Harry B. Weiss, *American Letter-Writers, 1698–1943* (New York, 1945).

tary's Guide; or a Speedy Help to Learning (mentioned above) even included illustrations of how to compose one's will, or gave "a Letter of Attorney from a Husband to a Wife upon a Voyage," or a letter from "A Wife to her Husband in Foreigne Parts." We know that many Virginians owned Hill's book.

Too much should not be made of these little guides, especially for the early years. Their subjects were the common interests of the age, and their turns of phrase its common property. The colonist who could indite a letter usually had a basic education in rhetoric and its principles entirely aside from what he may have learned from the letter-books. And from the nature of his new environment it was inevitable that he develop certain topics most fully.

I

Throughout the century the vast majority of letters are devoted to descriptions of the country, statements about the progress of agriculture and industry, analyses of factors which may have led to governmental shortcomings or failures, and discussions of the Indian problem. The official and personal letters of the reign of James I (1607–1625), particularly, describe the country and analyze the causes of failure to make rapid progress. The two subjects are of course interlocked, for glowing description might bring more settlers and solve a major problem of administration.

Perhaps what may be the earliest extant Virginia-Jamestown letter is a dedicatory epistle sent back to England with an account of the voyage just completed. It was composed by Robert Tindall, "Gunner," on June 22, 1607, two months after the first settlers landed, and is addressed to his friend and patron Prince Henry, whose interest in the colony was a source of comfort and pride to every venturer into the wilderness. Presumably, Tindall was not a man of much formal education. Yet his brief communication is rhetorically dignified. And it strikes the combined note of British manifest destiny and piety which were motivating factors throughout the colonial era.[2]

Other such early dedications are also in form and spirit open letters, such as that addressed "to the Reader" by R[obert] Rich in his *Newes from Virginia* (1610), a strong promotional tract. Rich, in his "blunt and plaine" style, cunningly urges Englishmen to plant themselves in the New World. There were to be a host of letters with the same intent.

Three more personal letters of the year 1608 inaugurate other patterns and purposes long to be followed in colonial epistolary communication. On June 16, Francis Perkins addressed a member of the household of Lord Cornwallis, analyzing the characters of the council in Virginia and soliciting the assistance of his addressee in obtaining for him a place among them.[3] On November 26, Captain Peter Wynne, a versatile young colonist, addressed a "Most noble knight" at home. Writing in an easy, loose, swinging prose, Wynne indicated that he was a man of some culture.

I was not so desirous to come into this Country, as I am now willing here to end my dayes: for I finde it a farr more pleasant, and plentifull country than any report made mencon of upon the River wch wee are seated I have gon six or seaven score miles, and

2. This letter is printed in Edward Arber and A. G. Bradley (eds.), *Travels and Works of Captain John Smith* (Edinburgh, 1910), I, xxxviii–ix. For other letters here mentioned, consult E. G. Swem, *Virginia Historical Index* (Roanoke, Va., 1934–36). For most seventeenth-century letters now in Europe, see the *Survey Reports* of the Virginia 350th Anniversary Celebration, Colonial Records Project (1956–65?), issued jointly by the Virginia State Library and the University of Virginia Library.

3. A. G. Brown, *Genesis of the United States* (2 vols.; Boston, 1897), I, 173–77.

so farr is navigable; afterward I travailed between 50 or 60 myles by land, into a Country Called Monacon who owe no subiection to Powaton; this Land is very high ground and fertill, being very full of very delicate springs of sweet water: the ayre more helthfull than the place wher wee are seated, by reason it is not subiect to such fogges and mistes as we continually have. the people of Monacon speak a farr differing Language from the subiectes of Powaton, theyr pronunciation being very like welsh so that the gentlemen in o^r Company desired me to be theyr Interpretor. . . .[4]

In October, Captain John Smith addressed a letter to the treasurer and council for Virginia which set a precedent for what was to be another persistent colonial trait. It gave fair warning that the colonial administrator would not then or later accept unfair or ignorant criticism from his superiors at home without answering back. In it Captain Smith answers point by point a series of accusations of intra-colonial quarrelling, summarizes the shortcomings of his rivals, Captains Newport and Radcliffe, and demonstrates the impracticability of certain schemes of exploration and gold hunting and the utter inadequacy of the provisions supplied. Smith begins by acknowledgment of the council's letter and by begging that they will pardon "if I offend you with my rude Answer." The rest is the reply of a man moved by righteous anger: "Though I be no scholar, I am past the schoole-boy; and I desire but to know, what either you, and those here [his Virginia detractors], doe know but that I have learned to tell you by the continuall hazard of my life. I have not concealed from you any thing I know; but I feare some cause you to believe much more then is true." His withering fire is then directed at Newport and Radcliffe. As to the latter, he "is now called *Sickle-*

4. M. P. Andrews, *Virginia: The Old Dominion* (Richmond, Va., 1949), 39–40; or H. M. Jones, *The Literature of Virginia in the Seventeenth Century* (Boston, 1946), 4.

more, a poore counterfeited Imposture. I have sent him home, least the company should cut his throat. What he is, now every one can tell you:. if he and *Archer* returne againe, they are sufficient to keep us always in factions." After several more such "suggestions," Smith concludes: "These are the causes that have kept us in *Virginia,* from laying such a foundation, that ere this might have given much better content and satisfaction, but as yet you must not looke for any profitable returne: so I humbly reste." Terse, bitter, ironic, bold, Smith's has been called "Hotspur rhetoric." The good captain was certainly master of at least two letter manual forms—the "Epistle Invective" and the "Epistle Accusatory."[5]

Other governors during Virginia's first decade also wrote personal as well as official letters home. Sir Thomas Dale analyzed the reasons for the troubles of the colony and suggested a series of frontier forts as one solution.[6] Sir Samuel Argall described the voyage over and, with some relish, the treacherous trick by which Pocahontas was betrayed into his hands.[7] Thus he anticipated what many considered the unscrupulousness of his later administration of the colony. George Percy, brother of the Earl of Northumberland, twice briefly governor in the colony, set a now familiar precedent by begging financial assistance from his elder brother at home.[8]

5. For information on Smith, see Arber and Bradley (eds.), *Travels and Works,* II, 442–45. For "Hotspur rhetoric," see Moses Coit Tyler, *History of American Literature, 1607–1676* (New York, 1878), 29. For examples of the types of letters, see Angel Day, *The English Secretarie* (London, 1592), Pt. II.

6. Sir Thomas Dale to the Earl of Salisbury, March 17, 1611, in Brown, *Genesis,* I, 501–508.

7. June, 1613. Sir Samuel Argall, *Purchas His Pilgrimes* (Glasgow, 1909), XIX, 90–95.

8. George Percy to the Earl of Northumberland, August 17, 1611, in Brown, *Genesis,* I, 500–501.

One should note also in reviewing these letters of the colonial administrators of the first decade that the best-remembered work of William Strachey, first secretary to the colony, is his account of a storm at sea included in a private letter in 1610 addressed to an "excellent lady." One of the widely read rhetorical prose descriptions of natural phenomena in English, it is generally conceded to be the source of Shakespeare's own *Tempest*.[9] Though the letter is connected as much with Bermuda as with Virginia, through Strachey's other writings in and about the mainland colony he has come to be accepted as one of the major writers of Virginia's first generation.[10]

Two other personalities of this first decade survive in several letters. One of these gentlemen, the Reverend Alexander Whitaker, has left in his communications what is perhaps our best evidence of the Puritan temper which dominated the religious outlook of the colony under James I.[11] He described Indian dances and Indian "witchcraft." He begged that young clerics who had refused to subscribe to the Act of Conformity come to the colony, where they would not be troubled.[12] Equally pious and far more introspective in his outpourings was that curious cavalier Master John Rolfe, father of the tobacco industry and, with his wife Pocahontas, ancestor of hundreds of thousands of today's Americans. To any reader accustomed to think of early Virginia character in terms of forthright men of action such as Captain John Smith, Rolfe's letter to his friend Governor Dale is one of the astonishing documents to issue from the colony. No Puritan judge

9. Argall, *Purchas His Pilgrimes*, XIX, 5–7.
10. See, *e.g.*, H. M. Jones, *Literature of Virginia*, 24–26.
11. George M. Brydon, *Virginia's Mother Church and the Political Conditions under Which It Grew* (Richmond, Va., 1947), 8, 22–29.
12. Brown, *Genesis*, I, 499–500; Alexander Whitaker, *Good Newes from Virginia* (London, 1613); Argall, *Purchas His Pilgrimes*, XIX, 95–102.

wrestling with his soul after the witchcraft trials could have probed for motive and justification more profoundly than did this Virginia planter preparing to marry an Indian maiden. Some of his mixture of motives emerge even in one sample paragraph among the eight long pages of text. This is also a fair representation of his language and prose style.

Let therefore this my well advised protestation, which here I make betweene God and my own conscience, be a sufficient witness, at the dreadfull day of judgement (when the secret of all mens harts shall be opened) to condemne me herein, if my chiefest intent and purpose be not to strive with all my power of body and minde, in the undertaking of so mighty a matter, no way led (so farre as mans weaknesse may permit) with the unbridled desire of carnall affection: but for the good of this plantation, for the honour of our countrie, for the glorie of God, for my owne salvation, and for the converting to the true knowledge of God and Jesus Christ, an unbelieving creature, namely Pokahuntas. To whom my hartie and best thoughts are, and have a long time bin so intangled, and inthralled in so intricate a laborinth, that I was even aweared to unwinde myselfe thereout. But almighty God, who never faileth his, that truely invocate his holy name, hath opened the gate, and led me by the hand that I might plainly see and discerne the safe paths wherein to tread.[13]

During the second decade of Jamestown history, when the affairs of the colony in London were in the hands of the Southampton-Sandys-Ferrar coalition, most of the extant letters were written by two "liberal" governors and two university-bred "literary" men. Voyagers, planters, burgesses, clergymen, and even an occasional indentured servant are represented, however, among the epistolarians. Perhaps most

13. Lyon Gardiner Tyler (ed.), *Narratives of Early Virginia, 1606–1625* (New York, 1907), 240–41; "Letters from John Rolfe to Sir Thomas Dale," *Virginia Magazine of History and Biography,* XXII (1914), 152–57. Rolfe's letters to Sir Edwin Sandys are in Susan Myra Kingsbury (ed.), *Records of the Virginia Company of London* (4 vols.; Washington, D.C., 1906–1936), III, 70–73.

interesting among the lesser officials was George Thorpe, formerly Gentleman of His Majesty's Privy Chamber and member of Parliament, and Virginia deputy in charge of the lands of the proposed college at Henrico, who survives in three optimistic letters concerned with the state of the colony in the two years before the 1622 massacre. Among other things, Thorpe documents the birth of American bourbon whiskey by mentioning that "wee have found a waie to make soe good drinke of Indian corne as I protest I have divers times refused to drink good stronge English beare and chosen to drinke that."[14]

Sir George Yeardley, several times governor and a champion of representative government, has left a correspondence which reveals him most fully for what we might guess he was from other sources—earnest, sincere, scantily educated, shrewd in business and as much concerned with building the first private fortune in English-speaking America as with his official duties.[15] His equally "liberal" successor, Sir Francis Wyatt, of better family and education, has left letters remarkable for their quiet calmness in a troubled period, for their dry wit, and for their remarkably able analyses of theories and practical problems in government. Wyatt shows the philosophic mind of Renaissance cast more frequently evident among those who did not visit America.[16]

The most entertaining in content and polished in style of the letters appearing in the colony's second decade, however, are those from the pen of that versatile gentleman John Pory. M.A. of Cambridge, M.P. for Bridgewater, author and translator, experienced lesser diplomat, Pory arrived in Virginia in

14. Kingsbury, (ed.), *Records*, III, 417–18.
15. *Ibid.*, 29–31, 297–300, 452–53.
16. "Letter of Sir Francis Wyatt, Governor of Virginia, 1621–1626," *William and Mary Quarterly*, Ser. 2, VI (1926), 114–21.

April, 1619, as secretary of the council and on July 30 became first speaker of the new general assembly, the first representative legislative body of English America. Pory remained in Virginia until August, 1622, exploring, talking, and writing. He came back again in 1624 and talked and wrote again. On his return to England after the second visit he became a professional letter writer!

Pory's letters show him to have been something of a tosspot and a worldly intriguer, but a graceful writer, and withal a man of charm and intelligence. Restless curiosity, real relish for the New World's strange and wonderful aspects and the consciousness that he must picture Virginia as "Earth's onlie Paradis" are some qualities of the man shown in his letters. These letters have been quoted again and again, but not even a brief consideration of Virginia's epistolary art would be complete without at least one famous passage from them. After acknowledging the uncouthness of this wild place where ships come in freighted more with ignorance than anything else, Pory rationalizes romantically: "At length being hardned to this custome of abstinence from curiosity, I am resolved wholly to minde my business here, and nexte after my penne, to have some good book alwayes in store, being in solitude the best and choicest company. Besides among these Christall rivers, & odoriferous woods I doe escape muche expense, envye, contempte, vanity, and vexation of minde."[17] One is reminded here of a sentence in a model letter included in Nicholas Breton's *Poste with a Packet of Madde Letters* (London, 1602), a manual Pory surely knew. "Now for my health, I thank God, I need no physicke, and for my Purse, it hath vent enough for letting my money grow rusty; and for

17. John Pory to an unidentified "Noble Lord," September 30, 1619, in Kingsbury (ed.), *Records,* III, 222.

my minde, to telle the truth, it is with God and thee."[18] Thus the Virginia legislator sits squarely in the rhetorical tradition.

After Pory came the 1622 massacre by the Indians. In the years immediately following the catastrophe, letters addressed to England reveal sharply the terrors and tensions of the survivors. Pathetic, even genuinely tragic letters from poor rustic indentured servants, hungry and frightened, are among them.[19]

During 1622–1623 George Sandys, who had arrived in the autumn of 1621 to be resident treasurer for the colony, addressed to friends and officials at home a series of personal letters reflecting his views of the desperate situation. Sandys, who was director of industry and collector of tobacco revenues, was also an Oxford-educated poet who spent what time he could snatch from "night and repose" in his verse translation of Ovid's *Metamorphoses*. The six extant personal letters in his autograph are the best surviving analyses of the state of affairs. They also suggest remedies, blame unsympathetic officials at home including his brother Sir Edwin and the two Ferrars, and present a trenchant appraisal of the personnel of the Virginia resident governing council.[20] These communications, with those of his nephew-in-law Sir Francis Wyatt, mark the end of the Jacobean period of Virginia history.

The beautiful rhetoric so characteristic of the age appears among these letters when certain situations call for dignity and formality; it is reduced to simpler and plainer forms when the writer is tense or angry or terror stricken. Quiet courage, the excitement of actual or potential discovery, despair, ill-

18. "A familiar letter to a friend in the Country," in Nicholas Breton, *Poste with a Packet of Madde Letters* (London, 1602).

19. See, for example, Kingsbury (ed.), *Records*, IV, 41, 58; also Richard Freethorne to friends and parents, *ibid.*, 38–39, 42, 59.

20. All these letters are reproduced in *ibid.*, III and IV; and in R. B. Davis, *George Sandys, Poet-Adventurer* (London and New York, 1955).

ness, and approaching death are all here. And piety as genuine and deep as that of Pilgrim or Puritan has left its unmistakable impression amid these natural outpourings of mind and soul. These letters represent the heroic pioneer age of Virginia colonization. After 1624, under the crown of Charles I and the Protectorate of Cromwell, Virginia entered into the era of settlement.

II

Few familiar letters are extant from the period of Charles I and the commonwealth. There are some official or semiofficial letters written by individuals in the 1630s, almost nothing save official records in the turbulent 1640s, and a handful of highly interesting, gracefully styled personal letters in the 1650s.

The two most interesting letters of the 1650–1660 decade were to and from Francis Yeardley, Virginia-born second son of Sir George Yeardley, and almost surely namesake of good Sir Francis Wyatt. The first letter was addressed to Yeardley, then living in Lower Norfolk near the Carolina border, by Mrs. Susan Moseley, wife of a recent European immigrant who had been a merchant in Rotterdam. Implicit in her discussion of business is a settled and quiet country (southeastern Virginia) in striking contrast to the harried frontier described or implied in earlier epistles. The reader notices too the relative simplicity of diction—as compared with that of earlier letters —with which Mrs. Moseley arranges a trade of cattle for the jewelry she and her husband brought from the Old World.[21]

The letter from Francis Yeardley was addressed to his father's old friend John Ferrar, then living in retirement at

21. "Families of Lower Norfolk and Princess Anne Counties: Moseley Family of Lower Norfolk County," *Virginia Magazine of History and Biography*, V (1897–98), 327–29.

Little Gidding in Huntingdonshire. This long communication, a link between founding father and mature first generation native-born American, is significant also as one of the earliest descriptive accounts of a portion of North Carolina. It pictures negotiations with the Indians under the happiest circumstances, the conversion of friendly chiefs, and the ethnological differences among the tribes.[22]

This is a courteous, graceful letter written by a man who had seen England only as a schoolboy. As in other letters of the decade, spelling was becoming more uniform, and rhetoric less florid and perhaps less picturesque. In these things, consciously and unconsciously, the Virginia writer was following English trends. Yet other things natively American were beginning to manifest themselves. George Sandys had once called the Indians the true Virginians. And Richard Freethorne had been bitter when he classified his fellow immigrants as the "old" and "new" Virginians. Now Francis Yeardley was proud to call himself a Virginian and to speak of the colony as his country. Yeardley was genuinely religious, but the Puritan piety of the earlier Whitaker variety seems to have been displaced by an emotion we may call patriotism.

III

From the Restoration to the end of the century, Virginia saw a rapidly increasing population and prosperity, the genesis and dissolution of Bacon's Rebellion, and the founding of the College of William and Mary. Most of the surviving letters are official or semi-official, but variety of subject increases even among these. At least four governors or acting governors were able epistolarians, two of them perhaps distinguished in the

22. Francis Yeardley to John Ferrar, May 8, 1654, from "Virginia, Linne-Haven." This letter has been reproduced several times, *e.g.,* in J. H. R. Yeardley, *Before the Mayflower* (London, 1931), 362–66.

art. Other significant letters were written by two secretaries of state, two or three clergymen, the wife of Nathaniel Bacon, a sea captain, a reformed Old World embezzler, and several plantation owners whose names survived in their descendants for many generations. Reports of the state of the colony, of battles with the Indians or Dutch, of scientific data, of the great Rebellion, love letters, begging letters, letters of introduction, and letters of advice to the youthful, as well as a growing and brisk business correspondence, enlarge the earlier trickle of literate communication into a mighty stream.

Governor Sir William Berkeley, a former court wit, scholar, and playwright, wrote letters on many topics over a fourteen-year period. All reveal a vigorous, even graceful stylist, and most of them demonstrate the cruel intransigence, impatience, and irascibility assigned to him by history and legend.[23] Another able administrator and acting governor, Nicholas Spencer, survives among the epistolarians chiefly for an early letter (June 13, 1672) to a relative at home describing in graphic and to us comic detail his "hypochondriac" symptoms.[24] His skill as a colonial official must be realized from other documents. Likewise Lieutenant Governor Sir Henry Chicheley is most entertaining when he indites a brief, homely letter to his niece in England;[25] his official correspondence is valuable for other reasons.

The most personally revealing among the gubernatorial epistolarians is Lord Howard of Effingham, a number of whose unpublished letters reached this country from two

23. Most of Berkeley's letters are reproduced in *Virginia Magazine of History and Biography*. See also Swem, *Index*.
24. "Letter from Nicholas Spencer to His Brother," *William and Mary Quarterly*, Ser. 2, III (1923), 134–136.
25. Sir Henry Chicheley to his niece, February 16, 1673/4, in Lady Newton (ed.), *Lyme Letters, 1660–1760* (London, 1925), 64.

different sources.[26] Effingham, who came to Virginia to make a fortune for himself and curb the unruliness of the colonial legislative assembly, has come down to us as a most unpopular viceroy. In his speeches, proclamations, and official letters Effingham addressed Virginians as though they were recalcitrant schoolboys, and the king as though he were divine master; but in the letters to his wife and to William Blathwayt, the secretary of the Lords of Trade and Plantation, he is much more attractive. These letters contain pleasant glimpses of plantation life, of religious habits, of Indian tribesmen. Once in a homesick mood he begs his wife to have her "picture drawn to ye knees or at lenth . . . by a good hand, & in some pritty neat dress, pray let it be as like y^u as possible wth ye Mole on yor brest." And after describing the jolly social life of his neighbors, he concludes that "So y^t any person y^t can content himself wth a Country life may live as happily here as in any p^t of England, & as plentifully, but I judge with little difference from charge."[27]

One of the most voluminous of extant correspondences is that of Thomas Ludwell, for many years secretary of state, a man who wrote regularly to officials and friends at home in behalf of the colony. Usually he is devoted to such matters as the state of the tobacco industry; a description of a battle between the Dutch and Virginia fleets in Hampton Roads; or a protest of the planters against the policy of sending over so many "Rogues and ill people." These accounts, with the exception of that of the sea fight, are not very lively. But when

26. One group, the Lord Monson Papers, is in the Manuscript Division of the Library of Congress; the other, the Blathwayt Papers, is in the Archives of Colonial Williamsburg, Inc., Williamsburg, Va.

27. Lord Howard of Effingham to his wife, February 28, [16]83, in Lord Monson Papers. Published with the kind permission of Lord Monson.

he describes natural phenomena or recounts explorations, Ludwell shows a realism and a dramatic sense which make pleasant, almost thrilling, reading. To Lord Berkeley of Stratton, the governor's brother, he presents in awesome detail the succession of "providences" which have put Virginia in a miserable financial condition. To Lord Arlington, secretary in the home government, he gives an entrancing account of an exploring expedition sent by Berkeley to the blue mountains.[28] Here the reader of American prose may in some degree anticipate the accounts of the great western explorations of the eighteenth and nineteenth centuries, and see also the mysterious white cliffs, stark mountains, and rising fogs of Poe's *Narrative of A. Gordon Pym*.

Since George Sandys' time the Virginia letter writer had communicated with collectors of curiosities and with scientists. Ludwell, for example, supplied much meteorological data. William Byrd I, John Clayton, and Alexander Moray, among others, sent back to the Royal Society and to individuals botanical specimens, small animals, Indian relics, and above all objective scientific descriptions. These letters are also significant for other things. For example, Moray's keen analysis of the Scottish character as it was and would be in America is remarkable self- and tribe-examination. And his yearning for the idyllic life is met with in several other literary documents of colonial Virginia. "Could a publick good, consist with a hermetick condition, I should prefere it before all others, but the nixt to it which is the settling in a wilderness of milk and honey: non can know the sweetness of it: but he who tastes it: one ocular inspection, one aromatick smel of our woods: one hearing of the consert of our birds in those

---

28. See Swem, *Index*, and *Virginia Magazine of History and Biography*, IV (1897), 230–245; XIX (1911), 30, 32, 33, 82, 353–56, 360–61; XX (1912), 19–22, 132–33, 357–59.

woods would affect more than 1000 reported stories let the authors be never so readible."[29]

By the latter third of the century the tradition of a landed gentry was firmly established in Virginia. Many letters represent in one way or another that tradition. For example, the courtesy book letter-of-advice-to-children form and idea are followed by the handsome and profligate Colonel Daniel Parke when from England he addresses one of his (legitimate) daughters in Virginia.[30] William Byrd I writes a similar letter to his more famous son, who was just then ready to begin his studies at the Inns of Court.[31]

The last and perhaps the best of the seventeenth-century epistolarians was William Fitzhugh. The series of letters this frontier Virginian wrote—and kept copies of—reveals how steady and painless a development the rise into the colonial aristocracy might be.[32] As Fitzhugh was a practicing barrister, his communications are concerned with legal business. But his interests were many. He was always a conscious stylist, referring frequently to his struggles with the written word, striving for felicitous phrase and well-turned sentence, at his best quite successful. "I must confess I want abilitys to polish & adorn my expressions with that Elegance & sweetness of stile your two letters I this year receiv'd are full freighted with, yet I'll endeavour to supply that defect with a true sincerity & ardent zeal to assure you of my most hearty af-

29. Alexander Moray to the Royal Society, June 12, 1665, *William and Mary Quarterly*, Ser. 2, II (1922), 159–61.
30. Colonel Daniel Parke to his daughter, 1697, *Virginia Magazine of History and Biography*, XX (1912), 275–76.
31. William Byrd I to his son, July 25, 1690, *ibid.*, XXVI (1918), 131.
32. See L. B. Wright, *The First Gentlemen of Virginia* (San Marino, Calif., 1940), 312–21; the Fitzhugh letters are in *Virginia Magazine of History and Biography*, I–VII; and in an annotated edition in R. B. Davis (ed.), *William Fitzhugh and His Chesapeake World 1676–1701* (Chapel Hill, 1963).

faction & real propensity which your generous worth obliges & obliging favours binds me to, & shall be always ready to court all occasion to demonstrate the same."[33]

With his correspondence this Virginia letter writer indicates that the settlement which followed the frontier was now grown into a confident, stable, moderately prosperous agrarian society. But he indicates much more. In Fitzhugh is the sense of public obligation, the love of the rural Horatian life, the study of the classics to bring aesthetic delight or to learn of the problems of practical government, the kind of loneliness that brings the country gentleman to communicate through his pen. In other words, the last of the seventeenth-century letter writers goes far toward explaining the mind, manners, and mode of expression, as well as the quantity and variety of that expression, of Thomas Jefferson.

33. William Fitzhugh to Nicholas Hayward, April 22, 1686, in *Virginia Magazine of History and Biography*, I (1893–94), 396–97.

⌐◦(IV)◦⌐

Chesapeake Pattern and Polestar:
William Fitzhugh in His Plantation World,
1676–1701

[Since this capsule portrait of a Virginia founding father was first read before the American Philosophical Society in Philadelphia, I have edited and published all Fitzhugh's known letters and speeches and his will. This sketch still seems pertinent, however, in a gathering of essays concerned with early society and thought in the colony, for it shows how a fortune and an aristocrat could be made in one generation. Fitzhugh may have been no more articulate or varied in his interests than such family-founders as Robert Beverley I or Richard Lee II, but it is *his* expressions of himself which survive. The curious reader can know Fitzhugh as he can never know the others. If the reader is a Virginian, he may have the blood of all three in his veins. Certainly Virginia history is in great part, through the Civil War, the record of the actions of the descendants of these men and a few dozen of their contemporaries mingled with the actions of lesser known men and women.

William Fitzhugh was a man of his time, shrewd and pious. An early land speculator, he made a fortune by the same sort of maneuvers through which his descendants pushed on into the West. He was a lawyer as well as a planter. Though the profession of law did not further his career in politics, it was a means of augmenting his fortune. In the long view, his combination of agriculture, law, and politics, guided by the principle of moderation, prepared the way for his descendants' continued rise in the world.]

THANKS TO AN admiring son or grandson who had his progenitor's letters copied into a bound ledger, we know today more about William Fitzhugh than perhaps about any other seventeenth-century American planter. The letters lead to Virginia colony and county records (which include letters to the commission of the peace, speeches in the house of burgesses, entries in litigation, etc.), which fill in some of the finer lines or colors of the epistolary self-portrait. It is possible now to present a faithful, and I think lively, picture of an individual planter and, what may be equally interesting, of the world in which he lived.

Fitzhugh's letters have been referred to in print for more than a century, and in the 1890s a badly garbled version of most of them, with little explanatory addenda, was published in a historical journal, copies of which are now hard to come by.[1] Since then they have been used in historical studies several times, notably by Louis B. Wright, Howard Mumford Jones, and Harvey Wish.[2] Only recently, however, with the bringing to light of the early copy, in the possession of a distinguished Philadelphia physician (Dr. Thomas Fitz-Hugh) has it been possible to assess the full significance of the letters and their contents accurately and comprehensively.

The story of William Fitzhugh is, from one point of view, the traditional American success story—Log-Cabin-to-White-

1. The first five volumes of the *Virginia Magazine of History and Biography* (1893–97).

2. Respectively in L. B. Wright, *The First Gentlemen of Virginia* (San Marino, Calif., 1940); H. M. Jones, "The Literature of Virginia in the Seventeenth Century," in *Memoirs of the American Academy of Arts and Sciences* (1946), XIX (2); and Harvey Wish, *Society and Thought in Early America* (New York, 1950).

House, Immigrant-Boy-to-Millionaire. It is also the story of the making of a southern aristocrat, or of the transplanted Englishman, or of the combination of mercantile, agricultural, and professional abilities and incentives which went into the making of individual success in the New World. But it is above all the story of one man in the shaping of a culture.

In 1670, about the date of nineteen-year-old William Fitzhugh's arrival in America, the Chesapeake civilization had existed for more than two full generations. Perhaps through family relationships in his native Bedford, Fitzhugh appears on the records first in a community which contained several Bedfordshire gentlemen—Westmoreland county in the Northern Neck of Virginia. His own family, mayors and aldermen of the city of Bedford and lesser gentry from the region about that county seat, were influential enough in a modest way to have moved emigrant fellow county-dwellers in his behalf, though later Fitzhugh was to insist that he had always struggled alone in the New World and had come to a moderate success, with God's help, through his own "mean endeavours."[3]

He came into a rapidly expanding and still frontier world such as America would remain until the end of the nineteenth century. The great difference between his frontier and the later (intra-continental) ones was the relative ease of communication with the center of civilization, London. For London ships could and did anchor off his own wharves in front of his dwelling house on the Potomac, and shipmasters brought the latest news, books, clothing, and other comforts.

Though Fitzhugh brought little or no property with him, he did bring a legal education which was to stand him in

3. William Fitzhugh (Virginia) to his cousin William Fitzhugh (London), May 18, 1685, in R. B. Davis (ed.), *William Fitzhugh and His Chesapeake World, 1676–1701* (Chapel Hill, 1963), 169–70.

good stead. In the early 1670s he appears in several of the Northern Neck county records, particularly in Westmoreland, as a practicing attorney. Then he married Sarah Tucker, the very young (she was between eleven and thirteen) daughter of a wealthy widow who was his client. Through his wife he was related to half the more prosperous families of Westmoreland and several counties across the Potomac in Maryland. By 1676 he was settled in neighboring Stafford, a real frontier county stretching up the Potomac beyond the present Alexandria and Washington—sparsely populated, and during his lifetime subject to Indian raids, alarms, and murders. Here he spent the rest of his relatively short life (he died at fifty) except for one possible trip to England in 1699–1700, seasonal excursions to Jamestown for the meeting of the general assembly and the transaction of legal business, and rounds of the neighboring county courts as practicing attorney. His letters indicate his steady rise economically, politically, and professionally. They reveal also a sense of proportion, an ideal of moderation, a genuine piety which he kept always before him. They show that the constant threat of the barbaric Indians and the wild loneliness of vast stretches of virgin forest could and did exist side by side with active and gracious, even sophisticated, social life; with busy free enterprises in both manufacturing and agriculture; with English common law administered calmly and judicially; with an almost serene practicing philosophical idealism rooted in the concept of the Horatian, or middle way.

Fitzhugh's friends, colleagues, and clients among his correspondents included large-scale planters like Robert Beverley and Ralph Wormeley of Middlesex; New England-born Isaac Allerton of Westmoreland, son and grandson of two of the more eminent *Mayflower* pilgrims; and Thomas Mathews, author of a history of Bacon's Rebellion. In his own county lived the two George Masons. In Jamestown his correspondents included two or three colonial governors, the attorney general, fellow lawyers, and members of the council and house of burgesses. He also corresponded with his factors and other merchants in London and Bristol, with several dozen ship captains, with officials and friends in Maryland, and after 1684, with his Fitzhugh relatives in England.

Like many another Englishman abroad, Fitzhugh for many years remained homesick. Again and again he offered his Virginia plantation for sale through his London friends so that he might buy a comparable estate in the mother country. In April, 1686, when he was thirty-five, he sent a description of his property to his brother-in-law, Dr. Ralph Smith (then on business in London), for possible use in negotiating its sale or exchange. Considering that the owner was at the time a prosperous man, but by no means the wealthiest man of his region, one may add to or deduct from the picture to visualize almost any Virginia or Maryland plantation of the period—a thousand-acre tract, seven-tenths wooded and the remainder fertile arable land. Three units or "quarters" for the Negroes were equipped with all necessary houses, fences, and livestock. A thirteen-room main dwelling contained four large rooms hung with tapestries, nine in all well furnished. This and the smaller "dependent" houses were equipped with good brick chimneys. There were four good cellars (the deep freezes of the age), a dairy, a dovecote, a stable, a barn, a henhouse, and a kitchen, all rather new. Nearby an orchard of 2,500 apple trees was entirely enclosed by a locust fence. A fenced one-hundred-foot-square garden, and a great "palisadoed" yard (perhaps as protection against the Indians) enclosed most of the dependencies, as well as cattle, hogs, sheep, horses, and household servants. About a mile and a half distant stood a grist-mill which more than paid its own way.

Two storehouses of food and textiles and farm equipment enough to last for two or three years completed the inventory.

There were twenty-nine Negroes in all. What he does not enumerate are the white indentured servants, many of them skilled artisans, and perhaps the bluecoat schoolboy who could keep accounts. When Fitzhugh died he had six men and one old woman in this status. One of the men was his own young cousin, another a carpenter, another a glazier, and another, a "signature" witness to his will, perhaps the former student of Christ's Hospital.[4]

Despite this early prosperity, Fitzhugh was sometimes uneasy and restless. As he explained to his friend Nicholas Hayward of London (January 30, 1686/7):

Our estates here depend altogether upon Contingencys, & to prepare against that, causes me to exceed my Inclinations in worldly affairs, & Society that is good & ingenious is very scarce, & seldom to be come upon except in books. Good Education of Children is almost impossible, & better be never born than ill bred, but that which bears the greatest weight with me, for I now look upon my self to be in my declining age, is the want of spirituall help & comforts, of which this fertile Country in every thing else, is barren and unfruitfull[.]

Contingencies kept him at worldly affairs all his life, and steadily he added to the worldly possessions which were his at this time. Charged against his tobacco credits with Bristol and Liverpool and London merchants were necessities of life and luxuries of gracious living. For plantation operation he ordered cart wheels, harness, saddles, two stills, a pewter cistern, cider "racks," and smaller things such as stone jugs and nails. For the great house he wanted tapestries, leather hangings, beds and bed furniture, curtains and valances,

4. William Fitzhugh to John Cooper, his London factor, August 20, 1690, in *ibid.*

matching chairs, leather and Turkey carpets, dress boxes, diamond-shaped panes for his windows, iron and brass andirons, iron backs for chimneys, an escritoire, picture frames, and a large looking glass. Of gastronomic and potable comforts he particularly wanted spice, fruit, sugar, Gloucestershire cheese, and cases of claret. For his wife and himself he ordered clothing of many kinds, including in his last years a black crepe gown and petticoat and pair of gallooned shoes for her, and a calico quilted morning gown, winter and summer suits, and two Carolina hats for himself. After many attempts he at last secured a light carriage which he called a *callash,* and later a larger coach.

As he grew more prosperous and more reconciled to living out his life in the colony, Fitzhugh ordered greater and greater quantities of silver plate (several pieces of which survive today in the possession of his descendants). As he observed, the silver would have a ready cash value and would be a secure and easily-divided legacy to his several sons. It also made the proper impression upon distinguished guests at his table; Lieutenant-Governor Nicholson, Fitzhugh wrote, had "first handsell'd" one recent silver importation. From 1687 to his last extant letters of 1698 he ordered candlesticks, snuffers, salt cellars, "basons," forks, (silver hafted) knives, castors, various sizes of spoons, porringers, plates, sugar bowls, ladles, etc., all to be engraved with his arms or crest, though in the last years he had a servant who could do the engraving.

Thus, William Fitzhugh provided against the turns of the fickle wheel of fortune and at the same time made himself more and more comfortable. As for religion, he did his best to secure a *sober* (perhaps in the sense of not quarrelsome—his neighbor Parson Waugh was anything but sober in this sense) and *learned* minister for his parish. For education, he sent his two older sons (the others were still quite young at the time of his death) to a French Huguenot clergyman in a nearby parish. So thoroughly were they saturated in Gallic atmosphere that he informed the Bristol merchant to whom he was sending the younger, eleven-and-a-half-year-old Henry (for British further schooling), that the boy could read and write only French and Latin. Over the years he ordered Latin and French textbooks for his children, and for himself with an eye to his children's future reading—scientific works by Boyle, Bacon, and Burnet; "Histories" of many kinds, including Rushworth and Acosta; and many religious works.

The ordinary concomitants of the lighter side of life, drinking and feasting, suited neither his physical nor his philosophical constitution. He mentions bacchanalian revels at Jamestown more than once, and drinking heavily with ship captains just before their departure, but he always speaks regretfully of the necessity of indulging. Near the end of his life, he wrote to a Virginian friend and brother barrister, Henry Hartwell, then (July 21, 1698) suffering from the gout in London: "I never much frequented Bacchus Orgyes, & always avoided Adoration of Ceres shrine, & never was one of Venus Votarys: To speak plainly to you, I never courted unlawfull pleasures with women, avoided hard drinking as much as lay in my power, & always avoided feasting & consequently the surfeits occasioned thereby, tell your Doctor this, & he will conclude I am not near being his patient yet."

But Fitzhugh clearly did enjoy in moderation the lighter side of social life. Guests were always welcome, for the relatively lonely life of the frontier planter was brightened by their presence. A travel account kept by a Frenchman named Durand in 1686–1687 gives an engaging picture of life at Fitzhugh's home estate, Bedford, near the Christmas season. Durand had already visited Fitzhugh's friend and correspondent Ralph Wormeley at Rosegill in Middlesex County, where he had been so warmly wined and dined that in holiday spirit he and some other gentlemen decided to continue the frolic by riding on to another abode of openhanded hospitality.

So we rode twenty strong to Colonel Fichous' but he has such a large establishment that he did not mind. We were all of us provided with beds, one for two men. He treated us royally, there was good wine & all kinds of beverages, so there was a great deal of carousing. He had sent for three fiddlers, a jester, a tight-rope dancer, an acrobat who tumbled around, & they gave us all the entertainment one could wish for. It was very cold, yet no one ever thinks of going near the fire, for they never put less than a cartload of wood in the fireplace & the whole room is kept warm. . . .

The next day, after they had caroused until after noon, we decided to cross this river. The Colonel had a quantity of wine & one of his punch bowls brought to the shore; he lent us his boat. . . .[5]

The accommodations for twenty guests, the flowing bowl, and the gleaming silver had been earned by hard work and clever management in several directions. Fitzhugh planted both Oronoco and Sweet-Scented tobacco and moved on to newly acquired fields as his topsoil became less fertile. He shipped for himself and his neighbors tobacco of all grades and kinds, experimenting with buyers and markets. He also exported black walnut plank, pipe staves, wheat, and a little Virginia cider. The largest number of letters he wrote was to the merchants who handled his shipments and the sea captains who carried them. To grow the tobacco, he operated the first plantation in Stafford to use Negro slave labor on a large scale, as the county tax records indicate. About him, certainly at the beginning of his years in Stafford, were many

5. Chinard Gilbert (ed. and trans.), *A Huguenot Exile in Virginia* . . . (New York, 1934), 158–59.

smaller farmers who used white indentured servants and few if any Negroes.

Tobacco led Fitzhugh and other large-scale planters into commission-merchant and storekeeping work, as his proposals to English firms suggest. His letters are full of schemes for partnerships with English merchants, ship captains, and friends. Since most of the tobacco buying at this period was entrusted to the ship captains themselves, the merchants frequently felt the need for agents in the colonies. In his double capacity as lawyer and planter, Fitzhugh acted for several of them. At the end of his life he was himself part owner of a tobacco ship. And he was always enthusiastic about the port towns for tobacco shipment and trade proposed by the colonial administration but successfully blocked by the British merchants, who wanted no middlemen to absorb their profits. Fitzhugh and his planter neighbors bought lots themselves in the laid-out town sites and tried to get various English tradesmen to settle upon them. There is no evidence that the southern colonial planter of this period felt that trade was socially demeaning; quite the contrary.

As a businessman, Fitzhugh was most active in land purchase and sale. All the Northern Neck county records include listings of his activities. He died in possession of some 54,000 acres in several tracts, the largest of which, Ravensworth, opposite what is now Washington, D.C., is today a gigantic residential subdivision. He once offered the Northern Neck proprietary agent a goodly sum for the whole county in which he lived, and at another time offered to buy a 100,000-acre tract. Later, when he himself was proprietary agent for Lord Halifax, he not only firmly secured for himself all the tracts he had previously bought with somewhat doubtful titles but also confirmed to certain fellow planters like Richard Lee enormous tracts of undeveloped land which they held for speculation. Dr. Douglas S. Freeman gives Fitzhugh the credit, or the blame, for doing much to encourage, if not to inaugurate, the speculation-in-lands policy which accompanied our frontier throughout its history. Fitzhugh's confirmations of lands, says Dr. Freeman, were full of evil potentialities.[6]

Fitzhugh apparently first gained fame in the Virginia colony as a learned lawyer. In his very earliest letters he is advising his clients and brother barristers on obscure technical points. His forte seems to have been in citing historical precedent. All through his life he appeared in celebrated Virginia cases as an expert on precedent, and, as a member of the house of burgesses, was clearly the authority on legal history. In his final session in the general assembly he was chairman of the committee for the revision of the laws. In commenting upon one vulnerable decision of a judge, he said: "By this you may see what precipitate judgment may be given of any Statute, without understanding the common Law, before the making thereof, which is the only guide, & which is only to be learn'd out of antient Authors, (for out of the old fields must come the new Corn) contrary to the opinion of the generality of our Judges & practisers of the Law here." [To Richard Lee, May 15, 1679.] The extant Fitzhugh speeches in the General Assembly, as well as his letters, afford evidence of his awareness of the difference in function and situation of colonial and British parliaments, and of the potential significance of this difference. He also pointed out to his fellow burgesses that the colonial legislature could never work effectively so long as the home government was dilatory or indifferent in observing and remedying patent injustices.

The limited space of an essay does not allow even a brief glance at the details of Fitzhugh's work as lawyer, farmer,

6. Douglas S. Freeman, *George Washington* (7 vols.; New York, 1948–57), I, 488.

chairman of the County Commission of the Peace, lieutenant-colonel of militia, provider of supplies for a frontier garrison, and staunch supporter of the Stuarts; nor is there space for further exploration of his moral, philosophical, and religious principles and practices.

But even an outline portrait of the man against his world is disproportionate unless one considers his ability as a writer and his urge to write. Fitzhugh, perhaps like many of his countrymen, might in another age or clime have been a poet, novelist, or essayist. For he loved written expression for its form's sake as well as its idea's sake. Always conscious of style, he mentions his own inferiority in this regard to Nicholas Hayward over and over again, e.g. (April 22, 1686): "I must confess I want abilitys, to polish & adorn my expressions with that elegance & sweetness of Stile your two letters I this year receiv'd are full freighted with. . . ." Yet he was too modest, for at his best he used consciously picturesque idiom and image. For example:

Necessity as 'tis the Mother of Invention, so it is the Nurse of Industry. . . . [To Captain Thomas Mathews, August 24, 1681.]

but to meet with a Concatenation of an Indulgent Husband, an obliging nature, and generous temper in one person is very rare. . . . [To Thomas Harris, January 30, 1686/7.]

& as certain you are not Yorkshire enough, to set the Course of your advice by the Compass of your Interest. [To Richard Lee, January 18, 1687/8.]

Yet would my Lord Fairfax there, take his turn in Shuffling & Dealing the Cards & his Lordship with the rest see that we are not cheated in our game, I question not but we should gain the Sett, tho' the game is so far plaid. . . . [To Roger Jones, May 11, 1697.]

Regarding the writing of letters, he observed to his friend Hayward in London:

[I] do fully agree with you in your Philosophical sentiments of y°. Simpathy of absent friends, as you in Laconick expression aptly deliver in your last, for which reason the first Inventer of letters deserves eternal Commendations, by whose means I have not only the opportunity, of the first acquaintance with so worthy & judicious a friend, but a continued Communication & Society, which I as really enjoy, whilst I am reading your most endearing letters, or answering them, as if happily present with you[.] [To Nicholas Hayward, January 30, 1686/7.]

Later Fitzhugh planned a long history of Virginia which might induce more colonists to go there, and he actually did write a short history of the colony as a preface to an edition he prepared of the Virginia laws. Much of his time was spent pen in hand, and clearly he would have preferred more leisure from other active concerns for this work at his desk.

Fitzhugh's death at fifty found him surrounded with most of the luxuries possible to a transplanted Englishman in the New World—a respected place in government and society, a congenial wife, and five sons who would carry his name and blood in distinguished examples into later generations. Without exception, the second generation married into the other great families of the Chesapeake community in Virginia and Maryland. Their descendants with *Fitzhugh* as Christian name or surname have been distinguished persons, from the Revolution to our own time. Perhaps no one of them has been at the same time more of a pattern and a polestar—for he is both type and leader—than this modest, kindly man who showed how the middle-class Englishman might realize himself in the American dream and remain a follower of Horatian idealism and Christian piety. Fitzhugh had been a hardpushing, driving farmer and a sharp businessman, as we have seen, but the enduring impression of the man is in his philosophy of living. Perhaps the statement of it he gave his mother just three years before his death is a fair final impression. It has in it, by the way, a beautiful serenity I do not find among the Puritans.

Before I was ten years old as I am sure you very well remember, I look'd upon this life here as but going to an Inn, no permanent being[.] by God's [grace] I continue the same . . . good thoughts & notions still. therefore am always prepared for my certain Dissolution, w.ᶜʰ I ca'nt be perswaded to prolong by a wish. [To Mary Fitzhugh, June 30, 1698.]

V

Arthur Blackamore: The Virginia Colony and the Early English Novel

[As a later essay will show, there were many more mute inglorious Miltons in early national Virginia than literary historians generally have acknowledged. Some allowed their works to disappear, as William Fitzhugh's history of Virginia. Others never found the time to compose or record on paper. A few, in the colony or in Great Britain, did write and even publish concerning the colony. Usually they were historians, such as Robert Beverley II, Hugh Jones, James Blair, and William Stith, the latter three of whom also published sermons. A very few colonists published their verses, and almost no one published prose fiction.

In the time of Daniel Defoe and Joseph Addison, however, a former member of the faculty of the College of William and Mary was writing sentimental forerunners of Samuel Richardson's kind of novel. Arthur Blackamore created scenes and characters based on his experiences in Virginia. He also wrote in Latin an "epic" on one of the great exploratory parties of the colonial Old Dominion, that of Spotswood in his transmontane expedition. At least part of Blackamore's fiction was probably composed in Williamsburg. Though hardly good literature, it, together with the author's dedications and his verse, shows him to have been a writer of some ability. A friend of William Byrd II and Governor Alexander Spotswood, he was not the only American colonial whose tragedy was his alcoholism.]

IF IT COULD be shown that either of the novels Arthur Blackamore published in London in 1720 and 1723 was composed in the colony of Virginia, our date for the first "American novel" would be set back at least half a century.[1] Both were written by an educated gentleman who had recently returned to England after many years in the New World. Both are dedicated in fulsome prefaces to living Virginians. One has a major character avowedly modeled on a Williamsburg matron. The other quite clearly is concerned with a religio-political struggle going on in the Old Dominion.

The 1723 volume is a significant forerunner of Samuel Richardson's *Pamela*. The 1720 work is a thinly veiled attack on personages, "parties," and perhaps sects in the colony, though the settings as such are not at all American. Both are more American than such literary works as George Sandys' *Ovid* or James Fenimore Cooper's *Precaution,* less American than John Smith's *Generall Historie* and *True Travels.* Because of the author's public and personal position in Virginia and the persons and problems with which he deals, he and his two books deserve attention in literary and general history.

Arthur Blackamore, the author, is at once pitiable and attractive. Son of a Londoner of the same name, he matriculated at Christ Church College, Oxford, in May, 1695, at the age of sixteen,[2] and in September, 1707 was sent to Virginia as

1. Though the 1789 *The Power of Sympathy* is generally accepted as the first genuine American novel written in this country, the 1776 *Adventures of Alonzo* (attributed to Thomas Atwood Digges of Maryland) may have some claim to this primacy. See Robert H. Elias, "The First American Novel," *American Literature,* XII (1941), 419–34.

2. See Edward Lewis Goodwin, *The Colonial Church in Virginia* . . . (Milwaukee, 1927); and William H. McBurney (ed.), *Four Before Richardson: Selected English Novels, 1720–1727* (Lincoln, Neb., 1963), xvi–xix, 5.

a schoolmaster. Shortly after his arrival he became master of the grammar school of the College of William and Mary, and, according to some accounts, "Professor of Humanity" in the college. Soon his alcoholic tendencies were clearly evident, and his name began to appear again and again in personal, academic, and gubernatorial records as a significant local problem, a man to be coped with or got rid of.

It is clear that he was accepted socially as a friend and equal by even some of the grandest of the Virginia planters. On June 7, 1709, William Byrd II noted that Blackamore, perhaps a congenial companion because of their common interest in books, came to see the master of Westover with Colonel William Randolph "because he did not dare come by himself, for I had reprimanded him for his being drunk. They both dined with me. . . . In the afternoon we played at billiards and I lost two bits." On June 24, Byrd records another visit from Blackamore "with Johnny Randolph." On October 28 the diarist notes that at a meeting of the board of governors of the college, "it was agreed to turn Mr. Blackamore out from being master of the school for being so great a sot." But the next day Blackamore petitioned for another chance, and it was agreed that he should be put "on trial, some time longer."[3]

Blackamore was still on probation when the new executive of Virginia, Lieutenant Governor Alexander Spotswood, arrived in June, 1710. In August of this year Spotswood wrote to the Bishop of London, observing that the failure of the newly appointed schoolmaster to come to the colony was providential, for "I understood that the present master of the grammar school is much reformed of late, and that he

3. L. B. Wright and Marion Tinling (eds.), *The Secret Diary of William Byrd of Westover* (Richmond, Va., 1941), 45, 52, 98.

gives good satisfaction in his business."[4] Presumably the governor was expressing a general hope that Blackamore now had his habit under control. Unfortunately such was not the case. Official and personal records of the next seven years show a succession of decisions to remove the schoolmaster, his promises to reform and a subsequent period of abstention, his relapse, and again the motion by the college board that he be removed. In April, 1711, Byrd notes that Spotswood was chosen rector of the college, "but he was displeased that we did not turn Mr. Blackamore out of the school and Mr. LeFevre in." During a stay in Williamsburg in 1712 Byrd observed that on an evening walk he "met Mr. Blackamore, who was drunk."[5] If we possessed the diaries for the next several years, we should probably find similar references to the unfortunate man.

By June, 1716, the college, the governor, and the schoolmaster together decided that probation and leniency had gone far enough. Perhaps as an effort to solve his problem, perhaps on his friends' advice and genuine desire to aid him, Blackamore decided to return to England and attempt to have himself ordained in the Anglican clergy. Then the board of the college gave him six months, on his own petition, to straighten out his affairs before he departed at the end of that period. The college would, if he behaved himself in the interval, forgive him certain debts and even buy his books and globes for the institution's library.[6] In reality they gave him a six-months further tenure as headmaster of the grammar school.

Within the six-months period Spotswood led his Knights

4. R. A. Brock (ed.), *The Official Letters of Alexander Spotswood* . . . (Richmond, Va., 1882–85), I, 4.
5. Wright and Tinling (eds.), *Secret Diary*, 335, 561.
6. "Proceedings of the Visitors of William and Mary College, 1716," *Virginia Magazine of History and Biography*, IV (1896–97), 170.

of the Golden Horseshoe across the Blue Ridge Mountains and returned in triumph. The expedition set out August 20, and returned to Williamsburg on September 17. The following November, when the college paid its annual "literary quit-rent" to the governor for lands held under its charter, two sets of Latin verses were submitted. Commissary James Blair, the bishop of London's representative in Virginia and president of the college, composed one of them on "The Suppression of the Late Rebellion." Mr. Blackamore, who was the author of the second tribute, made a hit with his lines on the recent journey of the governor's group in "Expeditio Ultramontana."[7] The poem is now lost, but the English translation by the Reverend George Seagood was printed in the *Maryland Gazette.*[8] A recent commentator suggests that the Latin verses were probably superior to the translation. At any rate, Blackamore became and remained a staunch supporter of the governor, who was by now having his troubles with certain members of his council and of the House of Burgesses, particularly with Commissary Blair.

In a letter of June 13, 1717, to the bishop of London, Spotswood records Seagood's arrival and the fact that he is sending a letter to the Society for the Propagation of the Gospel, which had recently elected him to membership, "by Mr. Blackamore."[9] James Blair, in a letter to the bishop a month

7. Arthur Blackamore, "Expeditio Ultramontana," in *William and Mary Quarterly*, Ser. 1, VII (1898–99), 30–36. This English translation of the poem was reprinted, edited by E. G. Swem, in Richmond in 1960.

8. The Maryland *Gazette,* June 17–24, 1729. Seagood, who arrived in Virginia just before Blackamore departed, had received the B.A. in 1702 and the M.A. in 1704/5 from Christ Church, Oxford, Blackamore's old college. They may have been friends in the University (see Goodwin, "George Seagood" in *The Colonial Church in Virginia*). Spotswood in a letter dated June 13, 1717, noted that "Mr. Seagood, being just arrived, is going to another parish on the Rappahannock," Brock (ed.), *Official Letters of Spotswood,* II, 253.

9. Brock (ed.), *Official Letters of Spotswood,* II, 253.

earlier, May 14, had thrown further light on the reasons for Blackamore's departure. Blackamore was going home with the idea of being admitted to holy orders and perhaps returning to America. Blair's long paragraph is interesting in several respects.

But the chief thing I am to lay before your Lo[rdshi]p is the case of Mr. Arthure Blakamore who is to wait on your Lop for Orders, and for that end brings a Testimonium under our College-Seal. No Testimonial in the usual form would fit his case, for to give one certifying his sobriety and good behaviour during the whole time of his residence at our College, it would never have past, every one of the Governours of the College being sensible of his very frequent failings in the point of sobriety; for he had received diverse warnings and publick admonitions to amend; other wise he was told that he must provide for himself, for the grammar School, of which he was Master, decayed apace; most of the gentlemen of the Countrey refusing to send their children to a school, where the Master gave so bad examples. Upon these admonitions he comonly reformed for a month, or two, or three, and was seemingly very penitent, and made vows with the solemnest imprecations that he would never more taste any strong drink. Many years were thus spent in scandalous acts of drunkenness, admonitions, endeavours of amendment, and relapses; and the governours of the College had abundance of patience with him, till at last the School was dwindled away to nothing; there were not ten Scholars left, and it was found that all further admonitions would be in vain; and at a meeting of the Governours of the College it was agreed by every body that there was no way to retrieve the School, but by changing the Master. Mr Blakamore understanding this, petitioned that he might hold it Six months longer, that in that time he might pay his debts, and desired the College to buy his books, and offered to resign: he hoped likewise they would give him a Testimonium to your Lop, for he designed to enter into holy orders. It was answered that if he abstained from drunkenness and behaved himself well for the remaining six months they would give him a Testimonium; but would put him in no further hopes of holding the School. And accordingly another gentleman who was known to have a very good talent at teaching, and to be a sober good man, was agreed to be invited to be Schoolmaster, and after the expiration of the six months this gentleman (by name Mr Mongo Ingles) was unanimously admitted, and the School under him thrives apace, there are already 26 scholars, and more dayly coming. But to return to Mr Blakamore, and to do him justice, the certain loss of his place, and the fear of want (for he had been a very bad husband) and the danger of going home without a Testimonium, and perhaps remorse for what was past, wrought so upon him, that he made the greatest and longest attempt towards a reformation that ever he had done; for he drank nothing but water or small beer, or ought any body knows, for five or six months together, only he unhappily broke out again into the former debauch a few days before another meeting of the Governours of the College which was held on the 23d of April last, at which meeting the Testimonium should have been granted. And that very day he was so in his cups, that he did not think fit to appear, and to sollicit his own business. I being at that time ignorant of this last relapse, and fearing there would not be another opportunity of a meeting of the Governours of the College, while Mr Blakamore was in the Country, proposed the business of his Testimonium to that meeting, where it was carried by a great Majority, and ordered to be prepared and engrossed, with the College Seal affixed, and we were all to put our hands to it. Some few indeed said then that they would never put their hands to it, for that to their knowledge he was now again as drunk as ever; but the greater part could not believe it: for most of us indeed were totally ignorant of this unhappy relapse at that time. But in a little time afterwards we found it too true, for he had been for several days and nights before, and was for 10 or 12 days afterwards so scandalously drunk, and talked madly in his drink, threatening what characters he would print of all the Governours of the College, after he got for England, and that he valued none of them, he had a friend that would be better believed than they all, with abundance more such stuff that I believe he gott very few hands to his Testimonium; he never had the confidence after this to offer it to me. I am told that it was signed by the Rector in the name of the Governours of the College, which he said he could not refuse to do, it having been carried by a majority at a General meeting, tho at the same time he declared if they would put their names every one for themselves, he would not put his. I thought it necessary to deal ingenuously with your Lop, and not to leave you in the dark in this affair. After all, perhaps if he were put into orders and put into some remote parish, where there is no temptation to drink, he might do well enough; for he has many serious fitts of devotion, and I often think he would fain break himself of this evil habit, if he could. But I will not promise for him, for I am sensible he has no command of himself, when exposed to temptation.[10]

Such was the "ingenuous" comment of a man who may have been absolutely sincere, but whom many of his contemporaries would have said was employing his usual devious means of routing his enemies. Some of it was undoubtedly true, as we have already seen. But Blair was going behind the governor's back, and perhaps also trying to make sure that Blackamore would not return to Virginia in Anglican orders.

With such testimonials, Blackamore was back in England by the end of 1717. Whether he took holy orders or not remains unknown, but certainly he did remain an orthodox Anglican churchman and a loyal friend of certain Virginians. And clearly he kept up with Virginia affairs, as the dedication to his first novel indicates.

Though Spotswood's administration got off to a good start in 1710, within a few years the able and strongly imperialistic lieutenant governor found himself at odds with his council, the upper house and general court personnel of the colonial legislature. In a long series of disputes with the "country" or "plantation party" which he frequently mentions in his letters to the Board of Trade, the bishop of London, and other

10. James Blair to the bishop of London, May 14, 1717, *William and Mary Quarterly*, Ser. 2, XIX (1939), 372–74. The first and last paragraphs of the letter are omitted.

officials, he insisted that Philip Ludwell and James Blair were leaders of a majority group in the council, a group buttressed by family alliances and blood relationship, a group which through Commissary Blair had procured the dismissal of at least two former governors when it found it could not control them. Of the group's power and resistance to further establishment of "the King's prerogative" there can be no question. Their motives may be another matter, not to be settled here.[11] Spotswood once polished them off individually to the earl of Orkney, the titular governor who never came to the colony: "the haughtiness of a Ludwell, the hypocrisy of a Blair, the inveteracy of a Carter, the brutishness of a Smith, the malice of a Byrd, the conceitedness of a Grymes, and the scurrility of a Corbin, with about a score of base disloyalists and ungrateful Creolians for their adherents."[12]

Though Spotswood and the commissary had disagreed violently on other matters, that to which Blackamore seems to be referring in his dedication took place largely after his departure from the colony. It concerned the right of collation, or appointment, of ministers to Anglican parishes, whether the right, clearly vested by law in the Crown, was to be exercised by governor, commissary, or parish vestry. The church historian George MacLaren Brydon rejoices that "the one greatest and most far-reaching service which [Spotswood] rendered the Church in Virginia lay in the strengthening of its solidar-

11. Brock (ed.), *Official Letters of Spotswood,* I and II; Cecil Headlam (ed.), *Calendar of State Papers, Colonial, America, and West Indies, 1717–1718* (London, 1930), items 588, 657, 759; Leonidas Dodson, *Alexander Spotswood, Governor of Virginia, 1710–1722* (Philadelphia, 1932), *passim;* George M. Brydon, *Virginia's Mother Church and the Political Conditions Under Which it Grew* (Richmond, Va., 1947), I, 327–60; Hugh Jones, *The Present State of Virginia, and the College,* ed., R. L. Morton (Chapel Hill, 1956), *passim.*

12. *Cal. St. Papers, Col., Am. & W. I., 1717–1718,* item 799, pp. 424–25.

ity by the defeat of the attack he made upon the right of the several parishes to select their own ministers."[13] Though there is not the space here to go into the details of the controversy— or to advance evidence for my view that Brydon's comment is distorted truth, if truth at all—there should be some explanation of the Spotswood "Tory" church policy and its supporters and opponents.

The governor, since there was no bishop in Virginia, held the legal right as the king's ordinary, to induct (give permanent tenure in individual parishes) in Virginia and claimed the right to appoint (collate) ministers to the parishes. The commissary, who represented the bishop of London and the Church in other matters, had no legal rights in regard to collation or induction. Vestries, which had usually chosen their ministers for many years, did not want them inducted, for that gave them permanent tenure, which destroyed the vestries' power over their ministers. The vestries preferred appointment on a year-to-year basis, preferably on their own recommendation. Because of the naturally consequent feeling of insecurity, the clergy had struggled to have the vestries present all ministers for induction.

Spotswood hesitated for a long time to exercise what he believed—and the king's attorney general had supported him in this belief—to be his own and the king's rights in both appointment and induction. His own strong convictions as to crown rights were in this case strongly supported by a majority of the clergy for the reason suggested above. The matter came to its first crisis in the Rainsford vs. Bagge case the year after Blackamore sailed for England. The clergyman Bagge probably sailed with Blackamore in June, 1717, so that

13. Brydon, *Virginia's Mother Church*, I, 344. Compare this with Dodson, *Spotswood, passim;* and Richard L. Morton, *Colonial Virginia* (2 vols.; Chapel Hill, 1960), II, 409 ff., especially 465–71.

he, Bagge, could have himself ordained priest (he had held deacon's orders previously).[14] When Bagge returned in 1718 he was reappointed to his old parish, then held by Rainsford, against the wishes of the vestry. In this case the governor won, and Bagge probably kept Blackamore informed of the situation. Blair, who saw his support in vestries (his fellow councilors among them) rather than in his fellow clergy, began or continued opposition to the governor's policies. By April, 1719, when a clerical convention was held at Williamsburg, a majority (though a bare one) bluntly declared their lack of faith in Commissary Blair by stating that they did not believe he had ever been formally ordained by a bishop in England, as law required, and asked him to furnish proof that he had been. This Blair never did. His categorical statement to the bishop of London that he had received episcopal ordination was true in only one sense, for certainly he had not received the legally required form.[15] His clergy, led by the intelligent young Hugh Jones, gave Blair a vote of *no confidence*. In 1720, the year Blackamore published his novel, the Blair-Ludwell faction and the governor agreed to present a test case before the general court. Governor Spotswood had accused Blair of accepting appointment as rector of Bruton Parish church by the vestry without coming to the governor for collation in the position.

The test case put Blair in a dilemma.[16] He seems to have resorted to his old delaying tactics, for when Spotswood was removed from office in 1722 the case was dropped. Almost surely the devious commissary had a hand in the governor's

14. Brydon, *Virginia's Mother Church*, I, 347–48.
15. As we now know, he could not have done so. He was ordained by a bishop of the Church of Scotland, not at this time a state church. (See Brydon, *Virginia's Mother Church*, I, *passim*; and Morton, *Colonial Virginia*, II, *passim*).
16. Morton, *Colonial Virginia*, II, 469.

removal, as did the "plantation party" of Council and House, though not necessarily because of the Blair case alone.

Whether Blackamore took holy orders or not, he was on the side of the clergy and of Governor Spotswood in this dispute. On June 23, 1720, he addressed a dedication of a curious little book, *The Perfidious Brethren, or, The Religious Triumvirate. Display'd in Three Ecclesiastical Novels. I. Heathen Priestcraft: Or, the Female Bigot . . . II. Presbyterian Piety: Or the Way to get a Fortune. III. The Cloven-Hoof: Or the Anabaptist Teacher Detected . . . London . . . 1720 . . .*

To the Honourable
The Lieut. Governour
    of
Virginia
Sir,
The following papers having chanc'd to meet the kind Approbation of some particular Gentlemen permit me to make a *Tender* of them to your *Honour;* as an Acknowledgment of the many Favours I have received from you, while I was, more immediately, under your *Protection.*

That I have presum'd to venture upon this Dedication to your Honour, without your Knowledge or Approbation, I hope, the Distance of *Great Britain* from the *Seat* of Your *Government,* will atone for: Especially if the Subject, on which I treat, shall happen to be grateful to You, so as to merit Your Perusal at a leisure Hour; when You shall think fit to relax Your Mind, from the Fatigue and Weight of Your other Affairs.

The Book, which I now offer to Your Honour's Patronage, contains three *Novels,* which are a sort of Comparison between the antient *Heathen Priests* and some more modern *Pretenders.* . . .

In continuing his summary of the little volume, the author declares that he does not say all Presbyterians and Anabaptists are as bad as two of his major characters, "neither can they say that all our Ministers" are immoral persons. Then he goes on:

Should I recount all the motives I have to this *Dedication,* the *Time* would fail me, and the Porch would be abundantly bigger than the House. But of the many, be pleas'd, *Sir,* to give me leave to mention one in particular; that I may take this Opportunity to Congratulate Your *Honour* upon Your *Continuance* in Your *Government,* notwithstanding the *united Force,* and all the *malicious Suggestions* of Your Enemies; but especially *One;* who should he be set forth as he ought, would appear to be a *false Priest:* like the worst of the following Triumvirate: of *equal Piety,* and as *black Example.*

It is with no small satisfaction. I reflect upon the Happiness *Virginia* has long enjoy'd, under the gentle *Influence* of Your *Command,* which has been severe to none, but such as have extorted a just Resentment from You. And if then a Party of Men, who have been Enemies to all Governours, and could never bear one above three Years (as a certain great Man, here, said of them) have felt your Displeasure, it was their own Obstinacy that drew it upon them; and the Disgrace they have suffered, is owing to themselves.

That the *Tongues* of your *Enemies* may be put to Silence; that *Virginia* may never want such a *Protector,* and that, Your Honour may long continue in that *Post* is the sincere and hearty Wish of

Honoured, Sir,
Your Honours
most oblig'd,
humble Servant,
A. B.

Dated at London.
June the 23d
1720.

The three short "novels" which follow are narratives exemplifying the perfidy of priests of varying religions and situations. The first, "Heathen Priestcraft: Or, the Female Bigot," is set in the reign of the mild and quiet Roman Emperor

Augustus Caesar (Spotswood?). It carries an old plot, of a virtuous husband and wife (Paulina), and her would-be seducer, Decius Mundus. A priest of Isis persuades the fervently pious Paulina that the god is in love with her and persuades her to give herself to him. Then of course she discovers that she has been betrayed into the arms of the importunate lover Decius Mundus. Ide, the female go-between servant, and the corrupt priest are hanged, for they, says our author, were more at fault than the seducer, whose "action began in generous love."

The second piece, "Presbyterian Piety: Or, the Way to get a Fortune," is the story of a London citizen who, restless in the "National Church," decides to look among the Dissenters for a wife. Sordidior is the Dissenting minister who aids him out of greed and not piety or brotherly love. In the end the heroine and her widowed mother denounce Dissenters (including Sordidior) and decide to return to the Church of England.

The third story, "The Cloven-Hoof: Or, the Anabaptist Teacher Detected," is again set in "the famous City of Augusta the grand metropolis of the Britannic Islands," in the vicinity of a famous college. One small "society" in the neighborhood is presided over by Whiskero, *"a dapper Blade* in Stature, but pamper'd like a Punchinello, with a Face like a *Full Moon,* and a *Belly* that discover'd that he was not much given to *Fasting,* or any other works of *Mortification,* whatever he might dictate to his *People."* Cornutus and his wife Flora are among Whiskero's auditors, and what plot there is concerns Whiskero's approaches to Flora, which end in her seduction and ruin. Whiskero, who "wrote," was really a Sensualist and a Chiliast, the author warns, and was corrupted by his own belief in pleasure, including carnal copulation.

Dialogue, sermons to the reader, and some good descriptive passages render this passable reading. One recalls that Blackamore's dedication suggested that he composed these "novels" from a variety of motives. Among them was certainly the orthodox Anglican's horror at dissent and his willingness to believe almost anything of its practitioners or followers. He knew too of Spotswood's troubles with Quakers and Presbyterians, and the governor's letters to the bishop of London suggesting means of obstructing their designs. But the author particularly singles out the "false priest," clearly James Blair, who had bedeviled the wise and good government of Spotswood.

Blackamore, a number of the Virginia clergy, and at times Virginia gentlemen like William Byrd were ready to believe the worst of the bishop's commissary. That he was an adulterer or panderer we have no record of in surviving accusations. That he was a Presbyterian in origin and allegedly sometimes in sympathies everybody knew. He had an enormous thirst for power and employed devious ways of obtaining it— as two governors before Spotswood and at least one after him were only too well aware. Blackamore felt, perhaps rightly, that Blair's siding with the vestry or people was for his own ends, not God's. As a good churchman, Blackamore was indignant that the commissary had managed to control lay and clerical government so that a strongly centralized or organized church under the crown was never to be visualized in Virginia.

If he had not already been accepted into holy orders, this little book would have been graphic evidence of his orthodox zeal, and might have persuaded his friends in Virginia to do something for him—perhaps to intercede again with the bishop of London. It is ironic that within two years the devoutly hoped-for continued government of Spotswood was to end,—surely partly because of the machinations of the priest Blackamore here attacks.

If not in holy orders, Blackamore was in these years pretty clearly attempting to secure favor with the Society for the Propagation of the Gospel in Foreign Parts. In 1722 he published a boiled down two-volume version of an eight-volume collection of Christian antiquities and laws, with the new title *Ecclesiæ Primitiva Notitia: Or, a Summary of Christian Antiquities* . . . (London), the first volume being dedicated to the S. P. G. and the second to his distant kinsman, Sir Richard Blackmore. He mentions that a friend, the Reverend Mr. Ley, Curate of Croydon in Surrey, has aided with the work, and that much of it was written as diversion while he, Blackamore, was conducting a school (presumably in England). It is militantly Anglican. In a section on ecclesiastical terms and definitions he defines the Quakers as "A brainless sect of fanatical Spirits that sprang up in *England about* the Middle of the 17th Century, in the Time of the Usurpation under *Oliver Cromwell*. . . ." This may be little more than hack work, but the flavor of Blackamore's prose is piquant, and the two volumes are not bad reading. But let us consider further Blackamore's fiction.

As literature, *The Perfidious Brethren* is miserable stuff. As a catchpenny pamphlet or chapbook it may have sold fairly well—we do not know. But the other work of fiction known to be his (there may have been yet more), *Luck at Last or The Happy Unfortunate* (London, 1723) is a different matter. Reissued at least once in the eighteenth century, it was reprinted in 1963[17] as a significant example of

17. The work was reissued in 1737 as *The Distress'd Fair, or Happy Unfortunate*. The modern edition is in McBurney (ed.), *Four Before Richardson*, 1–81.

the novel before Richardson and as a genuine forerunner of *Pamela* itself.

Blackamore borrowed his plot from a posthumous piece of Mrs. Aphra Behn published in 1698 as *The Wandering Beauty*.[18] It is at once a sermon exemplum on the subject of virtue and patience rewarded, and something of a sentimental novel of character. Silvia, the heroine, anticipates Pamela in her sensibility, prudence, and other practical virtues. The book had popular appeal for its combination of motifs of the runaway bride, the lost child, and the reconciliation-recovery.

The novel's recent editor insists on its "pervasive sense of realism," achieved through such exact details as servants, salaries, coaches, billiard tables, and bowling greens—the last two of which may have derived as well from Blackamore's remembrance of Byrd's Westover and Williamsburg as from contemporary Britain. There is also "a mild touch of bawdy" and some real beggars' idiom.

This air of realism as it is achieved through the Virginia references is the most interesting. The author this time dedicates his work to "Mr. David Bray, Merchant, of Virginia," suggesting that this gentleman knows him too well to believe the dedication is made out of flattery. He refers to the years in which he knew Bray's mother and father and their son, then a youth, so pleasantly. This is only a nosegay, a novel, but he wishes to present it as a remembrance of kindness, hospitality, and friendship: "But however this performance may appear in general, I flatter myself there is one particular character in it will not be displeasing to you; I mean the Lady Gratiana, because it so nearly resembles your late excellent mother in her parental care and Christian generosity that I

18. McBurney (ed.), *Four Before Richardson*, xvi–xix. McBurney discusses the literary qualities of the novel at some length.

think you can hardly read it without recollecting the alacrity and cheerfulness with which she used to supply the wants of her necessitous, sick, or distressed neighbors."[19] The gentleman thus addressed, born in 1699 and dying in 1731, was the only son of Colonel David Bray, who died in 1717 in the fifty-second year of his age, and his wife Judith, who had departed this life in 1720 in the forty-fifth year of her age. The handsome family monument recording these events still stands in the churchyard of Bruton Parish in Williamsburg. The family had been prominent for at least three generations. Colonel Bray had been nominated as a person suitable to serve on the Council[20] and his son was honored in like manner in the year of his own death.[21] That the family was on terms of some intimacy with Blackamore is suggested by the fact that the latter's friend, the Scot Mongo Inglis (or Ingles), who both preceded and succeeded Blackamore as master of the grammar school at William and Mary, married a sister of the elder Bray.[22]

Though the good lady Gratiana is sketched but lightly, in her quiet self-possession, deference to her husband's wishes, common sense, gracious hospitality, and warm natural affection for her offspring, she is easily an anticipation of the lovely

19. *Ibid.*, 4.

20. *Calender of State Papers, Colonial, America, & West Indies, 1708–1709* (London, 1922), item 216 (iii); *ibid.*, 1716–1717, item 452 (ix). William Byrd II records a visit to the widow Mrs. Judith Bray in May, 1720. On October 23 of the same year he notes "Mrs. Bray died this day of the flux," and the next day "we went to Mrs. Bray's funeral and I held up the pall." See L. B. Wright and Marion Tinling (eds.), *William Byrd of Virginia: London Diary (1717–1721) and Other Writings* (New York, 1958), 266, 402, 467.

21. "Bray Family," *William and Mary Quarterly*, Ser. 1, XIII (1904–1905), 268. He died without issue.

22. "Letter from Mongo Ingles," *William and Mary Quarterly*, Ser. 1, VI (1897–98), 88.

plantation mistress of the fiction of a century and a half later. The editor suspects that the description of Philaretus, the sentimental hero who marries her daughter Silvia, as "something swarthy," was based on the appearance of David Bray, junior, for swarthiness was an unusual physical characteristic in the conventional heroes of the period. The entire action takes place in rural scenes, again as suggestive of the James River plantation region as of eighteenth-century England (recall that Blackamore was apparently London born and bred), and again anticipatory of the sentimental endorsement of the country, as opposed to the city, to become familiar in *Tom Jones* as well as in *Pamela*.

Thus a poet and novelist who spent ten years of his troubled life in colonial Virginia continued to write and speak of the land he remembered with affection, exasperation, and perhaps some sense of shame at his own weakness. He left as a part of colonial writing a poem which survives only in translation. Though his fiction was almost surely not written in Virginia,[23] the dedications in both books seem to reveal a wistful yearning to be recalled to the colony. The books may have been written partly for that purpose. His contemporary, Defoe, had depicted something of Virginia from second-hand sources in his *Moll Flanders*. Blackamore drew from first-hand knowledge to produce works of fiction without labeled Virginia settings. But in one instance he presents the colonial church-and-state struggle and the two major personal antagonists as he saw them, and in the other, a fairly significant early novel, he recalls with warmth and sentiment a gracious

23. Blair's account of Blackamore's threats to write or print about the Council when he got to England may indicate that he already had some of the material for these novels, especially the first, when he sailed from Virginia in 1717.

Virginia lady and her son. In the latter work, incidentally, he insists on the fallacy of rigid class distinctions,[24] an idea far more prevalent in Williamsburg than in London. If he had remained in the colony he might have been our Swift or our Defoe. As it is, we must now assign him a place among those who wrote significantly and cogently about Virginia.

24. McBurney (ed.), *Four Before Richardson*, xix.

⌇⟨VI⟩⌇

William Byrd II:
Taste and Tolerance

[Despite some instances of poor business judgment, the second William Byrd added materially to the property he had inherited from his father and at his own death in 1744 left a great inheritance intact. Throughout his life he enjoyed what he had inherited—as a young blade, as a middle-aged widower in London, and as the owner and occupant of one of colonial America's finest houses. Apparently he designed Westover himself, and with the advice of his brother-in-law John Custis and his friend the naturalist Mark Catesby, laid out its beautiful gardens. Building on a good book collection bequeathed by his father, Byrd gathered one of the largest and most well-balanced colonial libraries.

Half his years were spent in Great Britain and he did some writing there. But his best composition was done in and concerning the Virginia he knew, in forms adapted from the current literary fashions of his day. Why he published so little is at least partially explained in the essay below. Certainly he wrote much. Newly discovered Byrd manuscripts are still being announced, even though most of the letters which have long been available have never been printed in an accurate form.

Yet newly found writings are not likely to change Byrd's image as a writer—those works printed for the first time in recent decades merely fill out a firmly outlined literary portrait. The subtitle of this essay suggests two of his most characteristic qualities as a Virginia gentleman and Anglo-American author.]

THE BEST KNOWN of southern colonial writers, William Byrd II (1674–1744) stands at the beginning of an intellectual and social golden age in the Chesapeake Bay country. Too often considered atypical of both society and literature in his time and region, he is more nearly archetypal, though he is not quite that. His earliest writing is close to the fashionable effusions of the English Restoration era in which he was born and educated, and his last bears clear resemblance in form and style to the literary composition popular in the reigns of Queen Anne and the first Georges. Yet his recorded interest in his native region—in poor whites, slaves, and Indians, in colonial society and government, in New World fauna and flora, in the economics of the agrarian way of life (including tobacco and investment in frontier lands), and in his country's future—mark him as genuinely American. Indeed, his interests are perhaps closer in character to those of the majority of writers in the new United States at the end of the eighteenth century than are those of any other colonial writer save Franklin.

Though a native Virginian, Byrd received all his education between the ages of seven and twenty-one in Europe, most of it in England. Sent by his father, the public official and Indian trader William Byrd I, to live with or near relatives in rural England, William II attended an excellent classical private school. He then studied business in the Netherlands with some of his father's associates, as well as in the counting house of the great London firm of Perry and Lane. In the 1690s he came under the protection of the statesman and scientist Sir Robert Southwell. In 1692, he entered the Middle

Temple and three years later was formally admitted to the bar. In the Temple he formed lifelong friendships with noblemen, playwrights, and a future chief justice of Massachusetts, among others. In 1696, probably through retiring president Sir Robert Southwell's nomination, he was elected to membership in the Royal Society and within a year had published an essay in its *Philosophical Transactions*. That same year, he was called home to Virginia for a short period, during which time he served a term in the House of Burgesses. In 1697, he was back in London on business both public and private. Among his political duties was service as attorney for Governor Andros in a hearing before the archbishop of Canterbury and the bishop of London, to answer Virginia Commissary James Blair's complaints that Andros was blocking the clergyman's ecclesiastical and educational program. Byrd remained in London until 1705, when he was called home at his father's death. In 1706, he married Lucy Parke, the handsome daughter of the profligate and dashing Colonel Daniel Parke.

Byrd settled for a time into the life of a Tidewater planter, improving his house and garden at Westover on the James, corresponding with friends in England, and now as a member of the governor's council (in addition to lesser offices) playing a part in colonial government he was not to relinquish until his death. His earliest extant diary gives the details of family, business, and official life. He had already begun to gather and arrange the library which was to be one of the greatest in the colonies in both quality and quantity. In 1714 or 1715, he returned to England for the second of his three missions as agent for the colony. His wife died there of smallpox.

Much of Byrd's time for the next several years was spent searching for a suitable second wife, preferably an heiress.

Many gallant—and despairing—letters and a second portion of the diary reveal much of these years. They record his daily life in the city of Addison and Steele and Congreve, including his amours with women of high and low degree. In 1718, he had an audience with George I, in which he represented the Virginia Council in a feud with Governor Spotswood regarding provincial courts. He spent much time writing, probably on the history of Virginia (of which he left copies with two noble friends) and the verses published under the pseudonym "Mr. Burrard." By February 13, 1720, he was back in Virginia.

In 1721, while on his third mission as Virginia agent in England, he married Maria Taylor, who brought him only the rather weak prospect of a fortune he never obtained. In 1726, he returned to America for good. He always planned to revisit the mother country; but financial concerns, a growing family, and finally age prevented him. From a literary point of view the last eighteen years of his life were the most interesting and fruitful. In 1728, he was the senior Virginia commissioner to settle the dividing line between Virginia and North Carolina. From the notes and official reports of the sea-to-mountains expedition he was in later years to shape his finest prose. In 1732, he visited various mines and in 1733 he surveyed, figuratively and literally, his recently acquired acres in Governor Eden's North Carolina. Working again from notes and reports, he wrote two travel-observation accounts of significance. In 1735–1736, Byrd once more acted as king's commissioner, this time to determine the true bounds of the Northern Neck, Lord Fairfax's proprietary. His record of this expedition, except for a letter or two, has disappeared.

Obtaining settlers for his vast frontier lands was the most difficult business problem of the last fifteen years of his life. The story of his attempts can be found in his letters and in a promotional tract published in German and signed Wilhelm Vogel—a polyglot assemblage of data from many sources. With his old friend the surveyor Mayo, he laid out on his own land the future Richmond and Petersburg, building in typical American fashion cities, instead of castles, in the air. About a year before his death he succeeded his venerable friend and former enemy Commissary Blair as president of the council, the most eminent political office a native Virginian was to achieve in that province during the colonial period.

Such, in barest outline (some of it will be filled out as his writings are discussed), was the social, political, and intellectual career of a southern colonial whom most literary historians have insisted was a biological "sport," a freak, the great exception among his contemporaries in the Chesapeake Bay region in the eighteenth century. This he distinctly was not. There were dozens of Virginians and Marylanders who had been educated in Great Britain or on the Continent. In his own time, Byrd's brothers-in-law John Custis and Robert Beverley II, along with Maryland Carrolls and Dulanys, were educated abroad. In later generations, William Stith, Robert Munford, Robert Bolling, Jr., the Lee brothers, the Wormeleys, Carters, Ogles, and many others, attended English classical schools—Oxford, Cambridge, Edinburgh, and the London Inns of Court. Some, like Sir John Randolph and his sons Peyton and John, visited England in public and private capacities more than once.

The Wormeleys, Carters, Dulanys, Randolphs, Blands, and a dozen others had impressive libraries, several of them apparently rivaling Byrd's; and two generations later there were greater libraries than his. Virginians Richard Bland, Landon Carter, and John Mercer are among those who seem to have written all their lives. In Maryland Dr. Alexander Hamilton, printer Jonas Green, and other rural and urban members of the Annapolis Tuesday Club apparently drove the quill steadily throughout their allotted years. Except for the clergy among them, most published even less than Byrd. Fortunately, some of their manuscripts survive. When they are published they will show not only these authors, but Byrd, in new perspective. Some parallel him in style, some in satiric intent, several in catholicity of interests, several in their representations of the needs and rights of the colonies before kings, bishops, or committees on trade and the plantations. The same men could be as gallant in their prose or metrical addresses to ladies as could the master of Westover. In other words, William Byrd II as writer is but the tallest tree in a forest of considerable size and modest variety.

I. Miscellaneous Minor Writings

William Byrd has been labeled belated Restoration cavalier and satirist, Queen Anne wit, pamphleteer, promoter, American Pepys, virtuoso, travel writer, and historian. He was most of these things in some degree. His varied interests, occupations, and recreations are represented in brief pieces he probably considered trifles or professional exercises of no literary significance. But even without his letters, diaries, and the well-known "Histories," his surviving compositions would entitle him to at least a minor place as a man of letters.

Too often Byrd's legal training and the literary uses he made of it are overlooked. During the three tours of duty in London as agent for Virginia he prepared arguments, petitions, and addresses which show him to have been an unusually able legal writer. In defending Governor Andros before the mature ecclesiastics at Lambeth in 1697 the twenty-three-year-old barrister acquitted himself well. His extempore remarks are preserved with the rest of the hearing in nine-

teenth-century print. But the formal defense of Andros he
had written out but never had an opportunity to deliver is
excellent legal prose in both style and reasoning. The next
year, as agent, Byrd submitted to the lords of trade and plantations "Proposals . . . for sending the French Protestants
to Virginia," a kind of petition in legal form on a subject
which was to interest him all his life, the settlement of continental Europeans in the great open spaces of his own colony.
A year later he wrote "Representation concerning Proprietary
Governments," arguing the abuses of fair trade and settlement under the proprietary colonial governments, including
the harboring of pirates, and urging that the control of these
governments be vested in the king as quickly as possible. Perhaps his most eloquent, effectively argued, and politically
significant legal piece is the brief address he delivered before
the lords of trade in 1718 on the subject of *oyer* and *terminer*
courts.

There are other politico-legal papers mentioned in the
diaries which do not appear to have survived. Byrd certainly
had a hand in several official addresses to and arguments before the governor and council during his long tenure in public
office. Closely related are the quasi-legal arguments in certain
letters to Governor Gooch, and in the official reports of the
1728 and 1735–1736 boundary commissioners, documents
which demonstrate the author's legal background and experience in public service.

Intensely conscious of his Virginia origin, especially when
he was in London, William Byrd tried his hand several times
at writing a history of his native province. Some time before
1708, Byrd had written a sketch of Virginia which was used
by John Oldmixon in the 1708 and 1741 editions of *The
British Empire in America;* in the second edition Oldmixon
acknowledged that he was indebted to Byrd for much of his

material in the Virginia chapter. One should recall that Robert Beverley's excuse for writing his own history of Virginia, first published in 1705, was that he had seen Oldmixon's manuscript and was so indignant at its errors regarding Virginia that he felt compelled to set matters straight. Since there was a considerable interval between Beverley's sight of the Oldmixon manuscript and its first publication, perhaps Oldmixon saw Beverley's book and asked Byrd for assistance in improving his own work. Or it may be, though it is unlikely, that Beverley believed Byrd to be the promulgator and perpetuator of error.

That Byrd was still working on or had completed a draft of his history of the Old Dominion is borne out by his diary entry of November 20, 1719, which mentions that he left copies of his "description of Virginia" for Lord Islay and his brother the duke of Argyle. Then there is the delightfully sardonic outline of Virginia history which forms the introduction to "The History of the Dividing Line" and does not appear in "The Secret History." As Louis B. Wright has pointed out in his introduction to *The Prose Works*,[1] the promotion tract published in 1737 as *Neu-gefundenes Eden*, the compilation already noted signed Wilhelm Vogel, may have been much the same as Oldmixon's source or the Islay-Argyle "description," though it seems unlikely. What evidence there is seems to point to the probability that from the beginning of the century to 1740, about the date of completion of "The History of the Dividing Line," Byrd worked at least intermittently on a fairly ambitious history of Virginia. It would be interesting to compare what he did compose with Beverley's *The History and Present State of Virginia*.

As Royal Society virtuoso or eighteenth-century son of the

1. L. B. Wright (ed.), *The Prose Works of William Byrd of Westover* (Cambridge, Mass., 1966), 17.

Enlightenment, Byrd had to be interested in science. His observations on botanical, zoological, ethnological, geological, meteorological, and pharmaceutical phenomena are scattered through dozens of letters, the two Dividing Line "Histories," the *Neu-gefundenes Eden* (though most or all of these are second-hand),[2] and the diaries. But there were at least two scientific pieces published in his lifetime. "An Account of a Negro-Boy that is dappel'd in several Places of his Body with White Spots" is the Royal Society published essay (in 1696) noted above. *A Discourse Concerning the Plague, with some Preservatives Against it,* By a Lover of Mankind (London, 1721), recently identified through the diary and internal evidence as Byrd's, is more significant. This is ostensibly a learned treatise, loaded with allusions to ancient and modern medical practices, and proposing that the government take specific precautions to prevent the spread of the plague. The principal antidote proposed is tobacco. Because tobacco has already been chewed, smoked, or snuffed in every rank of society since 1665, England is free of the plague. To insure further immunity, tobacco should be worn on the person, hung in coaches and apartments, burned in dining rooms, and chewed daily. Though the *Discourse* has been taken seriously as a medicinal-cum-tobacco-promotion tract, the ironic deadpan quality of Swift's *A Modest Proposal* or some of Franklin's essays is evident. It is difficult to believe that Byrd's contemporary reader could take him seriously, but then the readers of Swift and Franklin were frequently just as gullible.

The recently discovered commonplace book now in the

2. See Percy G. Adams, in "The Real Author of *William Byrd's Natural History of Virginia*," *American Literature,* XXVIII (1956), 211–20. Adams shows conclusively that all the materials and even phraseology of *Neu-gefundenes Eden* is drawn from earlier writers, but can offer no proof that Byrd did not compile the work purely as business propaganda, and with little thought of the matter of authorship.

Virginia Historical Society, clearly one of a number Byrd kept alongside the diaries, covers some of the years between 1722 and 1733. It contains a little of anything that interested its compiler, from love letters to Charmante to a random assortment of ribald anecdotes, epigrams, verse, and puns. There are even "Some Rules for preserving health" faintly suggestive of Franklin's rules in his *Autobiography*.

A Description of the Dismal Swamp and a Proposal to Drain the Swamp (printed in 1841 and 1922) is both a promotion piece and an engineering proposal. It was probably drawn from the same notes as the descriptions in the Dividing Line "Histories," and resembles them in style. The piece outlines a joint stock company and the necessary steps to set up the procedures for the draining operation.

Capable of reading more than half a dozen ancient and modern languages, Byrd wrote at least one letter in Greek and used Hebrew and Latin phrases when they seemed appropriate. His daily reading in foreign languages resulted in a number of translations, several mentioned in his diaries and a few actually preserved among his manuscripts. His version of "The Ephesian Matron" of Petronius is among his best.

Perhaps as early as his days at the Inns of Court, Byrd drew character sketches of his friends, his enemies, and himself, following a seventeenth-century tradition as well as a form popular among the Queen Anne essayists. Many of the early English caricaturists, as well as Theophrastus, La Bruyère, and Addison and Steele, were represented in his library. The works of Addison and Steele provided many of the tag names Byrd assigned the ladies in his sketches, or to whom he addressed his letters—names such as Sempronia, Clorinda, Amaryllis, Sabina, Cleora, and Monimia. There is good evidence that the tags were disguises for the names of real people.

His "characters" are panegyrics or sharp caricatures, though sometimes, as with "Dr. Glysterio" (Dr. Samuel Garth, poet-physician) he strikes a balance. "Cavaliero Sapiente" is an affectionate but accurate portrait of the amiable and able Sir Robert Southwell; but "Duke Dulchetti," his friend the duke of Argyle, is probably an overly favorable representation. The majority of Byrd's analyses are, however, satirical, a quality natural to both the man and his time. Byrd does not indulge in cruel invective. Normally he employs irony with an edge, expressed in those beautifully balanced antitheses he was to employ even more effectively in his later writings.

To the modern reader, his most interesting work is the relatively long self-analysis "Inamorato L'Oiseaux," the essential truthfulness of which is attested in his diaries and letters. He begins by lamenting his lifelong amorousness, or sexuality, which has been an embarrassment and—cryptically —a hindrance to his achievement of "Eminence in the World." His surface look of pride he recognizes and passes off with the comment "Hardly any body liked him that did not know him, and nobody hated him that did." He parades his good qualities such as sincerity, frugality, abstinence in food and drink, his perfectionism, his love of retirement, and his conviction that a taste for the company of the ladies is necessary to prevent a scholar's being a mere pedant or a philosopher a cynic. He notes his sympathy for "all brute creatures" who are without protection in a hostile universe." In summary: "His memory is in nothing so punctual as in performing of Promises. He thinks himself as firmly bound by his Word as by his hand & seal. . . . He knows the World perfectly well, and thinks himself a citizen of it without the . . . distinctions of kindred sect or Country. He has learning without Ostentation. By Reading he's acquainted with ages past, and with the present by voyaging and conversation. . . ."[3] Though these words taken out of context may seem to make Byrd pompous, in context they point up the whimsical irony of his attitude. Altogether he shows a sophisticated introspection, as indicative of his meditative cerebration as any of the self-probings of the theologically centered saints of New England. Nowhere else in his writing does this gentleman planter come nearer to lowering his guard, though in many places one learns more of his external self.

Most of these "characters" seem to be more British than American, though Byrd observes that one of them has an "Indian" way of expressing himself. They seem to have been useful preliminary exercises for the remarkably perceptive and ironic portraits he was to draw in the prose of his great American period.

His sincere religious belief, neither Presbyterian-puritan nor deistic, is spelled out in the "creed" written on the first leaf of his 1709–1712 diary. His was the moderate or middle way of his time, a fairly normal Anglican Trinitarianism with a rational tinge. The patriotism suggested in his legal pieces and in "The History" is nowhere more evident than in the epitaph he composed for the tombstone of the popular Governor Nott, Spotswood's predecessor, who died after only a few months in office. The final lines, unrecorded on the stone probably because of their reflection on Spotswood, are at once eloquent and patriotic: "Whoever thou art that readest the

3. Maude H. Woodfin and Marion Tinling (eds.), *Another Secret Diary of William Byrd of Westover, 1739–1741* (Richmond, Va., 1942), 280. This volume includes numerous letters, essays, and poems. Much of the material I quote in this essay is from Byrd's works still in manuscript or from excerpted passages in various journals. For a fuller bibliography than these notes afford, see Pierre Marambaud, *William Byrd of Westover, 1674–1744* (Charlottesville, 1971) and the Byrd items in R. B. Davis, *American Literature Through Bryant* (New York, 1969).

sad tydings of his death, if a Stranger, pity the Country: if a Virginian, thy self."

None of Byrd's minor writings is more in the spirit of Queen Anne's London than the few scattered verses attributed to him. One should recall that his diaries assure us he wrote more, such as lampoons upon the House of Burgesses or Williamsburg gentlemen, or amusing pieces to be read to a circle of ladies not too delicate to enjoy the sexual innuendos. Over a span of twenty years, from 1700 to 1719, he composed light *vers de société* on the ladies who thronged to watering places such as Bath and Tunbridge Wells. The surviving lines are gallant or mocking and quite conventional.

Of better quality is the elegiac poem on the deceased Malantha, or the elegiac acrostic (probably his) on his daughter Evelyn printed in the *Virginia Gazette*. The five and eight line pieces imbedded in letters to Facetia are worth studying to determine their intention. But there can be no doubt about the bawdy intent of "Upon a Fart," a burlesque of the Countess of Winchelsea's, "Upon a Sigh," both included in Byrd's letter to Bellamira.

Perhaps in imagery and meter Byrd's best verse is the eleven-line epigram on his former enemy Governor Spotswood, now his friend. Included in "The History of the Dividing Line," the verse is a compliment to Spotswood's efforts to christianize and educate the Indian youths of the colony. The balanced antithesis of his best prose is combined with apt historical and classical figures in this graceful, disciplined little poem.

II. Diaries and Letters

It was not known that Byrd was a diarist at all until 1939, when the discovery of one portion of his shorthand journal was announced, and it was not until two years later that the decoded work appeared in print.⁴ Two other sections turned up, and were printed in 1942 and 1958. The three diaries cover the years 1709–1712, 1717–1721, and 1739–1742. Other portions may yet be discovered. As it is, the three printed segments are historically and literarily significant in themselves, though they hardly raise Byrd to the rank of an American Pepys. In some ways they are most interesting as glosses or commentaries on his major work, the "Histories." And they combine with his letters to fill out the story of the life and times of one of the most eminent of colonial Americans.

Young Byrd, studying in England, must have been aware that many men kept daily journals, though he may not have known of those kept by his fellows of the Royal Society, Samuel Pepys and John Evelyn, one in shorthand. He is more likely to have seen the log-like records of men who had been at sea, records which in form remind us of Byrd's own. In America, New Englander Samuel Sewall kept a diary, as did Byrd's Virginia son-in-law Landon Carter, though both the puritan and the cavalier were more introspective and detailed than the master of Westover. There survive several other diurnal jottings from eighteenth century Virginia and New England.

As literary pieces *per se,* Byrd's diaries have little merit. They are merely thin segments of life, not the rounded, relatively complete story presented by an autobiography or a long, continuous diary. The schedule of the day's activities—from early rising, to exercise, to reading in one of his acquired languages, to the name of each food he ate, to the concluding

4. L. B. Wright and Marion Tinling (eds.), *The Secret Diary of William Byrd of Westover, 1709–1712* (Richmond, Va., 1941). The Woodfin-Tinling diary was printed in 1942. *The London Diary* (cited above, Chap. V, note 20) was printed in New York in 1958.

nightly prayers (or neglect of them)—becomes so monoto-
nous that one edition of the earliest diary completely omits the
methodical repetitions. Occasionally Byrd noted what he had
been reading. Sabbath observance is meticulously recorded,
whether it included reading Tillotson on a dreary day at
home; hearing a visiting parson at Westover, or Commissary
Blair in Williamsburg; or listening to a famous preacher in
London. Byrd's pre- and extra-marital sexual relations are
noted with the matter-of-factness of one who never expected
this personal data to be read by anyone other than himself.

The daily business life of the plantation, as recorded in
the diaries, embraced agriculture, health of slaves, shipping,
mining, and land purchases. Social life at Westover, Williamsburg, or London followed fairly regular patterns, though
the persons with whom Byrd associated were fascinatingly
varied, many of them prominent in the literary, political,
military, or fashionable circles of colony or kingdom.

Of the roughly nine years covered in the diaries, more than
seven were spent in Virginia. Almost all of plantation and
village-capital life is at least outlined here. Political and personal contention with Governor Spotswood and Commissary
Blair in the early years, and warm friendship with both when
he was sixty-five, are noted without comment. Arranging
books, laying out gardens, planning the new brick house,
playing games with the ladies, plying family, friends, and
servants with purgatives or quinine—the journals tell us a
good deal about plantation life on the James River. As a
record of life during "publick times" in the capital at Williamsburg, it is equally informative. Meetings of the council,
the general court, and the board of governors of William and
Mary, pleasant and unpleasant encounters with Governor
Spotswood, dinners and balls, are briefly observed, but often
with a personal anecdote which illuminates both the observer

and the thing observed. The diaries are rich in historical value; when taken chronologically they indicate the development of the colony from frontier fears to sophisticated political arguments in an established society—the record of a nation in embryo.

Byrd's sense of humor never deserts him, though in the diaries it is less evident than in his other writings. Cheating his first wife at cards and quarreling with her concerning her eyebrow-plucking are inherently comic situations, but Byrd's commentary is deadpan: "got the better of her, and maintained my authority." His curious dreams, faithfully recorded along with speculation as to their portent, were apparently taken seriously. But if the reader keeps in mind the age and Byrd's other writings, he can never be sure that the diarist is not smiling as he describes the figments of his subconscious.

The life of the London man-about-town (described in the second diary, kept during the interval between his two marriages) is as significant for the English social historian as for the American. It is interesting as an indication of how easily a Virginia colonial might slip into English high society, and it explains some of the habits, attitudes, and amusements of Byrd in America. He has been called a social climber, but there is no indication that the Virginian ever felt that he was not to the manor born, as that other diarist Pepys may have felt. Byrd's schooling, his intimacy with a score of noble and eminent men, his *entrée* to all the best houses and to the royal court—these seem to have been taken as a matter of course, though he took pride as well as pleasure in his friendships with Sir Robert Southwell and Sir Hans Sloane, and in being a member of the Royal Society.

Byrd hardly kept a diary out of mere narcissism or desire to create a public image. He enjoyed life, and by keeping a record of its fleeting days he could, as he grew older, reread his jottings and place events in their proper perspective. That he did reread he attests in his last diary and in his commonplace book. But probably his strongest motivation was the belief that some day, when he had the leisure time, and lacked hedonistic and business distractions, he would transform the diaries into more enduring prose. The fact that he did turn his notes and journals of most of 1728 and portions of 1732 and 1733 into such prose bears out this supposition. Perhaps he planned to utilize other portions of his diaries, such as the story of his English tour with Sir John Perceval, or descriptions of the literary and social activity surrounding the circle of London gallants who were also poets, scholars, and playwrights. But seventy years was hardly enough time for a writer such as Byrd, a reviser and perfectionist, to transmute the dross of daily trivia into the polished silver of prose in the age of Anne.

Byrd's letters scarcely compare in literary quality with those of his greatest British contemporaries, but among colonial American epistolarians he must be given high rank. The letters are a necessary complement to and gloss upon his other writings, especially the diaries. They fill gaps in his life which the extant diaries do not cover; they shed light on persons merely mentioned in the diaries; they give documentary evidence of his remarkably diverse interests; they indicate that he was a master of several epistolary forms; and they afford our best evidence of their author's concomitant love of England and patriotism for Virginia. They contain passages equal in style and feeling to the best of the "Histories," and they include a number of ordinary business and polite social notes.

Many of Byrd's epistles, most of them undated, follow the literary conventions of the late seventeenth and early eighteenth centuries. They are most often addressed to ladies.

Sometimes serving as mere frames for character sketches, they are in turn playfully flirtatious or piteously pleading for the lady's hand or for her favor. Preciosa, Vaporina, Zenobia, Lucretia, Fidelia, and the rest (as we have noted, actual ladies) were addressed in tones sharply satirical, mocking, semi-serious, or serious, though even in the last with sardonic overtones. The epistolary courtship of Facetia by Veramour (Byrd in his youth) is a series of pleadings interspersed with the malicious or droll gossip of the town. In middle age he addresses Minionet and the cruel Charmante in much the same fashion. In the same period, his epistolary wooing of Sabina reveals a serio-comic situation worthy of being turned into a sentimental comedy by one of his numerous playwright friends —if Byrd himself lacked sufficient detachment to undertake it. As Byrd observed in "Inamorato L'Oiseaux," he was usually at his worst—his most ridiculous—when he was in love.

But to others, such as Fidelia (Lucy Parke), the lady he won, or his kinswoman-by-law "Cousin Taylor," he is courtly, gallant, amusing, sure of himself. His letters to the latter are particulary witty and gently satiric—not of the lady herself, but of the rest of humankind. The balanced clauses, paradoxical images, alliterative phrases, the frequent reliance on assonance so characteristic of his fully developed style in the "Histories" is also here, from the letters of 1700 to the last forty-one years later.

Byrd was already an effective and witty letter writer by 1701, when he and the convalescent Sir John Perceval (later Earl of Egmont) began a tour of eastern and northern England and part of Scotland. Apparently Byrd's Scottish letters have not survived, but those giving his impressions of provincial England, scholars, antiquarians, university life, and the appearance of cathedral towns are almost as entertaining as his later travel accounts of the expedition from Currituck

Inlet to the Blue Mountains. Conversing frequently in French and sometimes relieving the tedium of horseback travel with Sir John's songs, Byrd mentions table talk with such still-remembered scholars as Humphrey Prideaux of Norwich and John Colebatch of Cambridge. In Cambridge, they were much entertained: "We din'd yesterday at Mr. Vice-Chancellor's, where Philosophy flew about the table faster than the wine." It is interesting to note the contrast with the picture of Oxford Byrd drew two years later in a letter to Facetia. He had stayed at Oxford while the troupe of players led by Mrs. Bracegirdle and Mrs. Prince were entertaining the undergraduates and the advanced theology students were contending for their doctorates. Though Byrd loved the theater, he found student rowdiness too much, and concluded, "I was perfectly sick of ye confusion & impertinence of Oxford, & thought every day a month til I coud return hither [to London]."

An observant lover of nature, Byrd continued to show in his letters as late as 1741 his enormously varied interest in the physical world about him in Virginia. He corresponded for at least thirty-five years (1706–1741) with Sir Hans Sloane, sending the great scientist boxes of seeds, plants, skins, live birds, and animals. He expatiated to Sloane on various medicinal plants, including ginseng and snakeroot. Byrd frequently alluded to the Royal Society, and sent its members boxes of plants to try in their gardens. In exchange, he asked for English flowering shrubs and trees for his own use. The great naturalist Mark Catesby frequently visited Byrd at Westover and gave advice on laying out his garden. Peter Collinson, the Quaker naturalist called Byrd's the finest garden in Virginia. Byrd corresponded with Catesby when the latter was back in England, with Collinson, and with the latter's friend John Bartram, who also visited him at Westover.

For thirty-five years Byrd begged Sir Hans Sloane to per-suade some young naturalist, preferably a physician, to come to the United States for several years of field work searching for medicinal plants. Both John Lawson of North Carolina and Mark Catesby did some of this kind of work, as did the two John Claytons and other "curious" gentlemen. But they had not gone far enough inland, Byrd felt, to have discovered significant new species. In his letters Byrd also showed his interest in minerals, meteorology, astronomy, and other phases of science, and commented upon them, much as he did in the "Histories."

Among Byrd's best letters, literarily and historically, were those addressed to his close friends and relatives. Among his London friends, in addition to the scientists and Sir Robert Southwell mentioned above, were Edward Southwell, secre-tary of state for Ireland; Sir Charles Wager, First Lord of the Admiralty; Charles and John Boyle, successively Earls of Or-rery; John Campbell, Duke of Argyle, and his brother Lord Islay; the Earl of Egmont; Lord Carteret; and Colonel Martin Bladen. It should be noted that all these were in some way men of letters, at least three of them having dashed off plays —all professionally produced—in their spare moments. Among Byrd's Virginia correspondents were his brothers-in-law, the horticulturist-planter John Custis and the historian-planter Robert Beverley II; Virginia governors Nicholson, Spotswood, and Gooch; North Carolina governors Burrington and Johnston; and his neighbors Benjamin Harrison and Sir John Randolph. English correspondents, most of them relatives of his second wife, were Colonel and Mrs. Francis Otway, Lady Sherrard, and Mrs. ["Cousin"] Taylor. With them all he shared the interests he displays elsewhere—with his Brit-ish friends his anxiety at the state of the empire, news and gossip about mutual acquaintances, and details of his own activities in a faraway corner of the world. With Custis he discussed family affairs and plants, with Sir John Randolph local politics and amateur theatricals at Williamsburg. Mrs. Taylor, Mrs. Otway, and Lady Sherrard were addressed with playful gallantry. To Mrs. Taylor, who appears to have enjoyed a spicy story, Byrd related the ribald tale of a Williamsburg actress who artificially enhanced her feminine charms, thereby coming to public grief.

In letters to England Byrd frequently jeered at the Saints of New England, who carried on a smuggling operation in the Chesapeake Bay region, sold Kill-Devil rum, and were the principal movers in the fiendish slave trade. Byrd, like James Fenimore Cooper a century later, considered the Puritans canting hypocrites. Even to his old friend and fellow Middle Templar Benjamin Lynde, chief justice of Massachusetts, he makes the charge directly, though in jesting tones. This anti-New Englandism shows up frequently in Byrd's Dividing Line "Histories" as well. His abhorrence of the slave trade is most trenchantly expressed to Lord Egmont (July 12, 1736), when he begins his discussion with "this unchristian Traffick, of making Merchandise of our Fellow Creatures. . . ."

Whether he addressed Sir Robert Walpole, his librarian at Westover, or a penniless fellow Virginian in London, Byrd wrote graceful phrases and witty anecdotes. So frequently did he write with tongue in cheek that the unwary must read carefully. One letter contains a sketch of a lady and a parson in a mail coach which might well match a Hogarthian print. The devastating irony of his letter to John Fox upon receipt of a volume of trifling verse Fox had without permission dedicated to him is worthy of comparison with Dr. Johnson's classic reply to Chesterfield. The playful irony of his "Most hypochondriack Sir" reply to librarian Procter's complaint about firewood and candles is as unanswerable as his letter to Fox.

Emotionally, and perhaps intellectually, the most appealing theme developed in Byrd's letters is his inner conflict as to whether he was Englishman or American, gay Londoner or busy and patriotic Virginian. He was one or the other according to his mood. The scale is definitely unbalanced, for most of his extant letters were written from Virginia to London friends, and he consciously and unconsciously rationalizes his rural existence as a sojourn in Eden.

But he wanted his first wife, on a visit to England, "to see the town [London] in all its glory"; and in later years he confided to the earl of Orrery that he longed to return once more "to that Enchanted Island," even with its smoke and fog. An earlier letter mentioned that his older daughters found the colony lifeless after the balls and masquerades of London. Begging for letters from "home," he wrote Mrs. Otway that "Our lives are uniform, . . . till the Season brings in the Ships. Then we tear open the Letters they bring us from Our Friends, as eagerly as a greedy Heir tears open his Rich Fathers will."

Nevertheless, the other side of the coin was usually uppermost. To Custis, from London, he declared that he longed to be in America, for "my heart is in Virginia"; a little later from the colony he described the second Mrs. Byrd's "first impression of the country in spring." Again and again he referred to "our sun-shiny country," where "the Heavens put on a Cheerful Countenance." A dozen times he portrayed himself in the role of *pater familias* in a natural paradise. This passage, from a 1726 letter, is fairly typical, including its biblical imagery:

I have a large Family of my own, and my doors are open to Every Body, yet I have no Bills to pay, and half-a-Crown will rest undisturbed in my Pocket for many Moons together. Like one of the Patriarchs, I have my Flocks and my Herds, my Bond-men and Bond-women, and every Soart of Trade amongst my own Servants, so that I live in a kind of Independence on every one but Providence. . . .

Thus my Lord we are very happy in our Canaans if we could but forget the Onions and Fleshpots of Egypt. . . .[5]

In a more pagan idyllic mood Byrd noted that "We [who] are banished from those Polite Pleasures are forct to take up rural entertainments. A Library, a Garden, a Grove, and a purling Stream are the Innocent Scenes that divert our Leizure."

Byrd's familiar letters then, like other epistles of the English Augustan age, offered instruction, advice, ribald entertainment, scientific information, and words of love and gallantry. His mood was sometimes playful, sometimes happily serene, but most often satiric. He liked to exercise the repartee of his time even in his letters: "I love to have the Ball tost directly to me & catch it before it reaches the ground." His turns of phrase were always graceful. He looked at himself and his fellow men with a certain equanimity, sometimes tinged with the cynical or the serene: "We play the Fool . . . 50 or 60 Years, what Prodigys then should we grow up to in double that time? And why should the figure of our constitutions be lengthened out when the odds are great, we should make a bad use of them." These words were written in 1739. Twenty years earlier he had been in a less disillusioned mood when he wrote: "God almighty is ever contriving our happiness, and does many things for good which appear to our short sight to be terrible misfortunes. But by the time the last act of the play comes on, we grow convinced of our mis-

---

5. "To Charles, Earl of Orrery," *Virginia Magazine of History and Biography*, XXXII (1924), 27.

take, and look back with pleasure on those scenes which first
appeared unfortunate. . . ."[6]

III. The "Public" Prose

William Byrd's four major works, "The Secret History of the
Dividing Line," "The History of the Dividing Line," "A
Progress to the Mines," and "A Journey to the Land of Eden,"
appeared together for the first time in 1966. This edition—
based on the original "Westover Manuscripts," the one manuscript of "The Secret History" in the American Philosophical
Society, and a few odd pages to fill lacunae—is the first tex-
tually satisfactory publication of these prose travel accounts.
Taken as a unit, this is the first classic work by a native
southern American. Some of the manuscripts were well
known in 1803 and 1817, portions were published in 1822,
1841, 1866, and 1900. A parallel-text edition of the two "Histories" first appeared in 1929, though a few pages of text
were left out which have since been filled in. A new printing of this edition, with the missing pages supplied, appeared
in 1967. There is still a need for a modern authenticated
text based upon a complete study of the variants among the
manuscripts in the Virginia Historical Society, the American
Philosophical Society, Colonial Williamsburg, Inc., and the
Henry E. Huntington Library, and the printed 1822 fragments of a different manuscript version of "The History,"
now apparently lost or disintegrated.

The reworked fragments of drafts in Byrd's own handwriting, especially when compared with the almost complete
fair copy of "The Secret History" in the American Philosophical Society and the fair copy of the other three travel ac-

---

6. "To Irene," in B. J. Lossing (ed.), *Recollections and Private Memoirs of Washington* (New York, 1860), 29.

counts in the Virginia Historical Society, graphically illustrate Byrd's habit of revising and filling out.

The Westover (Virginia Historical Society) version of "The History," a fair copy not in Byrd's hand but with emendations in his hand, was apparently nearly ready for the printer at the time of Byrd's death. As already noted, Byrd kept a diary during the Dividing Line expedition, the visit to the Germanna mines, and the excursion to North Carolina, he probably kept additional notebooks loaded with statistics and descriptions of fauna, flora, and topography. Among the sources for his expanded accounts of his travels were two documents, "A Journal of the Dividing Line Drawn between the Colonies of Virginia & North Carolina begun March 5: 1728 . . . [by] Col. Byrd & Others" (in the British Museum) and "A Journal of the proceedings of the Commissioners" (in the Public Record Office). These were rough reports submitted by Byrd in 1728 and 1729 as leader of the Virginia group of the expedition. There is no real evidence as to the date of composition of the shorter "A Progress to the Mines" or "A Journey to the Land of Eden," but they too were drawn from diaries and rough notes kept during the excursions.

Byrd probably waited several years before beginning at least one of the two "Histories." As early as 1728–1729, he gave Lord Orrery and others a capsule account of the expedition in his letters. Not until July, 1736 (in a badly damaged letter probably written to Lord Egmont) did Byrd mention that he was shaping his rough notes into a larger work, for he protested that his activity in founding the cities of Richmond and Petersburg, and promoting Switzer colonization along the Roanoke, had prevented his finishing the work identified in a manuscript note as "The History" (version unknown) and "A Journey." In the same month, in a letter to Peter Collinson, Byrd apparently declined to send a copy of the manuscript to Collinson: "I own it goes against me to deny you such a trifle, but I have one infirmity, never to venture anything unfinished out of my hands." Byrd does offer to send the rough journal, possibly "The Secret History," for it "is only the skeleton & Ground Work of what I intend, which may some time or other come to be filled out with vessels, & flesh, & have a decent skin drawn over all to keep things tight in their places and prevent their looking frightful. I have the materials ready, & want only leisure to put them together . . . ." A year later Byrd informed Collinson that he still intended to "cover this dry skeleton" and that, since the book would occasionally mention plants and animals, he would like for Mark Catesby to do the "figures," or illustrations, of them.

Internal evidence also aids in the conjectural dating of "The History." Byrd mentions in it a natural catastrophe occurring in 1736, but no one appears to have noted his comparison of throngs at an outdoor religious service to the multitudes who gathered in the open fields to hear George Whitefield preach. The great evangelist's first visit to America was February–August, 1738, though his preaching to great crowds had begun in England the year before. These two references may have been interpolations in a completed manuscript, but they do not so read, and neither appears in "The Secret History." "The History" was most probably begun about 1732 and finished some time between 1738 and 1740.

Almost surely "The Secret History" is the earlier version. It is half as long as "The History," omits the prefatory history of Virginia, uses tag names for the principal participants, and is much more sharply satirical, even sarcastic, than "The History." It includes several speeches by Byrd to the whole group of surveyors and assistants, and a number of letters and other documents which were passed between the Virginia and North Carolina commissioners, none of which appear in "The History." "The Secret History" could have been the skeleton he intended to flesh out, although the travel account he sent to Collinson may have been closer in content and tone to the longer "History."

What the two "Histories" have in common is that they are both travel accounts of the same expedition and both possess a mock-heroic quality—though in the case of "The History," mock-epic unobtrusively merges into genuine epic. Both may have been promotion pamphlets, though the propaganda quality is much stronger in "The History" than in "The Secret History." The latter apparently was written for the delectation of a private circle of American friends, as attested by the casual comparison of Moseley to "the Commissary" (James Blair), an allusion which might have been lost upon an English reader. The basis for most of the humor in both versions is sex, as in much Restoration and eighteenth-century English literature and in the works of neighboring Marylanders George Alsop and Ebenezer Cook. But sexual allusion is much more abundant and much coarser in "The Secret History." It is not difficult to visualize Byrd, with his kin and neighbors, the Harrisons, the Banisters, the Beverleys, the Stiths, and the Bollings, sitting before a winter fire in a plantation house along the James reading and laughing at "The Secret History."

The two works have certain stylistic qualities in common: antithesis; analogy; witty disparagement; puns; short, balanced, paradoxical, and epigrammatic statements. The two "Histories" share these qualities with the letters and character sketches. "The History" is in general the more urbane, sophisticated, and polished work, but has less of an air of spontaneity. In both pieces, the saints of New England receive a number of glancing blows—at their sanctimonious hypocrisies in trading, and in the instance of Puzzlecause (North Carolina Commissioner Little) at their debased and hypocritical lechery—with perhaps more anti-Puritanism to be found in "The History." Disparaging allusions to North Carolina frequently appear in "The Secret History," chiefly in the form of caricatures of that colony's commissioners and anecdotes about its people; but they are much more frequent in "The History." And more sweeping and generalized condemnations of Carolinians and other more northern colonists are employed in "The History" to accentuate Virginia as earth's only paradise for prospective settlers.

Whereas "The Secret History" was intended as witty social satire, "The History" was, at least in part, a redirecting of the same materials for propaganda purposes. The learned descriptions of unusual American plants and animals, from ginseng to buffalo and beaver; the detailed descriptions of beautiful rivers, flowery meadows, and odoriferous woods; the disquisitions on Indian life, customs, and costumes—these often appear in germinal form in "The Secret History," but the extrapolations (expanded versions) of these writings in "The History" are evidently aimed at the European reader, probably the potential emigrant. Yet "The History" remains essentially a work of art, the projection of a not-too-unusual colonial official enterprise into a travel-adventure symbolic of the frontier experience. Byrd adorned and furnished it from his wide reading in many languages and with even more of his personal experience than he had employed in "The Secret History."

The basic material for the two "Histories" sprang, of course, from the two-stage Dividing Line expedition of 1728, authorized by the king and implemented by the governors of Virginia and North Carolina to determine the exact location of the boundary between the two colonies. It was an old problem, at least once before having been undertaken with unsatisfactory results, involving such important matters as titles to land and squatters who evaded taxes from either colonial government. Byrd and two fellow commissioners from Virginia met their North Carolina counterparts at Currituck Inlet on the Atlantic Ocean. With them were surveyors, pioneers (engineer-chainbearers), and woodsmen-hunters. They began work in late February and stopped on April 9 as the snakes began to appear. They resumed their labors in September, and the Virginia party continued until late November in the foothills of the mountains, though they had long since been deserted by their Carolina colleagues. They had crossed sandpits and what is still the jungle quagmire of the Great Dismal Swamp, forded flooding spring rivers, endured torrents of rain and scarcity of food, visited Indian villages, narrowly escaped some potentially fatal accidents, and made observations of topography, red men, and fauna and flora. Byrd, as senior member of the Virginia party, had to prevent open conflict between members of his own group, endure some treachery, and occasionally mete out justice. According to his own modest statements and those of the two colonial governors, he showed his probity by awarding North Carolina more territory than it had ever expected, and his leadership by returning with all his men in comparatively good health and his instructions carried out. That he should profit personally by purchasing many thousands of acres in the territories he had first "discovered" was in no way incompatible with the spirit or letter of his mission.

As already noted, Byrd's friends who heard or read "The Secret History" must have found this account of the journey as entertaining as a Restoration or sentimental comedy. Byrd himself was Steddy, his Virginia compatriots Dandridge and

Fitz-William appeared as Meanwell and Firebrand, their surveyors as Orion and Astrolabe, and the North Carolinians Moseley as Plausible, Lovick as Shoebrush, and Little as Puzzlecause. The vignettes are apt and cutting, *e.g.*, "Puzzlecause [Harvard-educated] had degenerated from a New–England preacher, for which his Godly Parents design'd him, to a very wicked, but awkward rake." The vignette becomes a full portrait as the journey continues and Puzzlecause shows his wild and indiscriminate sexuality. Shoebrush is a merry, good-humored man who acquired his good manners while employed as *valet de chambre* to North Carolina Governor Hyde. Byrd treats Plausible, a learned and forceful character, with more respect; but toward the end Byrd professes himself disillusioned by this commissioner's "treachery." If the portraits of the Carolinians are unflattering, so are those of Firebrand and Orion, the one lascivious, vicious, and conniving, the other ineffective, untrained, sycophantic, and cowardly. Meanwell, the author's good friend and principal aide is portrayed sympathetically. But if there are any heroes other than the narrator in either "History," they are the rank and file, the men who cheerfully and uncomplainingly dragged the chains through quicksand and jungle, slept in soaked clothing, and in general "carried on." They were the frontiersmen who were making America, but they were also Virginia yeoman farmers who as hunters or craftsmen put their past experience to significant use. In "The Secret History" the villainy and knavery of Firebrand and Shoebrush were often in the foreground, but the same scenes also introduced the first-described American poor whites, inhabitants of Lubberland, where the men were indolent and boorish, the women careworn and slovenly. In both "Histories," Byrd refers to these latter folk as North Carolinians, perhaps because they do appear for the most part to have come first to the easternmost section of that colony; but actually they lived on both sides of the old and new boundary lines. Naturally, it suited his propaganda purposes in "The History" to label them as non-Virginians. But another point he makes implicitly, and occasionally explicitly, is that some of these people occupy good lands which, under the management of such thrifty immigrants as Swiss or German or French, might be turned into prosperous and perhaps eventually opulent farms. He makes the same point more explicitly in his letters promoting colonization.

Included in "The Secret History," as noted above, were Steddy's letters to various officials and his speeches to encourage his men. Both kinds of documents were certainly taken from notebooks or journals, the original rhetoric perhaps a little embellished in the retelling. The speeches suggest epic intent in that they roughly parallel the patriotic or council-of-war speeches Byrd knew from classical or Renaissance work in his library. All this documentation, the tag names, and the individual sexual adventures of certain members of the party are omitted from "The History," yet the latter is twice as long.

To flesh out "The History" Byrd used several devices. He added the rather long prefatory résumé of Virginia history, emphasizing the colony's steady shrinkage in size as broken promises carved from it new provinces. Thus he gave potential European readers a sense of the situation as his story opened. He took what is in "The Secret History" a brief entry about the Saponi Indians and expanded it into a detailed account of numbers, dress, hunting habits, and manners, some of it drawn from such sources as John Lawson's *A New Voyage to Carolina* (1709), some from Byrd's own experience. The well-known account of Bearskin the Indian hunter's religion occurs in both versions, but it is expanded and completely rewritten in "The History," with more picturesque adjectives and nouns throughout the discourse; it concludes with an observation not even suggested in "The Secret History":

This was the Substances of Bearskin's Religion, and was as much to the purpose as cou'd be expected from a meer State of Nature, without one Glimpse of Revelation or Philosophy.

It contain'd, however, the three Great Articles of Natural Religion: the Belief of a God; the Moral Distinction between Good and Evil; and the Expectations of Rewards and Punishments in Another World.

Indeed, the Indian Notion of a Future Happiness is a little Gross and Sensual, like Mahomet's Paradise. But how can it be otherwise, in a People that are contented with Nature as they find Her, and have no other lights but what they receive from purblind Tradition?[7]

Similar treatment was accorded the accounts of plants and animals, which Byrd amplified in "The History" from the scientific books in his library and his earlier observations in other parts of Virginia. His natural description was not always objectively scientific, for like certain of his contemporaries Byrd intensified or heightened the colors with a tall story, usually tongue in cheek or deadpan, but at times taken half seriously even by the sophisticated teller himself. He frequently employed literary allusion—to drama, verse, curious and learned tomes, and especially to the classics. Religion was taken seriously, at least by Byrd and Dr. Humdrum (Parson Fontaine), and its absence among frontier whites evoked serious concern and disdainful satire. Graphic figures emerged from his own experience: "We then kindled a rousing fire in the center of it, and lay round it, like so many Knights Templars," presents a vivid juxtaposition of frontier reality and

7. William K. Boyd and Percy G. Adams (eds.), *William Byrd's Histories of the Dividing Line* (New York, 1967), 202.

the memory of the round Temple church in London. Other emotions are rekindled in tranquillity. "The Secret History" 's already poetic commentary "I hardly knew how to behave myself in a Bed, after having lain a week in the Open Field, & seeing the Stars twinkle over my head," becomes in "The History," "A clear Sky, spangled with Stars, was our Canopy, which being the last thing we saw before we fell asleep gave us Magnificent Dreams."

The prose of "The Secret History" may be poignant, as the early "I often cast a longing Eye towards England, & sigh'd"; or piquant, as the "Commissioners of Carolina . . . [were] much better provided for the Belly than the Business." Perhaps "The History" suffers in liveliness as the author sacrifices this terseness for more explicit explanations of Carolinian uncouthness or ineptitude. But the pervasive ironic tone of "The History" displaces the shorter work's forthright satire and makes for an equality, or balance, between the two accounts. As more than one critic has observed, the two "Histories" complement each other. Most readers will find it more rewarding to read the parallel-text edition, despite the slight distraction of glancing from one page to the opposite one.

Similar in tone to "The History" are the two shorter pieces from the Westover manuscript, "A Journey to the Land of Eden in the Year 1733" and "A Progress to the Mines in the Year 1732." The former is really an appendix or afterword to "The History," detailing Byrd's experiences in surveying, with his friend Major Mayo, the lands acquired in the boundary region. The tone retains a slight tinge of irony, but the individual characterizations are less lively than those of "The History." For seeing and being instructed in the working of the mines of former governor Spotswood, "A Progress" is livelier—with portraits of such people as Miss Theky the old maid, entertaining anecdotes such as the story of the tame deer plunging into a full-length mirror, and interesting information on mining and smelting. Both add to our knowledge of the author and his world. But they are, after all, merely travel accounts.

"The Secret History" and "The History" are more conscious works of art. In the end "The Secret History" remains a remarkably lively comic satire, extremely personal, half London wit and half New World situation. "The History" is something more, a work superior in both intention and accomplishment. Here is the southern planter of the golden age seeing his native Virginia world through the eyes of European experience and education. He ornaments the picture with his learning and his knowledge of the world of men. Above all, he sees it as he should, as an actual journey which is also the symbolic progress of the American experience. As in Leatherstocking's gradual trek westward or Huck Finn's voyage down the Mississippi, the epic significance of the journey is largely implicit. But the epic quality, however shadowy, is definitely consciously intended. In both "Histories," Byrd playfully describes the founding of the noble order of Ma-ooty, with wild turkey beards as cockades, a spread winged turkey in gold suspended from a ribbon collar about the neck, and a Latin motto signifying that through this bird these chosen ones were supported in the wilderness. And in "The History," his last diurnal entry records his sense of the heroic quality of American destiny in the simile: "Thus ended our second expedition, in which we extended the line within the shadow of the Cherakee mountains, when we were obliged to set up our pillars, like Hercules, and return home."

Byrd wrote for a variety of reasons in a variety of forms. His entirely serious writings, including legal briefs and petitions, a proposal to drain the Dismal Swamp, business letters, and scientific epistles, afford evidence of his depth of learning, his eager curiosity, his practical sagacity, and his Christian rationalism. But he lived in an age when the comic spirit reigned, and the diaries, "characters," letters, and travel accounts, however factual, are marked by "an indulgent irony" which on rare occasions sharpens into somewhat disdainful but never cruel satire.

Byrd, like other great planters of his own and the succeeding age, lived by the golden mean—that is, he wished to see his world in balance. Others employed the yardstick of the middle way without humor—men like William Fitzhugh, Landon Carter, or even Thomas Jefferson. But the master of Westover found such deviations from the middle way droll— whether committed by pompous Carolina commissioners, lawless denizens of the boundary line, or the saints of New England whose practice differed so sharply from their professed pious morality. A talent nurtured in Queen Anne's London must shape incongruities into congruity by the mightiest of weapons, wit. Byrd's observant eye caught everything in Williamsburg, Westover, or the wilderness, and usually found it out of proportion. He was quite aware that he was laughing at himself when he laughed at things around him in Virginia. His mood and his intention thus sprang from his rationalism.

He united wit with utility. His wit might win a lady's favor, destroy a rival, or persuade Europeans that they should migrate to his Eden. He exercised the combination most effectively, as we have noted, in his most ambitious work designed to attract settlers. But the conscious artist in him would not allow him to limit "The History" to the function of promotion pamphlet. It was also planned to satisfy the natural curiosity of the European concerning the strange New World and to supply scientists with interesting data on every conceivable object of his regard.

Byrd was modest and, despite his satire or through it, tolerant. He could and did ridicule and accept in the same passage. One could wish him less modest and more detailed in both the "Histories" and the diaries—about what he was writing; his table talk with the coffee house immortals of his years in the London of Addison, Pope, and Swift; his founding of cities; his opinions of the books he was reading. Never does he pass critical judgment on a book he has read or on the abilities of a playwright or an actress he knew intimately; very rarely he ventures an opinion on such blurred or dim figures of the American past as Commissary Blair, Governors Spotswood and Gooch, or the distinguished Sir John Randolph. His diaries remain, at least when compared with those of Pepys or Evelyn or Landon Carter, curiously superficial. Byrd was not given to introspection even in the privacy of shorthand, perhaps because restraint went hand in hand with tolerance. Though he may have been as imaginative as his son-in-law Landon Carter, he did not possess the latter's sensitivity or sensibility.

Byrd was a perfectionist as a writer, as his quoted letters, rough drafts, and versions of the "Histories" demonstrate. An unfinished manuscript would never, if he could help it, go from his hands to the printer's. He wrote with grace and symmetry, in rhythms at once his own and his era's.

The aristocrat William Byrd, like that later Virginia aristocrat Jefferson, looked with sympathy at all kinds of his fellow Americans, and with perceptive curiosity at the uncouth and marvelous land in which they lived. More than the Massachusetts theologians, he projected the future United States, not as a city set upon a hill, but as a happy valley of plenty and a beehive of fruitful industry—despite the natural and acquired indolence of some of its inhabitants. And it is through William Byrd that the sprightly charm of eighteenth-century English literature entered colonial American writing.

⌐⟨VII⟩⌐

Samuel Davies:
Poet of the Great Awakening

[William Byrd was privately tolerant of man's manners and his foibles. Just after he disappeared from the Virginia scene, a quite different sort of person came forward in the colony to urge another kind of tolerance, a public one of religious differences—or of religious doctrines and organizations which were not Anglican. Like Byrd, Davies was a writer of prose and verse. Unlike Byrd, he published fairly voluminously in his own lifetime—a volume of poems, dozens of sermons, and many hymns.

For fifteen years after Byrd's death, Samuel Davies was one of the most distinguished colonists in Virginia. He assisted at the birth of the religious movement known as the Great Awakening, and he was in turn made famous by that movement. Though he did not introduce it, he firmly established the Presbyterian church in Virginia and in the South. He catechized and baptized hundreds, perhaps thousands, of blacks, and sent missionaries to the Cherokee Indians. He was easily the foremost southern pulpit orator of the period, a speaker whose discourses show how the principles and examples of Quintilian, Aristotle, Demosthenes, and Cicero might be fused with the prose rhythms of the King James Bible to produce impressive and persuasive rhetoric.

It was from Princeton, the college that Davies helped establish and of which he was an early president, that James

Madison was graduated. And it was from hearing Davies at Hanover courthouse that Anglican Patrick Henry is said to have acquired his forensic style. Yet as a man of letters Samuel Davies should also be remembered for his poetry, which owed something to George Herbert, Isaac Watts, and Philip Doddridge, but grew mostly out of the fervent and Calvinist spirit of Davies himself.]

ON APRIL 18, 1752, a clerk in the *Virginia Gazette* bookshop in Williamsburg recorded in his ledger the sale to Samuel Davies of one copy of Aristotle's *Art of Poetry*.[1] Other familiar names appear in the pages of this account book, such as Thomas Jefferson and George Wythe, who bought histories, plays, various editions of the classics, and many volumes of modern poems. Simultaneously, Davies' own *Miscellaneous Poems,* which had appeared three months previously, was being bought by many Virginians, possibly because it was published by William Hunter, printer of the *Gazette.*

This sale to Davies is interesting and perhaps significant in several ways. He had been a practicing poet for almost a decade, and his education in the classics would suggest that he had earlier been familiar with the book he now added to his library of more than five hundred volumes. But just at this time, and for more than a year later, Davies was engaged in an acrimonious debate in the pages of the *Gazette* with one "Walter Dymocke," who attacked "the Virginia Pindar" for alleged bad taste in diction and imagery, bad rhymes and meters, bathetic themes, "enthusiasm," and a dozen other weaknesses.[2] The acrimony was one-sided, for Davies ad-

1. *Virginia Gazette* Day Book (MS in Alderman Library, University of Virginia).
2. Between March 20 and June 12, 1752, eight long criticisms appeared signed with the pseudonym Walter Dymocke. Three replies, perhaps not by Davies, appeared May 22, June 25, and August 14. Davies

mitted freely certain real poetic deficiencies and replied to caustic criticisms courteously though sharply, pointing out that his adversary was unfairly lifting passages out of context and thus caricaturing his work. As we shall see, the poet usually compared himself with writers more recent than Aristotle; but perhaps he purchased the *Art of Poetry* because he wished to refresh himself on the principles of classical criticism, which his opponent was mixing with neoclassical dicta as weapons, or ammunition, in his attacks.

Both Davies and "Dymocke," who was actually an Anglican clergyman named John Robertson, made it clear in their arguments that more than good-versus-bad poetry was at stake. For four years Davies had championed the cause of religious toleration, and the right of his own Presbyterian group to hold meetings and have their own preachers in Virginia. Lieutenant-Governor Sir William Gooch and even the later executive Robert Dinwiddie encouraged him, but from the entrenched Anglicans of the Virginia Council and the king's attorney general, Peyton Randolph, he met with hostility and hindrances. The established clergy also were deeply alarmed at the inroads George Whitefield, Davies, and other preachers of the Great Awakening had already made in their parishes. The fact that Davies was the principal figure of the new evangelism in Virginia undoubtedly was a major reason for attempting to make him look ridiculous by attacking his verse, which was almost entirely religiously meditative and evangelical in character.

Samuel Davies was in 1752 already distinguished, and be-

---

himself answered in the July 3 and 10 issues. Other articles followed, though so many issues of the *Gazette* between late 1752 and 1755 are missing that we probably do not have all the essays for either side. For further discussion, see below; see also Craig Gilborn, "Samuel Davies' Sacred Muse," *Journal of Presbyterian History,* XLI (1963), 74–79.

fore his death in 1761 at the age of thirty-seven he was to become a nationally and internationally known figure. Born in Delaware in 1723 of parents of Welsh extraction, he attended the "Log College" at Fagg's Manor in Chester County, Pennsylvania, the academy-plus-college in which the New Light Presbyterians trained their clergy.[3] His teacher and mentor, in memory of whom in 1751–1752 he was to compose two elegies, was the able Samuel Blair. In 1746 Davies was licensed to preach, and in the same year he married. Early in 1747 he was formally ordained and sent as an evangelist-missionary to organize the scattered congregations in Hanover and adjacent counties of Virginia. In April he petitioned the General Court in Williamsburg for a license to conduct services at four different places, and his long struggle for toleration in a colony where the Anglican was the established church had begun.[4] Then and later he was primarily concerned that the British Toleration Act of 1689

3. George W. Pilcher, *Samuel Davies: Apostle of Dissent in Colonial Virginia* (Knoxville, Tenn., 1971). The best extensive study of Davies is still unpublished: George H. Bost, "Samuel Davies: Colonial Revivalist and Champion of Religious Toleration" (Ph.D. dissertation, University of Chicago, 1942). Briefer but useful summaries of his life and work are: John E. Pomfret, "Samuel Davies," in the *Dictionary of American Biography;* Samuel Finley, "Samuel Davies," in *Annals of the American Pulpit,* ed. William B. Sprague (9 vols.; New York, 1858), III, 140–46; Wesley M. Gewehr, *The Great Awakening in Virginia, 1740–1790* (Durham, N.C., 1930), 68–105; George M. Brydon, *Virginia's Mother Church* (Philadelphia, 1952), II, 154–77. See also William H. Foote, *Sketches of Virginia, Historical and Biographical, First Series* (Richmond, 1966) for his diary and an extended discussion of his career. The diary itself has been recently republished in a more careful text and with useful notes: George W. Pilcher (ed.), *The Reverend Samuel Davies Abroad: The Diary of a Journey to England and Scotland, 1753–1755* (Urbana, 1967). Manuscripts and letters are scattered, with notable collections in the Union Theological Seminary in Richmond, Princeton University, and the Historical Society of Pennsylvania.

4. See George W. Pilcher, "Samuel Davies and Religious Toleration in Virginia," *The Historian,* XXVIII (1965), 48–49.

should be in force in the colonies.[5] He got his license at the time, but he had to fight continuously to maintain it and to extend its privileges to other groups and individuals.

Meanwhile his first wife had died, and he had married Jean Holt of Hanover, who was related by marriage to William Hunter of the *Virginia Gazette*. This wife, who bore him six children and survived him for many years, is the "Chara" of several of his poems. From 1748 until 1753, Davies vigorously promoted the cause of Presbyterianism and, indeed, of evangelical Christianity in general. In Hanover and surrounding counties, he raised funds, established meeting houses, and won converts with his eloquent sermons. Often he preached in the open air because no building was large enough to hold the crowds who flocked to hear him.

In November, 1753, at the instigation of the trustees of the infant College of New Jersey (now Princeton), and in the company of Gilbert Tennent, Davies embarked for England on a fund-raising campaign designed to set the new institution on its feet. He also hoped to get a favorable and final interpretation of the Act of Toleration, though on this score he achieved little but advice from British dissenters. During his fourteen months away from home he kept a diary—a most meditative and introspective journal, though it contains interesting facts and shrewd character analyses. In England, he made himself a reputation as a pulpit orator which endured long after his death. The mission was successful beyond all expectations, and the two clergymen returned in early 1755 with funds enough to assure Princeton's future.

Meanwhile the French and Indian War had escalated along the frontiers of Virginia, which were populated in considerable part by Scotch-Irish Presbyterians. During the next

5. Gewehr, *The Great Awakening*, 68–105, sees Davies as contending for much more than this.

two years Davies' sermons, though concerned with the soul's salvation, usually related it to such current happenings as the Lisbon earthquake, the death of General Braddock, and the barbarities of the French and the Indians.[6] Through his pulpit the dissenting minister became the colony's best recruiting officer. His sermons, *Religion and Patriotism: The Constituents of a Good Soldier* (1755), *Virginia's Danger and Remedy* (1756), and *The Curse of Cowardice* (1758), equated zealous patriotism with sound Christianity.[7] In this period, too, he continued his efforts toward educating and christianizing the Negroes.[8]

By 1759, after eleven years of Davies' pastorate in Virginia, the New Lights had gained respect and permanence, the colony had long felt the full force of the Great Awakening, and the first phase in the struggle for religious liberty was completed.[9] Perhaps Davies was ready to move on when he received the urgent invitation to succeed his friend Jonathan Edwards as president of the College of New Jersey. He at first declined, and his presbytery and congregation fought against his removal, but through his synod he was persuaded—and authorized—to assume the academic position.

Before he went to Great Britain the college had conferred on him the degree of Master of Arts—in part an earned degree, for he had successfully defended a thesis before its

6. Finley, "Samuel Davies," 142.
7. One of these sermons, *ca.* 1755, contained the famous prophecy concerning "That heroic youth . . . Colonel Washington, whom we cannot but hope Providence has hitherto preserved in so single a manner, for some important service to his country."
8. In actual practice he was so successful in teaching a group of Negroes to read the Bible and the Catechism that his former pupils were for a generation afterwards frequently picked out to instruct their fellow slaves.
9. Bost, "Davies: Revivalist and Champion," 41.

faculty.[10] The success of his mission at that earlier time rendered him now more than an agreeable compromise to trustees torn by dissension over another candidate. Thus came Davies' opportunity to assure Presbyterians—though Princeton was open to all Protestant Christians—that they could secure an excellent collegiate education in this country in their own institution. The young clergyman set out at once to raise the standards for the bachelor's degree and to organize his faculty. Things were going well when he was struck down by pneumonia in February, 1761; he died after an incumbency of only eighteen months. Two funeral sermons in London and one in New York marked the fact that a great man had fallen in Israel.

In Great Britain and in this country, Davies is best remembered as an orator and composer of moving sermons. Samuel Finley, himself an eloquent preacher, testified that qualified critics pronounced Davies the finest pulpit orator of his generation. The noted English dissenting clergyman, Dr. Thomas Gibbons, edited and published the first three of a five-volume edition of Davies' *Sermons* in 1766 in London; two more volumes were added by 1771. This edition was the basis for the dozen or more editions which later appeared in England and America through 1864. Separate sermons were published in Virginia, Pennsylvania, New England, and Great Britain during Davies' lifetime and the years immediately following his death.[11]

Davies' style was hortatory (he once suggested a return to Demosthenes as model, then corrected himself to add that

10. Samuel Davies Diary, September 26, 1753, in Foote, *Sketches of Virginia*, 233.
11. See the bibliography in Bost, "Davies: Revivalist and Champion," 288 ff.; and additional items by Davies in the Union Catalogue, Library of Congress.

Scripture furnished similar or better models), but he denied that he was an enthusiast in feeling or method. He employed a variety of sounds and a whole spectrum of sublime imagery; but his effect was somewhere between the cool rationalism of the New England pre-Unitarians or Virginia Anglicans, and the extreme emotionalism of Whitefield and certain of Davies' evangelical countrymen, especially among the Baptists. It has been suggested that he is the grandfather, if not the father, of later southern oratorical and rhetorical style, the descent coming through Patrick Henry.[12] The theology of his sermons is from first to last orthodox Calvinism; his preoccupations are with eschatology, divine grace and man's salvation. Davies himself called Jonathan Edwards "the profoundest reasoner, and greatest divine . . . that America has produced"; but among the Presbyterians he ranked as Edwards' peer, if not his superior, in preaching, and not too far behind in reasoning. Sinful man and God's grace were the all-absorbing themes of Davies' sermons, and they carried over into his poetry. Or one may say his verse parallels his prose in theme and, to a considerable extent, in imagery.

Despite his relative youthfulness even in his greatest and final years, Davies was always venerable in appearance, dignified in sentiment and style, commanding and emphatic in delivery, and when he wished to be, learned in allusion. His references to Socrates, Plutarch, Horace, Vergil, Tacitus, Juvenal, and others earned him the appellation "Classical Champion of Religious Freedom."[13] To these he added the Church Fathers, and his sermons contain renditions in his

12. See Alan Heimert, *Religion and the American Mind from the Great Awakening to the Revolution* (Cambridge, Mass., 1966) for a number of significant comments on Davies. David Bertelson, *The Lazy South* (New York, 1967) makes suggestions as to southern attitudes.

13. Richard M. Gummere, "Samuel Davies: Classical Champion of Religious Freedom," *Journal of Presbyterian History*, XL (1962), 67–74.

own words from the Greek or Latin of pagan or Christian. Among later seventeenth- and contemporary eighteenth-century authors he refers to voyagers, essayists, preachers, poets, historians, and philosophers,[14] most notably Milton, Richard Baxter, Pope, Young, Addison, and Jonathan Edwards. In *Charity and Truth United . . . Six Letters to the Rev. Mr. William Stith, A. M.*, Davies gives his own poetic translations from Juvenal, Horace, and Cleanthes.[15] But more often he restrains himself at the moment he seems about to plunge into a series of learned allusions and is content with plain paraphrase; or he turns aside from the erudite to the hortatory and sublime. In this Calvinistic sublimity, a fusion of his Christian doctrine and belief with the means of expressing it, Davies is most effective in prose and verse.[16]

In the age of Burke, Alison, Blair and so many other forerunners of the full-blown Romantics who wrote and spoke in terms of the sublime, the American Calvinist clergyman gave the sublime a special place and a special definition, or at least interpretation. Since the effectiveness of any preaching had to depend on the individual soul, the Calvinist of the Great Awakening put the need to reach the human heart before rhetoric and imagery, the need for feeling before reason, though he believed in both. The Calvinist orator held in common with Burke and others that power, vastness, infinity, magnificence, and fear-admiration were among the elements of the truly sublime. Fear of God's wrath, God's infinity in time and space, the magnificence of the Almighty, and the

14. Bost, "Davies: Revivalist and Champion," 122.
15. *Samuel Davies, Charity and Truth United . . . Six Letters to the Rev. Mr. William Stith, A. M.*, ed. Thomas C. Pears, Jr., *Journal of Presbyterian History*, XIX (1941), 193 ff. The brief translations included in the tract are not reproduced in my recent edition of Davies' verse.
16. For a discussion of the sublime in late colonial Calvinistic oratory, see Heimert, *Religion and the American Mind*, 217–18, 226–27, 233–36.

rugged majesty of the Christian concept were the qualities Davies felt he could and must stress. Stylistic felicity was important, but never so much as clarity, a clarity through terms and figures calculated to reach deep into the hearts of men.[17]

In his prose and poetry Davies reflected the influence of the somewhat older English dissenting clergy who were hymn writers—men like Isaac Watts and Philip Doddridge—for he shared their idea of the sublime and its expression. In one of his replies to the Anglican "Walter Dymocke,"[18] Davies defended Watts's sensuous paraphrase in verse of a sensuous passage from the Old Testament. Davies acknowledged using Watts's paraphrase as a model for a poem-hymn: "These, Sir, are not the wild Rants of *Fanaticism,* or the Reveries of *Enthusiasm,* that would affect a *presumptuous fondling Intimacy* with Heaven; but the *Language of divine Inspiration* in sacred Poetry." Here is more than a statement of the Calvinistic idea of the sublime: it is an acknowledgement of some of its sources, in the rhetorical cadences of the King James Bible and, in this particular case, of the Song of Solomon as paraphrased by a Renaissance poet, George Sandys. In other words, at the same time the evangelical Calvinist denied the excessive fanaticism of some of his contemporaries, he returned to an older age for his rhetoric, imagery, and concept of the duty of religious verse, thus denying that the neoclassical rationalism and liberalism of some other contemporaries was an acceptable way in which to approach the matter of the soul's salvation. In common with other writers both earlier and later, this Calvinist believed that awe could produce sublime emotion—a kind of tranquillity tinged with terror—which might reach the souls of men.

Davies' poetry is sublime in aim, imagery, and theme. Its form is derived from the hymns of Watts and Doddridge,

17. *Ibid.,* 218.   18. *Virginia Gazette,* July 3, 1752.

from Milton, Pope, the Bible, the classics, and what his age called the Pindaric ode. In genre it belongs with the seventeenth-century poetry of meditation, which was especially pervasive among religionists.[19] Davies' sermons reveal that he knew Baxter's *The Saints Everlasting Rest* (London, 1650), as any educated Calvinist should have. This treatise on meditation argues for the unceasing self-examination which was part of the Presbyterian as well as the New England Puritan heritage. The few poems which may not be classed as meditations are the generally descriptive and patriotic verses growing out of the poet's concern with the French and Indian War. Even these exceptions, in their use of fear, awe, and death, show the qualities of the sublime in a more secular nature and application.

Of the ninety-odd poems, fifty, published in *Miscellaneous Poems* in January, 1752,[20] are in one way or another self-examinations, even the poem on "Conjugal Love and Happiness" and the "elegy" on the expected death of Samuel Blair. Reflections on the death of a pious parishioner and the description of a storm are also meditative, employing the themes and images of sublimity. Of the remaining once-scattered pieces, the majority, including the hymns, are concerned with self-dedication, self-examination, and the transcendent excellency of Christ. "A Father's Reflections on the Birth of a Son" and translations from Dr. Watts's Latin belong to the same meditative tradition. The odes on peace and science are still contemplative, though not at all in the melancholy tone

19. See, for example, Louis L. Martz, "Foreword," in *The Poetry of Edward Taylor*, ed. Donald E. Stanford (New Haven, 1960); and Louis L. Martz, *The Poetry of Meditation* (Rev. ed., New Haven, 1962).

20. The poems were announced as "Just Published" in the *Virginia Gazette* of January 17, 1752. These and miscellaneous other poems from scattered newspapers, magazines, books, and manuscripts have recently been collected and reprinted with notes as R. B. Davis (ed.), *Collected Poems of Samuel Davies, 1723–1761* (Gainesville, Fla., 1968).

of most of the group. But the sublimity-fear motif produced by great storms is reflected in the two or three written at sea.

Davies, in his verse and in his sermons, is neither a happy Calvinist like Edward Taylor nor a gloomy depicter of final doom like Michael Wigglesworth (though this is oversimplification of both Puritans). Davies veers between extremes, from ecstasy in his contemplation of Divine Goodness, to fear concerning his own eligibility for salvation, to dejection. His phrasing and imagery have been criticized as hackneyed, neoclassical, and stiff—his works are certainly not couched in the homespun gnarled language of Edward Taylor. But a comparison with one of Davies' mentors, Alexander Pope, reveals a relative simplicity, combined with the majesty of Biblical phrase, which neither Pope nor his British imitators display. Though some of Davies' diction is often derivative, especially in his hymns, it frequently, as in his storm descriptions and depictions of Indian massacres, displays a power of combination which appears to be his own.

In his diary Davies observed how music and harmony affected him emotionally and even intellectually. His later "Odes" were set to music by a Princeton graduate, and for his earlier hymns he always carefully indicated a familiar tune. Thus he must have composed most of these poems with particular musical settings in mind. This may explain the close resemblance of some of them to the work of Doddridge and Watts, who used many of the same tunes. In this he was exceptional in the America of his time, which usually employed an older psalmody. He is usually cited as the earliest hymn writer of colonial Presbyterianism.[21]

21. Louis F. Benson, "President Davies as a Hymn Writer," *Journal of Presbyterian History*, II (1904), 277–86, 343–73 contains the fullest discussion of the subject. Also see Edward S. Ninde, *The Story of the American Hymn* (New York, 1921), 42–46; Henry W. Foote, *Three Centuries of American Hymnody* (Hampden, Conn., 1961), 149–53; and Gilborn, "Samuel Davies' Sacred Muse," 63–79.

In his Preface to the *Miscellaneous Poems,* the poet conventionally and modestly speaks of his "fortuitous" compositions. He quotes "that antiquated Wit, Herbert," in observing that "A Verse may hit him whom a Sermon flies./ And turn Delight into a Sacrifice."[22] So he affirms that his poems were meant to represent religion and virtue, as he felt some other "poetasters" meant to do and all should do. He mentions Pope's *Messiah,* Edward Young's *Night Thoughts,* and James Thomson's *The Seasons* approvingly, because the spirit of devotion breathes through them. He admits he has occasionally imitated Milton and "the noble *Licence* of Pindar (the last of which is most natural for me.)" And he concludes that religion and daily life must be considered as one.

As we have noted, the themes are familiar to anyone fairly well acquainted with Calvinistic and Puritan thought. In the meditations which are not hymns he employs the decasyllabic or octosyllabic couplet, and sometimes he varies the length within a variety of stanza forms in a manner suggestive of several contemporary British poets. Imagery, as in "Solomon," is strongly representative of the Solomonic passages of the Old Testament. As one critic has remarked, there is remarkably little fire and brimstone in any of his verses, even when his theme is the future life.

"The Invisible World" is somewhat suggestive of George Herbert. Thomson's *The Seasons* and other pre-Romantic poems may be echoed in the storm poems, but Nature's thunderous majesty clearly fascinated Davies personally. Whether writing about the wind and rain of a Virginia summer day or the mountainous waves of the winter Atlantic, Davies considered storms the creator's grandest symbols of sublimity.

22. R. B. Davis (ed.), *Collected Poems of Davies,* v. See also *Virginia Evangelical and Literary Magazine,* II (1819), 538 for a letter to a friend in which Davies quotes a stanza from Herbert as the inspiration for a particular composition.

Elegies and epitaphs suggest the saintliness of the subjects. They are interesting primarily as effective examples of a form and theme popular with Anglican and Puritan alike. The birth of his son brings alarmingly to his mind the question of whether this "infant man" is destined to doom or glory, a Calvinist question always gnawing at Davies' mind. The other miscellaneous poems speak largely for themselves as representative of their author's patriotism, his interest in learning, his knowledge of Greek and Latin.

But it is Davies as hymn writer who is most significant as poet. Themes and models have been discussed, but from the point of view of American literary history the particular occasions for writing them, and their relation to his sermons, is their most interesting quality, especially since we have become acquainted with Edward Taylor.

For like Taylor, Davies composed most of his hymns to accompany sermons on the same subjects. He tells us that some of them "came" to him on Saturday nights, as he relaxed for a half hour from the labors of preparation for his Sunday sermons. Others were written before or after the sermon, in certain instances perhaps to accompany it in its separate printed form, but probably more often as a means of sharpening and harmonizing the ideas presented in the longer prose exegeses.

Many of Davies' sermons were published separately; occasionally, though not frequently, one was published with the related hymn. Benson tells us[23] that Davies' first editor, Dr. Thomas Gibbons of London, almost surely had hymns appended to a great number of sermons when he received them in manuscript. Gibbons in his *Hymns Adapted for Divine Worship* (London, 1769) published sixteen of Davies' hymns,

23. Benson, "President Davies as a Hymn Writer."

and the Baptist John Rippon in *A Selection of Hymns* (London, 1787) printed seven. These, and others in the *Miscellaneous Poems,* were "annext," as their titles often indicate, to sermons concerned with appropriate subjects.

There are hymns for sermons about a Virginia summer drought, the ordination of a fellow clergyman, the deaths of British heroes in the French and Indian War, the need for soldiers to defend the frontiers—though in the verse these contemporary affairs are seldom referred to directly, as they are in the sermons. Most interesting of all, a fair number of hymns were apparently composed to accompany discourses preparing Davies' flock for the sacrament of the Lord's Supper. The Presbyterian "Preparatory Meditations" do not equal the Puritan Edward Taylor's verse—this is due perhaps as much to the poetic conventions of their respective eras as to Taylor's natural superiority as a poet. But Davies' versified admonitions to his congregations were effective, as witness the fact that they were used by several denominations as "Communion Hymns" for a century after their composer's death.

Davies wrote most of his poems, including the hymns, in the "highly literate environment in colonial Virginia which fostered literary expression."[24] They were bought and read by stout Anglicans as well as Presbyterians, as the *Virginia Gazette* account books and copies in many libraries testify; and they were copied in newspapers and early magazines from South Carolina to New Hampshire. Several of the poems were printed in British magazines, some accompanying the British editions of his individual sermons. The controversy as to the merits of the completed volume (carried on in the *Virginia Gazette* for about two years) indicates local interest in the man as well as his work. His verse had its champions,

24. Gilborn, "Samuel Davies' Sacred Muse," 66.

among them many who were not dissenters. Davies' Anglican adversaries wrote too, usually on such frivolous subjects as a lady's appearance, or in satires ridiculing men and manners of the community.[25] But none of their poetry ever received the attention his did.

His verse may not be great poetry—and by no means is all of it good poetry. But it was the rhymed representation of a significant American movement, the Great Awakening. And with all due allowance for the *Bay Psalm Book*, Michael Wigglesworth, and a number of New England fugitive religious poets, it was Samuel Davies who brought Polyhymnia, the muse of sacred poetry, before the American public.

25. See R. B. Davis (ed.), *The Colonial Virginia Satirist* (Philadelphia, 1967).

⤙VIII⤚
The Intellectual Golden Age in the Colonial Chesapeake Bay Country

[Throughout the colonial period, the sister Chesapeake Bay colonies Virginia and Maryland had many interests and characteristics in common.* They were maritime and tobacco colonies, they were strongly Anglican and yet in the later years almost as strongly Presbyterian, they had charming little capital villages of architectural distinction and artistic liveliness, and they were centers for astute politicians and for gentlemanly intellectuals. Both were founded in the first half of the seventeenth century, and by mid-eighteenth century both had developed a planter aristocracy. They had also produced individuals and groups of men who not only had superior minds but employed them in pursuits beyond the functions of everyday living.

The northern historians who until recently have written most of the history of colonial America have not considered all of the existing material or looked for additional information on the mid-eighteenth-century Marylanders and Virginians. These colonists have been written off as non-intellectuals, perhaps because they did not demonstrate their cerebral powers by struggling with the knotty problems of Calvinist theology. This paper is an all too brief attempt to show that the intellectual may be measured by other yard-

* This paper was originally delivered at the 1971 meeting of the Virginia Historical Society.

sticks than theology, and that by these other yardsticks the planters along the Chesapeake show an intellectual ability as profound as and perhaps more diverse than that of their New England contemporaries. For more detailed evidence for one of the two colonies see J. A. Leo Lemay's *Men of Letters in Colonial Maryland* (1972).

A major point, perhaps more implicit than explicit, is that without the sustained intellectual exercise of these mid-eighteenth-century planters, merchants, and professional men the colonies would not have been ready for the leadership they exercised nationally in the Revolutionary era. These men made a significant beginning in polemical political writing. But the products of their artistic and intellectual creativity— beautiful architecture and gardens, verse in many forms and traditions, prose satire, annotated editions of laws, persuasive and eloquent sermons—show distinctly that these men are worth considering for their individual talents.]

AMERICAN HISTORIANS for almost a hundred years now have been attempting to explain how the agrarian society of the Chesapeake Bay region was able to produce, in the crucial decades at the beginning of our national life, such men as Washington, Jefferson, Madison, Paca, the younger Dulany, the Lees, the Randolphs and the Carrolls. Actually no one has ever explained them. Henry Adams, W. J. Cash, and our own Clifford Dowdey have shown how military and purely political leaders came into existence and fruition, men like George Washington, Light-Horse Harry Lee, George Rogers Clark, and John Eager Howard. But none of these historians explains the men of mind and vision who argued for, logically constructed, and then led the nation in its first steps. In fact, the most commonly held theory is that they were not natural products of the Chesapeake society, that the few "intellectuals" who did exist were biological "sports" or freaks in a world which normally produced soldiers or farmers. One contemporary historian stated the generally held negative concept fairly succinctly:

Those who have appointed themselves custodians of the historical reputation of this fascinating region have generally insisted that it produced that which, by its very nature, it could not produce—a developed intellectual and artistic culture rivaling that of any other part of the colonies . . . . [The writer suggests that this impotency was because it lacked cities.] Thomas Jefferson and James Madison were as nearly unique in 1776 as William Byrd in 1720. For each there were dozens of gentlemen by whom, as a contemporary perceived, "the ingenuity of a Locke or the discoveries of a Newton were considered as infinitely inferior to the accomplishments of him who knew when to shoulder a blind cock or to start a fleet horse . . . . It is really affecting to consider what a prodigious number of men have not the least spark of taste, have no relish for the fine arts." They led a gracious but not a cultured life . . . . [and in conclusion] the Chesapeake Society produced a unique bourgeois aristocracy with more than its share of great and noble men; they were, however, men of intellect, not intellectuals.[1]

What this historian and others mentioned above are denying, explicitly or implicitly, is a habit of *sustained* cerebration and of rationally developed good taste among the people of the Chesapeake region. By implication or assertion, these were not thinking people as were their New England or Pennsylvania contemporaries. On the contrary, for the two generations preceding the Revolution and the decade thereafter, that is, from about 1720 to 1789, there was in actuality a strong expression of discriminating taste in the arts, as high a proportion of well-educated men as existed anywhere in the

1. Carl Bridenbaugh, *Myths and Realities: Societies of the Colonial South* (Baton Rouge, 1952), 51–53. Bridenbaugh quotes Josiah Quincy's "Journal" of the 1770's.

colonies, frequent discourses on religious doctrine and application, a creativity in belles-lettres, and a dynamic and reasoned political expression springing from scores of thoughtful and sophisticated minds. In other words, during the period when great families such as the Lees, Fitzhughs, Randolphs, Carters, Lloyds, and Ogles were producing a golden economic and social age, their kinsmen, friends, clergy, physicians, or schoolmasters were producing an intellectual golden age. My own observations suggest that there was at least as large a proportion of educated men at this period in Virginia and Maryland as anywhere in America, that they had better than average taste and a *variety* of interests—agriculture, history, politics, architecture, and religion. That variety gave them a sophisticated, perhaps urbane (in the best sense of that word), basis for their oral and written expression, and an ability to deal with men and affairs which the narrow ecclesiastically or theologically trained New England intellectuals *as a whole* did not possess.

Space limitations allow me to touch upon only a few aspects of the intellectual life of the Chesapeake region. Genuine achievements in botany, medicine, anthropology, cartography, meteorology, historical writing, and the careful study of their Indian neighbors, recognized even in Europe, cannot even be considered here. Other matters that demand whole volumes for complete elucidation can only be mentioned.

Few persons realize the widespread opportunities for education which existed in the Tidewater region. During the period covered in this essay, Maryland was establishing parochial, county, and charity schools in every part of the province; free grammar and other private academies appeared in various parts of Virginia, and plantation tutors and village schoolmasters worked in both colonies. Among the last were the diarists, poets, and essayists like John Harrower, James Reid, and Philip Fithian. Many planters' sons were sent to English or Scottish schools. Many more went to the universities of Great Britain, to Leyden, if Catholic to St. Omer's on the continent, and of course to William and Mary. By the end of the pre-Revolutionary period the majority of American medical students at Edinburgh were from Virginia and Maryland, and a large proportion of the young lawyers at the Inns of Court came from the same region.

Contrary to the negative assertion in the quotation given above, visual evidence of the Tidewater appreciation of the fine arts lies everywhere about us—in the graceful lines and bonded-brick patterns of the mansions of the Chesapeake Bay region; in the surprisingly large number of surviving houses with majestic chimneys, beautifully carved mantels, and balustrades; in fine churches, governors' palaces, and public and college buildings. The ingenious designs of the landscape gardens of the Maryland Eastern Shore, the Northern Neck of Virginia, or the Williamsburg and Annapolis mansions are as convincing examples of intellectual ingenuity (and good taste) as anything ever produced in the fine arts in America. Boxwood in mazes and other geometrical patterns, exotic flowers and shrubs, proportioned sunlight and shade, required and received as much mental pondering in the Chesapeake area as did any tangled knot of theology among the saints of New England. In Virginia, William Byrd and John Custis, the Lees, the Carters, and the Taylors, planned and cultivated their gardens—as did Daniel Bowly, Horatio Sharpe, the Ogles, the Carrolls, and the Dulanys in Maryland. Wherever there is extant correspondence, there is evidence of ingenuity, eager curiosity about the new and strange, and a taste for the beautiful among these gentlemen gardeners. Equal evidence is afforded for an interest in the visual arts—there are works by native painters and journey-men limners from the Old World, religious scenes in churches, Hogarthian prints, portraits of families, ancestors, and friends in England.

Music was everywhere. There were public orchestral performances and private concerts. In Maryland there was music composed by the Reverend Thomas Bacon and others; in Virginia by Bruton Parish organist Peter Pelham. Councillor Robert Carter was a musicologist and performer of great versatility. Merchant Henry Callister of Oxford in Maryland played at least three instruments and frequently performed in concerts with Bacon and others at the governor's or his own house. In Williamsburg, John Blair had gathered a group who played upon spinet, harpsichord, violin, and flute. Governor Lord Botetourt joined in group singing on the household steps. Governor Fauquier was the organizer of a group of amateurs who gathered for weekly ensemble playing—young Jefferson, Councillor Carter, and John Tyler the elder among them. Landon Carter confided sourly to his diary that he had heard that in Williamsburg "from every house a constant tuting may be listened to upon one instrument or another."[2] Recently a musical historian who has assembled a voluminous record of activity in colonial Virginia has concluded that by 1776 "the ground appeared to have been fertile for the development of a musically erudite civilization whose taste and participation in art music would have been equal at least to that of many European countries."[3] And one may recall that Jefferson and John Randolph, Jr., as well as

2. Jack P. Greene (ed.), *The Diary of Colonel Landon Carter of Sabine Hall, 1752–1778* (Charlottesville, 1965), II, 618.
3. John W. Molnar, "Art Music in Colonial Virginia," in Francis B. Simkins (ed.), *Art and Music in the South: Institute of Southern Culture Lectures at Longwood College 1960* (Farmville, Va., 1961), 63–108.

the St. George Tucker family, were constantly practicing and performing musicians.

The much-discussed colonial theater need hardly detain us, except to note that Virginia had the first permanent theater in America, that Maryland and Virginia were the principal supporters of the most distinguished company of actors in America before 1800, and that villagers and country people in a dozen vicinities had for three decades the opportunity to see popular contemporary plays, the earlier Restoration drama, and Shakespeare, performed by a first-rate company. The *Gazettes* of two colonies contain our first dramatic criticism, from the time of William Byrd to that of the Reverend Jonathan Boucher in Annapolis; both these gentlemen contributed personally to the criticism.

Most intriguing is the little we know of private theatricals and the production of locally authored plays. There is rather sound evidence that Byrd was the actual coauthor of a famous play heretofore attributed to Colley Cibber, and that Byrd produced the play and took the leading role.[4] Two decades later Robert Munford of Mecklenburg wrote and helped to produce in private houses his two timely plays, *The Candidates* and *The Patriots*. In Annapolis and Williamsburg, genteel amateurs performed in such tragedies as Addison's *Cato* (a play with significant political and moral implications which made it popular long after the Revolution). In Williamsburg, a contemporary comedy was acted out by Mayor Nicholas, former London playwright Dr. Henry Potter, Dr. George Gilmer, and other citizens. Students at William and Mary had given public dramatic performances since early in the century.

4. See Carl Dolmetsch, "William Byrd: Comic Dramatist?," *Early American Literature*, VI (1971), 18–30.

In the Chesapeake society, religious or theological thinking was never as dominant as it was in theocratic New England; for from the earliest times, especially in Virginia, the church was under the secular control of local vestries and Crown- (or Proprietor-) appointed governors. In Maryland the Church of England, though soon established, never included the majority of the populace, and in Virginia in the eighteenth century it encountered strong Presbyterian rivalry. Yet despite these conditions, and contrary to general historical opinion, the Tidewater society developed a considerable and in many ways distinguished body of theological and religious expression, ranging from sermons to the politico-ecclesiastical tracts of the 1760s. The Anglican sermon of the eighteenth century survives in perhaps two hundred examples, most of them as yet unprinted or uncollected since they were first printed. On the whole, they contradict almost everything Perry Miller and other historians of the New England mind have said or implied about them. Clearly the sermons have not been read.

In Virginia, they survive in such forms as the forty-eight-item sermon book of Robert Paxton, a preacher whom William Byrd heard and approved; the loose sermons of James Maury, Jefferson's old teacher and an essayist of ability; one family homily by Peter Fontaine, Byrd's Huguenot chaplain on the Dividing Line expedition; three separately published discourses by historian and college president William Stith; and five volumes of *Our Saviour's Divine Sermon on the Mount* . . . (London, 1722–1723) by James Blair. In Maryland, there is in the Diocesan Library the largest collection of unpublished sermons surviving from the colonial South, containing the work of such able and godly men as Henry Addison, Thomas Chase, Thomas Cradock, John Gordon, and John Humphrey, among others; and among many printed discourses are able exhortations by Cradock, Thomas Bacon the musician, and the former playwright James Sterling.[5]

In dedicating the first (1722) edition of his discourses to the bishop of London, Commissary Blair summarized the qualities of the typical Chesapeake sermon of the period. After declaring that he did not find it necessary to preach against deists, atheists, Arians, or Socinians as one did in the mother country, he continued: "Yet we find Work enough . . . to encounter the usual Corruptions of Mankind, Ignorance, Inconsideration, Practical Unbelief, Impenitence, Impiety, Worldly-mindedness, and other Common Immoralities. For which Reason, the Practical Part of Religion being the Chief part of our Pastoral Care, I was easily inclined to fix my Meditation on *our Saviour's Divine Sermon on the Mount.*" Blair's sermons pleased the noted English clergyman Dr. Daniel Waterland, who in a preface for the 1740 edition concluded by calling Blair learned in theological scholarship but above all one who had the happy talent of "deciding Points of great Moment, in a *few* and *plain* Words, but the Result of *deep Consideration,* and discovering a great *Compass of Thought.*" In other words, he is "a compleat practical *Divine.*"

So one might characterize the sermons of Fontaine, Maury, and Stith of Virginia, and Addison, Bacon, and Cradock of Maryland, along with the discourses of a dozen others. They are at least as plain in style (both of organization and language) as the plainest Massachusetts Bay sermons. Though their authors do not, from choice, grapple with complex doctrinal problems, they show wide learning and inexorable logic with remarkably effective homely illustration.

5. For bibliographical and biographical studies of the Maryland clergy, see Nelson W. Rightmyer, *Maryland's Established Church* (Baltimore, 1956).

Then there were the (usually) printed sermons on special occasions—thanksgiving, war, funerals, legislative gatherings —comparable in quality to the election and execution sermons from New England. Frequently sermons were concerned with more than the daily problems or the special celebrations of the church's communicants. Thomas Bacon left *Four Sermons* addressed to slaveowners as to their care of these black human beings, *Two Sermons* addressed to the black servants themselves, and a powerful plea for a charity working school in his parish. Thomas Cradock, erudite scholar and poet, preached on education, fraud, wealth, and in perhaps the most courageous sermon of colonial America, on "A Corrupt Clergy," citing specific instances around him. The same man on a quite different occasion preached from the text "A merry Heart doth Good like a Medicine," one of two homilies celebrating British victories over France and interpreting them as triumphs for liberty and religion. He included, principally in the imagery of music and musical instruments and wine red in the glass, an eloquent plea for Christianity as properly a religion of laughter and joy. A brief excerpt will illustrate his tone and his point:

And can a gloomy untoward Soul answer the ends of [Christ's] coming: can a morose Pharisaic Temper be suitable to so blessed a Design of our Lord's? . . . .
Besides, were we not form'd for Society? Were we not born to be sociable? And can that Society be carried on without a chearful and benevolent Disposition? How can a Man be desirous to promote the Happiness and Benefit of his Neighbour, when he has not a Soul susceptible of generous Sentiments; When he's wholly absorbed in himself, and looks with an evil Eye on every Thing hearty and sociable? Can the Soul promote Harmony that hath no Harmony in itself? Will the Violin please the Ear with it's Voice, when it's Strings are broken; or who can say the Hautboy joins the Concert, when in the Hands of an unskilful Player?

No, the morose, surly, unchearful Man can never answer the End of his Creation; he can never be a good man, nor the good Christian; the good Neighbour, or the good Friend: He may say what he will, but if he wants a *merry Heart,* he wants a very great characteristic of the human Mind.[6]

In Virginia, Stith's occasional sermons, all preached before the General Assembly between 1745 and 1753, were of high quality. The last was one of the very few polemical or doctrinal sermons from Tidewater Anglicans, *The Nature and Extent of Christ's Redemption* (Williamsburg, 1753), a reply to a tract by Presbyterian Samuel Davies. The latter's final word in the dispute, *Charity and Truth United,* has been published only in this century (Philadelphia, 1941).

Nine out of ten of these Chesapeake Anglican sermons deserve reprinting or first printing, both for their literary and religious quality and as a refutation of the allegations of almost total irreligion sometimes ascribed to the colonial Anglican South. But Presbyterianism also had its place in Virginia-Maryland religious expression. Francis Makemie the pioneer, Old Light preachers John Craig and John Thomson, New Lighters including Gilbert Tennent and John Blair from Pennsylvania, preached as eloquently, in as plain style, and usually for a much longer time than did the Anglicans. The greatest of the New Lights was of course Samuel Davies, who recently has begun to receive the attention he has always deserved as both literary and religious figure. Though he was born in Delaware and died as president of Princeton, Davies married a Virginia woman, spent the years of his active ministry largely in Hanover County, and left descendants in Virginia. As poet and essayist, this New Light Presbyterian

6. Thomas Cradock, *Two Sermons with a Preface,* (Annapolis, 1747), 2–3. (MS in Maryland Diocesan Library, Maryland Historical Society, Baltimore.)

preached in the Calvinist plain-style tradition, but in a rotund and rolling rhetoric all his own. (See Chapter VII for a fuller discussion of Davies.) Curiously enough, though the Great Awakening had apparently as great an effect on conversion in the Chesapeake region as in other parts of America, it did not provide a theological pamphlet warfare such as appeared in South Carolina and in parts of New England. Not a single pamphlet is known to have been composed in Maryland as a result of the confrontation of Whitefield and the Anglicans. In Virginia there was the Stith-Davies exchange and some paper debates between New and Old Light Presbyterians. The Annapolis and Williamsburg *Gazettes* impartially carried attacks upon and defenses of Whitefield, as they did of Davies and his religious poetry.

But perhaps the most significant, because most characteristic, form of religious tract in the Chesapeake Bay country is that which was partly political. In Maryland it was as old as the periods of the Commonwealth and the Bloodless Revolution. For four years early in the eighteenth century (1728–1732), Commissary Jacob Henderson and Daniel Dulany, Sr., exchanged opinions in a now obscure (even after reading the newspaper and magazine diatribes) quarrel on orthodox Anglican doctrine and government. In Virginia the most famous exchange grew out of the Two-Penny Act and the Parsons' Cause, a flaring up of the ever-present tension and conflict between the people and the established clergy. Patrick Henry's speech in the James Maury test case at Hanover made him famous. But from a literary point of view, or a religious one, the long series of pamphlets exchanged between the Reverend John Camm of the College of William and Mary and two Anglican vestrymen most deserves attention. Landon Carter, whose diary is already a classic of our literature, opened the war in 1759 with *A Letter* to the bishop of

London. Richard Bland—antiquarian, historian, parliamentarian, and poet, called affectionately but half facetiously by Jefferson "the wisest man South of the James River"—soon followed in 1760. Camm replied to both men in 1763. Carter returned with a new pamphlet in 1764; Camm rejoined the same year. Bland then came up with one of the great politico-religious essays of colonial history, *The Colonel Dismounted: Or the Rector Vindicated*, a mock defense of the clerical position which is overwhelming in its combination of logic, sophisticated satire, irony, and cogent facts. Later, in a more purely political connection, Bland published *An Inquiry into the Rights of the British Colonies* (1766), but *The Colonel Dismounted* is usually considered the abler work. Few Tidewater colonists went to bed chewing on a morsel of Calvin, but clearly many carried with them to their couches the problem of church in relation to state. Their cogitations were to produce interesting results.

Belletristic writing in eighteenth-century Virginia and Maryland is almost a *terra incognita*. One of the most startling and pleasant research experiences for me in recent years was the discovery that from 1720 to 1790 the Tidewater inhabitants produced an amazing number of poems, familiar essays, journals, and autobiographies. Maryland especially produced an astonishing amount. Verse from both colonies appeared frequently in British journals and in the magazines and newspapers of all the colonies. It was written on all sorts of subjects in all sorts of forms by rural and town clergy, planters and their wives and daughters, schoolmasters, tobacco merchants, physicians, lawyers, indentured servants, and public officials.

In Maryland, Ebenezer Cook (1670–*ca.* 1732) wrote *The Sot-Weed Factor* (first edition 1708), a poem about Bacon's Rebellion, as well as elegies, and occasional pieces. His contemporary Richard Lewis (*ca.* 1700–1734), Eton-educated schoolmaster and promoter of a system of public schools, has recently been labeled "the best neoclassical poet of colonial America."[7] His meditative, nature, and occasional verses will appear in the future in many anthologies.

But the most active, versatile, and humorous group of genuinely gifted writers were the members of the Annapolis Tuesday Club from 1745 to 1756. Their "Record" (or minutes) and the "History" drawn from them, both composed by Dr. Alexander Hamilton, secretary,[8] offer striking parallels in form and quality to the two Dividing Line histories of William Byrd. When they are published from the manuscripts, southern colonial literature will have another book worthy to lay beside Byrd's masterpieces. Both "Record" and "History" contain mock elegies, speeches, songs, musical scores, amusing conundrums, and other material by various members of the Club. Like the Byrd *personae*, the members appear in one version under such pseudonyms as Signior Lardini (for Thomas Bacon) or Slyboots Pleasant (a Dulany). Founder Jonas Green was known as P.P.P.P.P. (poet, printer, punster, purveyor, and punchmaker), and the visiting Benjamin Franklin was dubbed Electro Vitrifico. Virginia-Maryland planter William Fitzhugh was Colonel Comico Butman. Most of the poems appear to have been written by Green and Hamilton.

For us one of the interesting features of the club, and of Annapolis and Maryland society, is its direct connections with Virginians, especially those who lived along the Potomac.

7. J. A. Leo Lemay, "Richard Lewis and Augustan American Poetry," *PMLA*, LXXXIII (1968), 80–101.

8. Hamilton was also author of the *Itinerarium*, twice printed in this century, and of literary criticism. See Carl Bridenbaugh (ed.), *The Itinerarium of Dr. Alexander Hamilton* (Chapel Hill, 1948).

Families such as the Fitzhughs, Lees, Chews, Diggeses, and Bruces left representatives in both colonies. One learns from Hamilton's minutes of December 31, 1754,[9] that William Fitzhugh (of Roubsy Hall in Maryland) produced a charter or commission for a branch society at his Virginia estate known as the Hickory Hill Club, and that it had been holding regular sessions since 1750. One would like to locate *its* minutes. Also through Bacon and one of the Calvert governors there had been pleasant exchanges of visits between the two capitals, and a successful campaign in Williamsburg to raise funds for Bacon's charity working school. Northern Virginia essayists and poets published almost impartially and indiscrimately in the Annapolis and Williamsburg *Gazettes,* and the two newspapers frequently exchanged materials.

Virginia and Williamsburg had from William Byrd's time a number of more or less gifted belletrists, including the poet and later novelist Arthur Blackamore; the Reverend George Seagood, whose "combined" *Expeditio Ultramontana* appeared in the *Maryland Gazette* in 1729[10] before there was a Virginia newspaper; John Fox, King William County poet and journalist; educator and clergyman William Dawson, whose volume of verses appeared in 1736; New Kent attorney John Markland,[11] widely known for his *Typographia* (Williamsburg, 1730), celebrating the arrival of the printing press; Dr. Henry Potter, the above mentioned poet who had left his musical comedies behind in London and who was to

---

9. The minutes or "Records" and the "History" manuscripts survive in various parts in the Maryland Historical Society, the Library of Congress, and the Evergreen House Library of Johns Hopkins. See also R. B. Davis (ed.), *The Colonial Virginia Satirist* (Philadelphia, 1967), 6 *n.*

10. There is a new edition of Arthur Blackamore and George Seagood, *Expeditio Ultramontana,* ed. Earl G. Swem (Richmond, 1960).

11. J. A. Leo Lemay (ed.), *A Poem by John Markland of Virginia* (Williamsburg, 1965), 5–12.

die in frontier Spotsylvania; Joseph Dumbleton, renowned for "The Paper Mill" and "A Rhapsody on Rum;" public official Benjamin Waller, poet and patron of poets; political and legal theorists Peyton Randolph, George Wythe, Richard Bland, Landon Carter, George Mason, John Mercer of Marlboro, and a score of others whose names are yet to be connected with their trenchant essays. These come into the Revolutionary generation, in which were also poet-playwright Robert Munford and well-known versifier (in English periodicals) Robert Bolling, Jr., former schoolmates in Yorkshire but native Virginians. St. George Tucker was just beginning his amazing career as poet, legal scholar, scientist, progressive educationist, inventor, dramatist, and book collector, Scottish tutor James Reid was a poet, satirist, and prose moralist; and John Randolph, Jr.'s *Treatise on Gardening* (written between 1758 and 1775) has become a classic of horticulture.

In Maryland other establishments succeeded the Tuesday Club, the most famous being the Homony, of which the Tory parson Jonathan Boucher was president in the early 1770s. At the Harmony meetings, verses, joviality, and politics might be thoroughly mixed with the punch (the Tuesday Club had forbidden political discussion, but several others did not). Between 1750 and 1775 the versatile Thomas Bacon published his *Laws of Maryland at Large* (Annapolis, 1765), a legal monument and the most beautiful example of colonial typography; another parson-poet, the Christian hedonist Thomas Cradock, brought out *A New Version of the Psalms* (Annapolis, 1756); customs inspector parson James Sterling, erstwhile Irish dramatist and friend of Swift, appeared in almost every American (and many British) newspapers and magazines as poet and prophet of Empire,[12] and as "Philo-

12. L. C. Wroth, *James Sterling: Poet, Priest, and Prophet of Empire* (Worcester, Mass., 1931). See also Sterling's sermons, listed in L. C. Wroth, *A History of Printing in Colonial Maryland* (Baltimore, 1922).

Musaeus," Dr. Adam Thomson printed poems, familiar essays, and, in other connections, treatises on smallpox.

Much of the Tidewater verse is mediocre; a considerable amount of it, especially the satiric and the elegiac verse, is competent. At the very moment when a northern scholar was stating in his fairly comprehensive *American Colonial Verse*[13] that there was no elegiac tradition in the colonial South, a young southern scholar was completing his thick volume of examples of the elegy of the southeast before 1775, most of them eighteenth-century elegies from the Chesapeake Bay country. The poems possess a unified secular and classical tone, as distinctive as the rigid or lugubrious Calvinism of New England graveyard verse. The same northern anthologist stated that there was no southern colonial nature poetry indicating a genuine love for the region (though he actually included two pieces which belie his statement). He was apparently unacquainted with the works of Richard Lewis, John Fox, Charles Hansford, and Robert Bolling, men who showed that the land of pine and blue sea and sunshine was appreciated in rhyme.

And this brings us to the major intellectual expression of the Revolutionary generation of Maryland and Virginia. One who scans the individual belletristic imprints from 1763 to 1780 or the verses in the Annapolis and Williamsburg newspapers finds them fewer in number and, with few exceptions, poorer in quality than in preceding generations. One finds also that some of the better minds—men who thought long and deeply like Daniel Dulany, Jr., Jonathan Boucher, and John Randolph, Jr.—could not go all the way to independence and ended their lives in the silence of seclusion or exile. But for two glorious decades they, like their erstwhile friends, cousins,

13. Kenneth Silverman (ed.), *American Colonial Verse* (New York, 1968).

or neighbors (now called patriots), poured forth in pamphlet form or in the pages of the *Maryland* and *Virginia Gazettes,* essays reprinted from Boston to Savannah and in Dublin, Edinburgh, and London. One scholar who has read every extant American periodical essay of the period before 1781 finds in the *Virginia Gazette* of the 1760s and early 1770s the finest expressions of political and social philosophy, often as they applied to manners and morals, produced on this continent in our colonial era. Those of Maryland are also superior. As far as my reading enables me to, I agree with this judgment.

Quality and effectiveness, which go hand in hand in these expressions, are seen clearly, in part at least, in the breadth of classical learning, the knowledge of history and the interest in human events, a tradition of freedom in theological specu-lation and church government—or really a combination of these. The power to express these qualities was learned from the rhetorical manuals but above all in the bodies politic— the legislatures and general courts—of the Chesapeake Bay region. One may still be moved by *reading* the words of Richard Henry Lee or Patrick Henry. One may be moved, or convinced, by the imaginative logic of another kind of rheto-rician—of the Tory Daniel Dulany, or the patriots Charles Carroll of Carrollton, Thomas Jefferson, George Mason, Ed-mund Randolph, or James Madison, among many dozens. Jefferson's *A Summary View of the Rights of British America* (1774) shows a texture and movement of mind fashioned by two preceding generations of humanistic and legal thinking and learning. So do the political tracts of Bland, Carter, and a score of others of those anonymous or pseudonymous writers of the 1760s in the capital-village newspapers of Tidewater. And one can trace kindred qualities on through the slightly later writings of Jefferson, Pendleton, Mason, and Edmund

Randolph to a sort of culmination in the *Federalist* essays of James Madison.

Perhaps it does not take intellectuals to make a great age, as the historian quoted at the beginning of this paper *seems* to suggest (he might deny this was a great age). It is, of course, partly a matter of definition. But all my dictionaries, and my own pondering of the nature of *homo sapiens Americanus,* would define an intellectual as one who puts things of the mind, the reasoning power, ahead of matters of emotion and will. Certainly there was much sensuous and sensual delight to be experienced in the Tidewater country before the adoption of the Constitution; and perhaps a majority of the colonials, as in most other sections of the world, were directed by their wills and emotions. But by any concept of taste in the fine arts, of interest in religion and theology in relation to the state and the individual, in creative urge and rational argument—by these standards, there were scores, actually hundreds, of men in the eras of Spotswood, Gooch, Ogle, and Sharpe who were far, far more than mere men of intellect. All these men knew what it meant to ponder in depth. These two generations constituted the great age of colonial Virginia and Maryland in power and wealth. But the period's true greatness, the golden quality which was to gleam in America for at least one full generation later, came not from the color of money or tobacco, but from the manner of mind of a major segment (no more a majority than were the theocrats of New England in their region) of the literate inhabitants of Tidewater. If they could be assembled, these men in long columns might march for several hours, or thousands of pages, before they would all pass before us—these schoolmasters, farmers, lawyers, parsons, physicians, and planters who were, in a real sense, intellectuals.

⤙ IX ⤚

James Reid:
Colonial Virginia Poet and
Moral and Religious Essayist

[Though there is no proof that James Reid was a Presbyterian, his attitude towards Virginia upper-class worldliness is similar to that of Davies or later Calvinist divines such as John Holt Rice. Reid was a Scot, with the same love of learning exemplified in Virginia by such men as schoolmaster Donald Robertson, Jefferson's great teacher William Small, dozens of clergymen, and members of the faculty of William and Mary. Reid was himself almost surely a tutor, and an indentured one. In these respects he was a fairly characteristic example of one of the new ethnic or national factors in eighteenth-century Virginia life which were altering the colony's complexion.

Reid saw the wholesome hedonism of the colonial squirearchy as boorish, arrogant, and unpardonable ungodliness. His own admission that he was awkward and clownish when he attempted a minuet is one key to his attitude toward English-bred social graces—an attitude he shared with the members of other Calvinist and evangelical sects. But like his fellow middle-class moralists, he looked with disgust and indignation at the white planter's miscegenation and general treatment of his black slaves.

But Reid lived with an aristocratic planter family he respected and loved. And he was born to write. His major known work, the prose satire on the worldly esquires (assqueers, he calls them) of King William county is a perceptive if prejudiced indictment of his neighbors, a powerful piece of prose. A selection from it has already crept into a recent anthology, although it was not printed for the first time until 1967 (see page 171 and note 2 below). The present essay presents more newly discovered verse and prose by this sensitive and learned man, who reveals the warm cordiality of the domestic circle of which he was a part, a tenderness and sympathy for youth, a shy and shrinking nature in society, a real sense of humor, and a genuine piety. He expressed these qualities in poetry which ranges from the merely conventional to the highly personal and lyrical. "To Ignorance," though it includes some hackneyed and stilted eighteenth-century phrases and imagery, is all together a strong plea for intellectualism. Here is a Virginian who on the threshold of the Revolution was concerned not at all with politics, but with human and humane values.]

THOUGH IT APPEARS that no official records or documents have survived which could reveal to us the personal life of James Reid, recently there have come to light manuscript and printed writings by this eighteenth-century Virginian which show that he was a facile and somewhat versatile poet, a thoughtful commentator on and explicator of the Scriptures, a trenchant moral and social satirist, and withal a scholar of wide learning. All his known work was composed within two years, 1768 and 1769. But he may have arrived in the colony several years before and continued to write many years after. His most ambitious work existed only in manuscript until 1967. His newspaper publications in the *Virginia Gazette* are identified as his for the first time in this essay. Other writings may later be connected with his name.

The work we do have is another of the examples steadily coming to light that there were in this southern colony during the half-century preceding the Revolution a much larger number of gifted writers than has been recognized in published accounts of the cultural and literary history of the period. Certain verses of John Markland, William Dawson, and Charles Hansford have been published or republished in the last few decades, though relatively little is known of their work as a whole. Other poets and prose writers have barely been touched upon.[1]

1. J. A. Leo Lemay, "Richard Lewis and Augustan American Poetry," *PMLA*, LXXXIII (1968), 80 *n*–81 *n*. Lemay's essay is primarily concerned with a forgotten Maryland poet, but he points out that Virginia also had a number of almost or totally forgotten writers. When Ralph L. Rusk edited *Poems on Several Occasions by a Gentleman of Virginia* (Williamsburg, 1736) in 1930, he did not know that the author of the volume was William Dawson. Many poems of Dawson's in the *Virginia Gazette* have not been identified as his, and there are other materials in the Dawson papers at the Library of Congress. Dawson, though a prominent clergyman and the president of the College of William and Mary, is not even in the *Dictionary of American Biography*. Quite recently James A. Servies and Carl R. Dolmetsch edited the hitherto unknown manuscript of the *Poems of Charles Hansford* (Chapel Hill, 1961). Lemay himself edited *A Poem by John Markland of Virginia* (Williamsburg, 1965), by the author of an even finer poem, *Typographia* (Williamsburg, 1730), reprinted in an edition by Earl G. Swem in 1926. Unfortunately both of Markland's poems are in limited editions hard to come by. I published John Mercer's "Dinwiddianae" and other poems from manuscript in *The Colonial Virginia Satirist* (Philadelphia, 1967); other works of prose and verse familiar to Mercer's contemporaries have not yet been identified, though every legal historian knows his work on Virginia law. Verses by Benjamin Waller and a Goochland County friend remain in manuscript at Colonial Williamsburg. Dr. Henry Potter, who published two operas before he came to Virginia during Governor Gooch's administration and who seems to have worked in the colony for several years and to have died there, was apparently the author of two essays in the *Virginia Gazette* and probably wrote a great deal more for that and perhaps other American and British journals. Robert Bolling of Buckingham County published verse in quantity in at least one London magazine and in the *Virginia Gazette*, though only now have his impressive manuscripts begun to be edited. Their publication will add another significant poet to the colonial American list. This is merely the beginning. Buried in the columns of the *Virginia Gazette* and in manuscript repositories are the writings of many others whose names are not yet known, as well as the so-far unattributed verse and/or belletristic essays of such well-known men as William Byrd,

Before I published Reid's prose satire, "The Religion of the Bible and the Religion of K[ing] W[illiam] County Compared" in *The Colonial Virginia Satirist*,[2] in 1967 I searched for some years in this country, in England, and in Scotland for details of Reid's life. I found nothing positive in the King William County records,[3] the Virginia State Library, the University of Virginia, the Virginia Historical Society, or the Library of Congress. It was necessary to rely on internal, or internal-external, evidence in Reid's satiric-essay book. This manuscript, written in December, 1769, was dedicated to an unknown clergyman (half the dedication page is lost). Indications are that Reid was Scottish and probably from Edinburgh, for he was a classmate, in either grammar school or the university, of the blind poet Thomas Blacklock.[4] Reid asserts that he has never been a landowner, that he has spent most of his life immured in "the lonely, forsaken habitation of books." He avows that he tries to act always according to reason; and he adds details which may indicate that he was an Old Light Presbyterian, for he was not a member of the Church of England and not an Enthusiast. As for his life at Sweet Hall in King William County, he had the good fortune to live with a gentleman who suppled him with food, noticed

---

Richard Bland, and Landon Carter. For tantalizing excerpts from otherwise unknown manuscript prose and verse, see Moncure D. Conway, *Barons of the Potomack and Rappahannock* (New York, 1892).

2. R. B. Davis, *The Colonial Virginia Satirist* (Philadelphia, 1967) includes only Mercer's "Dinwiddianae" poems and Reid's prose satire, with extensive introductions and notes. The manuscripts of Mercer's poems are in the Brock Collection, Henry E. Huntington Library, San Marino, Calif.; Reid's prose is in a manuscript book in the Southern Historical Collections of the University of North Carolina at Chapel Hill.

3. Many or most of the King William County records were destroyed by fire in 1885. See John H. Gwathmey, *Twelve Virginia Counties* (Richmond, 1937), 79.

4. R. B. Davis, *Colonial Virginia Satirist*, 70, n. 50.

before Reid himself did when he needed clothing, and paid him wages.

Sweet Hall, built between 1710 and 1720, is today the oldest surviving mansion in the county. A fine Georgian brick structure with certain seventeenth-century Stuart architectural features such as its chimneys, it was built by one of the famous Claiborne family descended from doughty William Claiborne, first-generation colonist and official. Presumably one of his descendants lived there in Reid's time.

Thus the satirist was probably a tutor in an affluent family —just possibly, despite his wages, an indentured one. He may profitably be compared with other contemporary tutors, the indentured Scot John Harrower or the Princeton graduate Philip Fithian, both of whom taught the children of Tidewater Virginia planters.[5] Harrower possessed neither the learning nor the sagacity of Reid. Fithian, who seems to have been accepted on *nearly* equal social terms with the Carter family for whom he worked, likewise did not display Reid's abilities, thoughtful and observant though he was.

Since Reid's longest and most ambitious work, "The Religion of the Bible," was recently printed with a discussion of its theme and purpose, I need only to summarize the work here. It shows the author as a religious and moral man who reflects with "the glass of satire" the foibles of his fellow county-dwellers. He hits the King Williamites at their most vulnerable points—worship of money or wealth; overweening personal pride; extravagant social gluttony; inordinate love of horse and minuet; love of "meaningless" titles such as "Es-

5. Edward Miles Riley (ed.), *The Journal of John Harrower, an Indentured Servant in the Colony of Virginia, 1773–1776* (Williamsburg and New York, 1963); Hunter Dickinson Farish (ed.), *The Journal and Letters of Philip Vickers Fithian, 1773–1774: A Plantation Tutor of the Old Dominion* (Williamsburg, 1943).

quire;" and perhaps above all, arrogance (distinct from the pride mentioned above), which is unbearable to the learned Scot.

Reid's work is a satire, its form derived from such models as Montesquieu's *Persian Letters* and Goldsmith's *Citizen of the World*, but suggesting also several other kinds of social criticism prevalent in the eighteenth century.[6] Sometimes it descends into invective, sometimes it becomes mere sermonizing, as other satires do. It may have sprung purely from moral indignation and the desire to improve the public morals, as Reid declares. But it may also have been a weapon in a struggle among the members of the vestry of the local Anglican parish, St. John's—a struggle which continued through 1772.[7]

In its eighty-four manuscript pages in thirty-four chapters[8] the author reveals, as suggested above, as much about himself as about the quality of his moral indignation. He had his

6. R. B. Davis, *Colonial Virginia Satirist*, 43.

7. This last suggestion comes from Dr. Malcolm Harris of West Point, Virginia, a historian steeped in King William County history. The struggle is recorded in official state documents; see John P. Kennedy (ed.), *Journals of the House of Burgesses of Virginia, 1770–1772* (Richmond, 1906), 164, 169, 171, 199, 207–208, 225–26, 227–31, 242, 285, 288. The Claibornes and most other families of the parish were involved. Actually the missing dedicatee for James Reid's "The Religion of the Bible" (printed in R. B. Davis, *Colonial Virginia Satirist*) may have been the local rector, the Reverend Henry Skyren, an almost universally admired clergyman whom all sides wanted to retain, and did, until 1787; see *Virginia Magazine of History and Biography*, XXVI (1918), 85; and Edward Lewis Goodwin, *The Colonial Church in Virginia . . .* (Milwaukee, 1927), 307. Skyren seems to have been touched by the Great Awakening and to have been more evangelical than most of his Anglican contemporaries; see George M. Brydon, *Virginia's Mother Church and the Political Conditions Under Which It Grew.* (Philadelphia, 1952), II, 150.

8. Parts of chapters VIII and XI, and all of chapters IX and X (pages 22–29) are missing from the manuscript book of Reid, "The Religion of the Bible," Southern Historical Collection.

Bible beside him and quoted from it fairly accurately. Numerous classical references and modern literary allusions may have been quoted from memory, for they are frequently inexact. His reading in French was varied, perhaps again remembered rather than directly referred to (except in the case of Fénelon's *Télémaque,* which he quotes accurately at length). He seems to have enjoyed Voltaire, Fénelon, Montesquieu, and the French Huguenot writers somewhat indiscriminately. The references to Boccalini's *I Ragguagli di Parnasso* may indicate knowledge of one of several English translations rather than the Italian original. Reid's quotation from his friend Blacklock's verse must have been from memory, for the quotation does not appear in the same form in any printed edition by that author. Clearly Reid knew much about history, ancient and modern; he was acquainted with Young's *Night Thoughts;* Addison's *Cato* and *Spectator;* the works of Erasmus; and other material one might expect an educated man of his time to know. His knowledge of Parsee or Zoroastrian lore was in itself a little unusual, but the device of an Oriental commenting upon Occidental *mores* was familiar to Reid from the many works of French and English literature with which he was acquainted. Either the library at Sweet Hall was good, or Reid had an unusual memory.

More of this Scottish-born Virginian's writings came to my attention through a friend[9] who had read *The Colonial Virginia Satirist* and noticed the dateline from Sweet Hall in certain pieces in the Virginia *Gazette.* Early in the year 1769

9. J. A. Leo Lemay, whose *Men of Letters in Colonial Maryland* (Knoxville, 1972) was recently published, has also been engaged in making a census or checklist of poems published in the colonial newspapers. He caught the Sweet Hall name, which is not listed in Lester Cappon and Stella Duff's *Virginia Gazette Index, 1736–1780* (Williamsburg, 1950).

four items appeared, signed "Caledoniensis" and dated from Sweet Hall or Sweethall. Their style, theme, and content indicate that they are indubitably Reid's. But also in the Virginia *Gazette,* beginning in September, 1768, were other items signed "Caledoniensis" but datelined from "Mayfield, near Petersburg" (in Dinwiddie County). Since there were many known Scots in Virginia, and many were schoolmasters, the pseudonym did not necessarily connect the two places. But after some search it was discovered that, during the winter of 1768–1769, Colonel Robert Ruffin of Mayfield sold his Dinwiddie estates and moved to Sweet Hall or to the adjoining plantation of Windsor Shades, in King William. At one time Ruffin almost certainly owned Sweet Hall, for Bartholomew Dandridge informed George Washington (who often crossed the ferry at Sweet Hall—sometimes called Ruffin's—on his way to the House of Burgesses) that Colonel Ruffin had bought Sweet Hall for half its value.[10] Roger Gregory, presumably acting as Ruffin's agent, offered the plantation for sale in the *Virginia Gazette* of December 2, 1773.[11]

10. Bartholomew Dandridge to George Washington, December 30, 1773, in Stanislaus Murray Hamilton (ed.), *Letters to Washington, and Accompanying Papers* . . . (5 vols.; Boston, 1898–1912), IV, 300. Dandridge does not say when Ruffin "bought Sweethall for half of what it must be really worth" (see notes 11 and 12 below.) The advertisement is in both the Purdie and Dixon edition and the Rind edition of the *Virginia Gazette* of this date.

11. Dr. Malcolm Harris, in an interview with the author, suggested that Ruffin bought at least the land and ferry at Sweet Hall in 1767–68. He probably did not do so until later (see notes 10 and 12). Gregory, a relation of the Claibornes, apparently did not succeed in selling the estate, for it remained in the Claiborne family until after the Revolution. It is just possible that Ruffin *bought* the estate as late as 1773 and presented it to a daughter married to a Claiborne, perhaps an original Claiborne owner who was in dire financial straits. This would explain Ruffin's living next door at Windsor Shades and yet at one time owning Sweet Hall; see note 12 below.

Colonel Ruffin moved to be near two of his daughters, who had married or were to marry Claibornes.[12]

Thus Colonel Robert Ruffin is the connecting link to indicate that the "Caledoniensis" of Mayfield was the same man as the writer of Sweet Hall. Theme, style, and form in both poems and prose of 1768 show that the earlier work was done by the man who resided in King William in 1769. But the *Virginia Gazette* material also reveals that the newspaper contributor, though profoundly religious and moral in outlook, had a lighter side not evident in "The Religion of the Bible." Between September 15, 1768, and March 30, 1769, "Caledoniensis" published in the *Gazette* four essays and nine or ten poems. Two of the essays are explications of Biblical passages; another argues that there is in the Old Testament much "to prove" the future state; and one discusses the uses

12. *William and Mary Quarterly*, Ser. 1, XVIII (1909), 252. The two Claibornes who married Ruffin girls lived in Dinwiddie and Sussex when their nuptials took place. In the *Virginia Gazette* (Purdie and Dixon) issues of December 1, 15, 22, and 29, Ruffin advertises for sale his extensive holdings in Dinwiddie, Mecklenburg, and Brunswick counties. In Dinwiddie were two plantations, with "commodious buildings and an ordinary" (the last of which he rents). The other properties are likewise extensive. The advertisement begins, "As I have thoughts of moving to King William. . . ." It is interesting that the December 1 notice appears at the bottom of the same column in which Reid's poem "A Billet Doux" appears.

One of the marriages definitely took place after Ruffin's removal. A notice in the *Virginia Gazette* (Purdie and Dixon), November 25, 1773, announced: "Marriages: Mr. Herbert Claiborne, of Sussex, to Miss Molly Ruffin, of King William." An otherwise blank preliminary page of the "Religion" manuscript has faintly legible the name Ruffin preceded by two initials, one an M. The hand is different from that of the manuscript.

It is also worth noting that Sterling Clack (a brother or close relative of Mrs. Ruffin), who died in 1751, left in his will many volumes of the *Spectator* and *Guardian*, Pope, Addison in other works, Ovid, etc.; see *Virginia Magazine of History and Biography*, VIII (1900), 61. Sterling continued to be given as a Christian name in the Ruffin and Claiborne families; see *William and Mary Quarterly*, Ser. 1, XVIII (1909), 252–258. Ruffin married in 1751, according to *William and Mary Quarterly*, XX (1911), 198.

and misuses of language. Of the poems, two are addressed "To my Pen," with another between the two, perhaps Reid's, a kind of rejoinder to the first, as the second is a rejoinder to it; another represents the lamentation of a young lady on the loss of a favorite bird, and the later "Epitaph" may be on the same theme; others have the titles "To Ignorance," "The Sports of Cupid," "A Play upon the words Fire, Ice and Snow," "A Billet Doux in the modern taste," and "Ode on Christmas Day 1768." Except for "To Ignorance," all the poems were written at Mayfield.

The first of the essays, dated from Mayfield, November 17, 1768, and published on December 15, occupies the honored position in the first column and a half of page one. It discusses Jude, verse 9, "Yet Michael the Archangel, when contending with the Devil he disputed about the body of Moses, durst not bring against him a railing accusation, but said, the Lord rebuke thee." Reid modestly advances a "personal" interpretation. He cites several other possible explanations, demonstrating considerable knowledge of the Old Testament and of Roman history. He argues that Moses' body was kept free from corruption not because the Jews wished to deify him; that it was beneath God's dignity to bandy words with Satan; and finally that God had Moses buried in a private place so that at Christ's Transfiguration, Moses' body, free from corruption, could stand with Elias beside the Son of God. "God could have raised him from the dust to be present there, but it is contrary to the laws of God and nature to perform by a greater act what can be done by a less miracle. Nature always acts in the shortest way. . . ."—thus reasoned the pious son of the eighteenth century. He was probably not a whit abashed when "W," in the *Gazette* of January 12, 1769, asked that "Caledoniensis" be told that Stackhouse's *History of the Bible,* volume II, page 1619, contained the same interpreta-

tion of the passage,[13] for Reid had in his essay asked for suggestions and corrections.

On February 9, 1769, in another biblical explication from
Sweet Hall dated January 29, "Caledoniensis" again occupied
a column and a half in the honored position on page one of
the *Gazette*. This time he was concerned with Genesis 1:26,
"Let us make man in our image, after our likeness." Reid
argued that God had really said, "Let us make man a Trinity
like ourselves." This Trinity consisted of Spirit, Soul, and
Body, an image of God "which is stamped upon every thing
in the creation." For even a rose has shape, color, and smell,
all coeval and indivisible. Like the sun, another form of the
Trinity of God, man has body, heat, and light. Holiness or
purity, the secondary image of God upon man, the original
righteousness, was lost by the fall. But the primary image of
God, the resemblance to the Trinity, remains. "This doctrine
makes man a glorious being, and cuts off every pretence that
the Deists can have of placing him among the brutes, and of
cavilling against a Trinity." Reid went on to equate the spirit
(light, etc.) with the conscience, which returns to God at
the separation caused by death. Several scriptural passages
were cited to support his conclusions.

Again from Sweet Hall, writing on March 4, 1769, Reid
published in the issue of March 16 (this time on pages two
and three) an argument against statements that in the whole

13. Thomas Stackhouse, *A New History of the Holy Bible, from the
Beginning of the World, to the Establishment of Christianity. With Answers to Most of the Controversial Questions, Dissertations upon the Most
Remarkable Passages, and a Connection of Profane History All Along.
To Which Are Added Notes, Explaining the Difficult Texts, Rectifying
Mis-Translations, and Reconciling Seeming Contradictions* (2 vols.; London, 1737). "W's" reference was to the first edition or one of those between 1742 and 1754, all of which are paged continuously and in two
volumes. Most of the later editions, perhaps all, are in a smaller format
in six volumes.

of the Old Testament there is "not one single text that will prove a future state." He endeavored to show that there were indeed "tacit" if not "absolute" proofs of that state in various places. One of his "proofs" was an ingenious interpretation of portions of the Book of Job. For example, he saw the story of Job's children as one of the "tacit proofs."

The fourth *Gazette* essay, in the issue of March 30, 1769, again occupies part of the front page and is again dated from Sweet Hall. But this article is moral and linguistic rather than religious in subject. "Caledoniensis" is concerned with his contemporaries' misuse of language, especially in folk and colloquial expressions which do not say at all what they mean. "Hectoring bully," for example, is an unjust aspersion on the great Trojan hero, who was never arrogant or overweening. "An ungrateful dog" conveys an idea inconsistent with the nature of that faithful animal. "Born a gentleman," a term employed by the rich, is opposed to fact; for all are born equal, helpless, naked, and poor, and those oftenest called *gentle men* are not so. The wise Chinese knew the value of truth and of his reasoning, Reid avers. Finally, he cites the use of "damn'd" as a qualifying adverb, employed universally by those around him, as meaning nothing at all. This essay is close in subject, style, and intent to the later satire, "The Religion of the Bible," a work which Reid was probably already composing.[14] In the later work, for example, he also castigates the boorish use of the indiscriminate "damn'd," which was a typical blasphemous habit of the King William Ass-Queers (Esquires).

If one takes the subjects and content of the poems written at Mayfield as indicative of the author's attitude towards life, Reid enjoyed himself; he was perhaps happier in the Din-

14. The dedication to Reid's "The Religion of the Bible" is dated December 2, 1769.

widdie household and society than he was in the King William. Colonel and Mrs. Ruffin had a number of children growing up besides the two girls married to Claibornes.[15] Apparently Reid entertained the whole family with his verse and wit, and was an accepted part of their social circle. His initial contribution to the "POETS CORNER" of the *Gazette* for September 15, 1768, the first of the verses titled "To my Pen," indicates something of this:

> Thou dear companion of each idle hour,
> With joy I view thee, and confess thy power;
> Not showers to larks, nor sunshine to the bee,
> Are half so charming as thy touch to me.
> The miser, brooding o'er his much lov'd gain,
> Feels not the pleasure which thou dost contain;
> The beau, O pen, so proud of outward show,
> Tastes not the raptures that thou dost bestow;
> The lover, folded in his mistress' arms,
> Finds not felicity beyond thy charms;
> The vain coquette, adorn'd in pride of dress,
> Does for her ornaments less love express
> Than I, when from the busy world set free,
> Am in my closet left alone with thee.
>   From foolish subjects, O my pen, keep free,
> With ill tim'd satire ne'er conversant be;
> Immodest words admit of no defence,
> And want of decency is want of sense;
> Religion's tenets be thy constant care,
> But in disputes be candid and sincere;
> True love to mankind in your writings show,
> Nor vent thy spite and malice 'gainst thy foe;
> Defend your cause with all the skill you can,
> And, though you hate his errours, love the man;
> Let every injur'd fair in thee still find
> A wise protector, and a stedfast friend;

15. See note 12 above and *William and Mary Quarterly*, Ser. 1, **XVIII** (1909), 252 ff.

That young and old may in thy praise combine,
The virtues of humanity be thine.
 O friendly pen! how much by me admir'd!
I'm of thy lov'd assistance never tir'd;
By thee to distant friends I tell my mind,
And in thy friendship we true friendship find;
In foreign climes, where I some friends have found,
By thee I make the circling laugh go round;
By thee, without a blush, I can unfold
Things which with equal ease could not be told.
Farewell my pen, and still assured be
My chiefest joy will center'd be in thee.

The Mayfield mansion, probably built in the mid-eighteenth century, also still stands. Perhaps even more than Sweet Hall, it is a fine example of Georgian architecture.[16] Both the main buildings are modest in size, though they were once surrounded by smaller structures such as plantation offices, smokehouses, kitchens, dairies, and schoolhouses.[17] In such a smaller "dependency" Reid probably lived and taught, though like other tutors and educated staff members, he probably had his meals with the family. He corresponded with friends at "Home" in rhyme, as other Virginians did with each other,[18]

16. The Dinwiddie house is now within the grounds of the Central State Hospital in Petersburg, Virginia. For a description and photograph, see Edward A. Wyatt IV, *Plantation Houses around Petersburg in the Counties of Prince George, Chesterfield, and Dinwiddie, Virginia* (Petersburg, 1955), 37. Mayfield, being of a later date, does not, of course, include seventeenth-century architectural features such as those found at Sweet Hall.

17. For information about the outbuildings at Mayfield, see note 12 above. Mr. N. R. Palmer, owner of Sweet Hall in 1964, recalled that when he bought the place in 1920 a very ancient detached schoolhouse stood in the yard. Reid may have taught in it. John Harrower (see note 5 above) lived alone in his schoolhouse, a building twenty by twelve feet, and had his meals with the family of his master, Colonel Daingerfield; see Riley (ed.), *Journal of John Harrower*, 57. Fithian slept with his older male pupils in one of the larger "offices" which also served as a schoolhouse; see Farish (ed.), *Journal and Letters of Fithian*, xli.

18. See Benjamin Waller manuscripts, Colonial Williamsburg.

and he wrote amusing verses for the entertainment of the Ruffin family and their friends. His rules for his pen are strictly neoclassical and moral. Though he was to write the *prose* satire already noted, it was not "ill turn'd" verse, either in form or vindictive spirit.

On October 13 a writer who signed himself "Your Pen. From the Inkstandish at Mayfield, near Petersburg," replied with "To Caledoniensis, from his Pen." He ridiculed "Caledoniensis" for thinking he could write effective moral verse, or that he could move others from vice to virtue with his pen. The tone was more playful than malicious, however, and this second poem *may* have been written by the author of the first, though the lines are somewhat cruder in form.

On October 27 "Caledoniensis" replied in another "To my Pen," referring to the October 13 verses as Bavius' bark. Reid denied that "Your Pen" was written from Mayfield, and averred that its author was merely jealous. The ridicule was effective, concluding with his throwing the dog a bone and observing: "Lie hid, poor cur, for since thou seem'st at rest, My anger's fled, and all my threats are jest."[19]

Following this half serious exchange, "Caledoniensis" turned to a lighter theme, again characteristic of its age in its mock-elegiac quality, "The lamentation of a young Lady for the loss of her favourite Bird." These lines appeared in the *Gazette* of November 3, datelined from Mayfield October 22. Pope, Gray, Goldsmith, scores of other English poets wrote on such subjects in a similar tone. Like their work, this verse almost certainly referred to an actual incident, probably a recent catastrophe in the Ruffin household:

> O woeful day! a day of woe to me!
> And, wretched I, who live this day to see!
> When that dear bird, the pleasure of my eyes,

19. The poem has fifty lines.

Robb'd of its precious life before me lies.
Confounded be each noxious mouse and rat,
Which makes us in our houses keep a cat;
That cruel quadruped.

. . . .
O lovely bird! still lovely though now dead!
Amongst the sweetest flowers thou shalt be laid.

Thirty-eight lines altogether were expended, perhaps to console or distract one of the younger members of the plantation family. On November 10 (dated October 23 from Mayfield) another mock-elegy appeared, perhaps inspired by the same incident, but written in a different mood and tone. Here Reid departed from the couplet form which he had used heretofore:

Epitaph

Below this turf a being lies
    Who was nor saint nor sinner,
Yet men such company do prize,
And wish them of a larger size,
    If hungry, when at dinner.

For as the belly has no ears,
    And singing cannot relish,
So hunger drives off other cares,
Man minds not how his fellow fares,
    If he himself don't perish.

The breathless corpse which lies below
    Met an untimely end,
Yet not from an avowed foe,
Nor yet from one that was not so,
    Nor, thirdly, from a friend.

For in the dark the murderer cruel
    Attack'd the creature mild,
Yea instantly did him embowel,
And robb'd of life my darling jewel,
    As tigers would a child.

> O all ye parents, far and near,
>   Who of my loss do read,
> With sorrow my afflictions hear,
> And, with the sympathetick tear,
>   Show that your hearts can bleed.
>
> Young Ladies, see your charmers fled;
>   Wives, see your husbands gone;
> Yourselves, old men, see on death's bed;
> Ye young, perceive your sweethearts dead;
>   And then, like me, you'll moan.

The next week (November 17) Reid was represented by two poems in the "POETS CORNER," both playful occasional verses on love, in the neoclassical fashion. The first, "The Sports of Cupid: or, The Fever and Ague of Lovers," begins

> Ah! teach, ye Nine, me justly to unfold
> Love's different ailments, changes, heat, and cold!
> When Celia begs, and for her swain's love sues,
> Then Damon flies and doth her suit refuse;
> When Damon next entreats the comely fair,
> The nymph disdains to hear his humble prayer:
> Love burns in both, and each for other lives,
> But still his fever her the ague gives.

So the poem of paradoxes goes on for twenty more lines. Perhaps suggested by phrases included in the above, Reid followed immediately with a short poem, "A Play upon the words FIRE, ICE, SNOW."

> Lately when suffering by a fire,
> Julia's kind aid I did desire;
> With snow and ice the haughty dame
> Attempted to destroy the flame.
> What colder is than ice and snow?
> Yet these my fire did higher blow;
> For ice and snow, from Julia sent,
> Gave to my fires a stronger vent.
> Ah me! Where shall I seek for rest?

For cold but more inflames my breast!
Ah! Julia, neither ice nor snow
Can quench my fires which fiercer grow;
But come with equal fires, no doubt
One fire will drive the other out.

In the *Gazette* of December 1, "Caledoniensis" continued his conventional assaults on the heart of a fair lady (dating his poem November 8), with "A Billet Doux in the modern taste," a piece of sixty-eight lines. A sample is sufficient.

Dear Madam, let this letter tell
   The dictates of my mind;
And let thine eye propitious be,
   And to its author kind.
Let his chaste wishes warm thy soul,
   And turn thy lovely mind
Upon thy amorous swain, that he
   His wish'd for prize may find.
Open my heart, thou sprightly maid,
   Keep up a lover's flame;
For thee I wish, for thee I sigh,
   I've pleasure in thy name
. . . .
And whilst my heart before thee lies,
   Both fervent and sincere,
Listen whilst I do yield it up
   With this laconick prayer:
Dear Madam, hear a dying swain,
   Redeem me from the grave;
And while I live I shall remain
   Your very humble slave.

Whether it was inspired by a living maiden or desire to compose an exercise in a fashionable form, this was the last of Reid's lighter poems from Mayfield. He did write one more poem in Dinwiddie County, on December 16, 1768, published in the *Gazette* on December 29. It was appropriate to the season:

Ode on Christmas Day 1768[20]

Arise, my muse, with warmth divine,
No subject mean I am to sing
   Arise without delay,
In lofty strains teach me t'unfold
That heavenly bounty shown of old
   Upon first Christmas day.

The God of Nature, he who said
The word, and straight all things were made,
   That do this earth adorn,
This day, in favour of mankind,
Was born, and acted as a friend
   To men the most forlorn.

He who, of all the worlds around
Which through immensity are found,
   Was by one word creator,
Yet from his heavenly throne of bliss
Vouchsafed to appear in this,
   As God, Man, Mediator.

When blood of bulls for sacrifice,
And that of goats, could not suffice
   T'appease offended Heaven,
Then said our Lord, behold I come
To free the wretched slave from doom,
   Myself the ransom given.

The angels these good tidings spread,
A star the eastern Magi led,
   Who forthwith presents bring;
Myrrh, teaching us the child was man,
Incence, by which we God him scan,
   And by the gold a King.

20. The microfilm copy from the Institute of Early American History and Culture and photostat copy from the Massachusetts Historical Society are both defective here, but the Virginia Historical Society copy is perfect in the area of the poem.

Yet see from Herod's cruelty
This infant King soon forc'd to fly,
  For shelter and relief;
And with amazement too! perceive
That from his manger to his grave
  He was a man of grief.

At last to 's heavenly father's will,
Which he had sent him to fulfil,
  He paid a due submission;
His life he for us sinners gave,
And by his sufferings we have
  Of sins the full remission.

He paid the debt which we did owe,
For us his precious blood did flow,
  For us who did rebel!
From hence all blessings we receive,
By it, at length; we hope to have
  A sure release from hell.

When thus our great Redeemer trode
The wine-press of the wrath of God,
  And trode it out alone,
The Sun, amaz'd, his face did hide!
Earth from her inmost centre sigh'd!
  And Nature gave a groan!

The temple's veil was rent in twain!
Darkness did universal reign!
  The graves gave up their dead!
'Twas then, O serpent, thou didst feel;
The seed, of whom thou 'adst bruis'd the heel,
  Then sorely bruis'd thy head.

Forbid it, Lord, that we offend
This so divine and heavenly friend,
  Or former faults renew,
Since by such conduct we again
Do give our blest Redeemer pain,
  And torture him anew.

Let love and gratitude inspire
Our souls with pure seraphick fire,

> T'adore this best of friends;
> On goodness such let us not trample,
> But wisely follow his example,
> Until our lives he ends.

Though he published several essays between this devout ode and his next verses, "Caledoniensis" did not appear in the "POETS CORNER" again until March 16, 1769. By then he had been at Sweet Hall for at least two months. As the writer made clear in this final published poem, as well as in the satire "The Religion of the Bible and the Religion of K[ing] W[illiam] County Compared," he did not find the new environment to his liking. Either as part of the household of Ruffin or of a daughter who had married a Claiborne, he found himself surrounded by a large, proud, and wealthy circle of Wests, Foxes, Blands, Littlepages, Quarleses, Roanes, Robinsons, Braxtons, and Wallers. As "The Religion of the Bible" illustrated, Reid never appreciated the fine qualities of political and legal acumen and independence of spirit that later made several of them leaders in the Revolution. He was apparently unaware that one of them, John Fox (of a slightly older generation), was, like himself, a poet, with a reputation in England as well as in America.[21] In this last poem Reid showed his dislike, even indignation, at his personal treatment in their society. For he seemed to admit that on the ballroom floor he was out of place; that he was laughed at for his shabby clothes; and that he was generally considered an eccentric. This poem was far more personal than his prose satire, but both showed the sensitive and learned colonist

21. Kenneth B. Murdock, "William Byrd and the Virginia Author of *The Wanderer*," *Harvard Studies and Notes in Philology and Literature,* XVII (1935), 129–36.

In the Maryland Historical Society is a manuscript poem by Fox on Thomas Bordley. Fox probably was also an anonymous or pseudonymous contributor to the *Virginia Gazette* many years before Reid.

reacting against a dominant society which he was sure misunderstood or at least failed to appreciate him.

To Ignorance.

Hail Ignorance! thou source of all content,
In pleasures gay, in raptures innocent;
Though old as Chaos thou thy power maintain'st,
And happy every breast is where thou reign'st:
The smiles, the graces, and the sports attend
Where'er thy easy snow-white footsteps bend;
Light as a feather thou can'st trip along,
No heart-felt sorrow to thy sons belong;
Polemick doctrines never vex their brain,
The tree of knowledge never gave them pain;
Blest in themselves, they need no foreign aid,
Nor are of any outward woes afraid;
Joy, mirth, and pleasure, always on them wait,
Advance their merit, and support their state;
Fortune to them delights in being kind,
But to dull sons of science still is blind;
She, though a female, constant doth remain
To thee, O Ignorance! and all thy train;
None call her fickle but the learn'd and wise,
Because from their dull seats she always flies.
Thy foes their constant joy of heart express
By looks and actions, words, and airy dress;
In them it is, and them alone we find
The smooth forehead an index of the mind;
No furrow'd wrinkle on their visage grows,
Nor from their eye e'er drops the tear of woes;
The day with melody they merry keep,
And, free from care, all night they soundly sleep:
For they alone do Morpheus' kindness share
Who, sons of Ignorance, are free from care,
Nor have their cheek e'er sully'd with a tear.
   Not so the man who from his eager breast
With care and pain hath got thee dispossess'd;
By loss of thee he lost his greatest friend,

And brought on toils and troubles without end:
Wrapp'd up in dreary thought, he neither knows
What is around him nor which way he goes;
Like one amaz'd, he wildly stares and talks,
And frights thy darling children in his walks;
Shabby from head to foot, he cannot show
Himself in presence of a sprightly beau;
Hear how they cry when clumsily he dances,
"See, see, how that strange bear or camel prances!"
Thy old child LAUGHTER, holding both her sides,
The aukward wisdom of thy foes derides;
A hearty laugh, or in or out of season,
O'erthrows the strongest arguments of reason;
A scoff, a sneer, is loaded with such magick
As bids defiance to all rules of logick;
A well tim'd grin can baffle all the rules
So much admir'd by the dull sons of schools,
Who losing thee thus lose their greatest good,
 Alas! 'tis lost not full understood;
By this, unfit for company, they hide
Among their books, and in their cells abide,
And, as asham'd of day, take their night tour,
With bird of Athens, at the moonshine hour,
When heavily along their footsteps tread,
For loss of thee makes them despise their bed;
Such cares oppress, such griefs afflict their mind,
That day nor night they no true pleasure find;
By flights of soaring fancy vainly toss'd,
They are in mazes, endless mazes lost;
Strangers to joy, wrapp'd up in anxious thought,
Yet ne'er arriving at the end they sought.
  Blest IGNORANCE! who giv'st us halcyon days,
I'll raise a monument unto thy praise;
Around it all thy wanton sons shall play,
And incense offer there from day to day,
From day to day thy praises there resound,
And sing this theme to all the world around:
" 'Tis IGNORANCE alone from which we find
"Our body's safety, and our peace of mind;

"She keeps from care, and shelters us from strife,
"And makes us feel the real joys of life."

Thus in a period when the planter aristocracy wielded the pen, and wielded it effectively, against the Pistole Fee, the Two-Penny Act, the Stamp Act, and tobacco taxes, one finds in James Reid a southern late-colonial writer concerned almost solely with what men were and what their relation to their God was. Politics, political rights, and political institutions were not his themes. He did compose some conventional, light occasional verses, as did his Virginia contemporaries, including especially the planters themselves. But like the great Presbyterian Samuel Davies in two earlier decades, Reid's prose and his verse represent a tradition outside the political which has persisted throughout the South. This tradition finally flowered in the twentieth century in that region's pervasive exploration of the individual in relation to his immediate society, his cosmos, and his God. Reid's temper is closer to Faulkner's or Robert Penn Warren's than it was to Jefferson's. For he was a southern puritan, not Puritan, as was Alexander Whitaker in the first generation of Virginia colonists and as are dozens of the section's writers in the mid-twentieth century. Out of necessity, he expressed himself in the accepted forms of his neoclassical age—the periodical essay, the long prose satire, and the religious, occasional, or satiric poem.

Thomas Jefferson
as Collector of Virginiana

[From the days of the Virginia Company at Jamestown in the 1620s to C. Waller Barrett in the 1960s and 1970s, groups and individuals in Virginia have been gatherers or collectors of books. Now as in the past, their reading has usually been purposeful or pious. Even in the seventeenth century there are records of hundreds of private libraries, including a half dozen fairly large ones. In the eighteenth century Ralph Wormeley, Landon Carter, Richard Bland, Sir John Randolph, and, above all, William Byrd II, John Mercer, and Thomas Jefferson brought together great libraries. Byrd's was perhaps half a collector's library, one of the earliest in America, but he did read an enormous number of his several thousand volumes. Mercer's included a large percentage of legal works, but the Irish-born Virginian's many-sided interests brought books on almost every conceivable subject into his library at Marlborough on the Potomac.

Jefferson's three or four collections varied in nature and quantity, the second, which was sold to the nation as a nucleus for the Library of Congress, being the greatest of them. The master of Monticello was a "curious" man in the eighteenth-century sense of wanting to know something about everything. He brought together books he could and did use for all sorts of guidance, from shoeing horses to weighing political and diplomatic questions. The books came by purchase from shops in several countries and from the libraries of at least a half dozen of his fellow Virginians, including John Banister, William Byrd II, Richard Bland, and Jefferson's Randolph relatives. His old teacher George Wythe bequeathed an interesting group to him.

In collecting materials concerning his own state and colony, Jefferson followed a tradition as well as a real interest. For soon after its appearance John Smith's *Generall Historie of Virginia* was in colonial libraries, as were Hakluyt's *Principall Navigations* and Purchas' *Pilgrims* and *Pilgrimage,* though all the latter were not concerned directly with Virginia or written after Jamestown was established. The histories by Oldmixon, Beverley, Hartwell-Blair-Chilton, Hugh Jones, and William Stith had been acquired by Virginians as soon as they appeared; and they survive in remnants of many colonial libraries, as do many poems and sermons. A few of the earlier libraries also contained manuscript records of the early days of the settlement.

But as the present essay shows, Jefferson went far beyond any of his predecessors as a collector of published and unpublished Virginiana. Some of the material he salvaged from innkeepers who were about to use the paper to kindle fires; some items were presented to him by friends or acquaintances who knew of his interests. All American historians are indebted to him for the preservation of unique manuscript records of our early history, and of copies of unpublished literary-historical materials which are now part of the American literary canon. Jefferson was not a systematic philosopher, nor a student of Calvin, but his considered weighing of written record and authority in the scales of experience mark him as another Virginia intellectual, perhaps the greatest of them, as he determined courses of action for "his own country," Virginia, or for the nation.]

ON MARCH 29, 1764, a clerk in the bookshop connected with the *Virginia Gazette* office in Williamsburg recorded the purchase by Thomas Jefferson, for ten shillings, of a copy of "Stith's History of Virginia."[1] This is the earliest surviving record of the acquisition of an item of Virginiana by the young man who was later to gather in his library the most significant material pertaining to his native state ever assembled by an individual. "When young, I was passionately fond of reading books of history,"[2] he commented in 1787. In 1789 he added that "[I am] sensible that I labour grievously under the malady of Biblomanie."[3] Still later he agreed with a fellow Virginian "that it is the duty of every good citizen to use all the opportunities which occur to him, for preserving documents relating to the history of our country." That "our country" here is his native state is proved by his next sentence, for William Waller Hening's *Statutes at Large,* to which Jefferson alludes, pertains only to Virginia: "That I have not been remiss in this while I had youth, health, and opportunity, is proved otherwise, as well by the materials I furnished toward Mr. Hening's invaluable collection of the laws of our country."[4]

These statements afford a glimpse of the complex motivations behind this particular activity of Jefferson. He said several times that he was assembling a library which would

1. *Virginia Gazette* Day Book (MS in Alderman Library, University of Virginia, Charlottesville). There is a photostat copy at Colonial Williamsburg.
2. Thomas Jefferson to the editor of the *Journal de Paris,* August 29, 1787, in Lipscomb and Bergh (eds.), *The Writings of Thomas Jefferson* (20 vols.; Washington, D.C., 1903), XVII, 148; and in Julian P. Boyd *et al.* (eds.), *The Papers of Thomas Jefferson.* (Princeton, 1950–), XII, 62.
3. Jefferson to Lucy Ludwell Paradise, June 1, 1789, in Boyd *et al.* (eds.), *Jefferson Papers,* XV, 163.
4. Jefferson to Hugh P. Taylor, October 4, 1823, in Lipscomb and Bergh (eds.) *Writings of Jefferson,* XV, 473.

be useful to him as a lawyer and as an American statesman. Since he was a Virginia lawyer and eventually a Virginian in national office, much of the material gathered to assist him in his profession was Virginian. And many items of Virginiana came to him incidentally or accidentally through his personal and public reputation as a scholar and author of *Notes on the State of Virginia* and through his positions in national as well as state government. Americans and Europeans who had anything to say about Virginia frequently sent him copies of their books, with autographed inscriptions. Many actually dedicated the books to him.

But Jefferson the collector of Virginiana was first of all an eighteenth-century colonial gentleman building a library which would answer all his needs. Like his distinguished predecessor William Byrd, he planned and gathered a general collection representing all fields of knowledge. Like his kinsmen Sir John and Peyton Randolph, he brought together those law books, some of them two centuries old, which might be practically useful.

During his long life Jefferson gathered three libraries for himself and another for the University of Virginia. In his youth he inherited forty-odd books, useful ones, from his father. He added to these judiciously[5] until by 1770 his library was valued at £200. On February 21 of that year he lamented to his friend John Page the loss of his mother's house by fire, and his own loss, "of every pa[per I] had in the world, and almost every book" (*Papers*, I, 34). Thus ended his first gathering.

From this moment he began the steady accumulation of his

5. See the *Virginia Gazette* Day Book's list of Jefferson's purchases in Williamsburg during 1764–65; or, more conveniently, see William H. Peden, "Thomas Jefferson: Book Collector," (Ph.D. dissertation, University of Virginia, 1942), Appendix.

greatest collection, in quality and quantity—which he would sell to Congress in 1814 to replace the national library destroyed by the British. The trouble, expense, and care which went into this collection were reflected in the wistfully proud letter of 1814 to Samuel H. Smith, who was negotiating the sale to Congress:

You know my collection, its condition and extent. I have been fifty years making it, and have spared no pains, opportunity or expense, to make it what it is. While residing in Paris, I devoted every afternoon I was disengaged, for a summer or two, in examining all the principal bookstores, turning over every book with my own hand, and putting by everything which related to America, and indeed whatever was rare and valuable in every science. Besides this, I had standing orders during the whole time I was in Europe, on its principal book-marts, particularly Amsterdam, Frankfort, Madrid and London, for such works relating to America as could not be found in Paris. So that in that department particularly, such a collection was made as probably can never again be effected, because it is hardly probable that the same opportunities, the same time, industry, perseverance and expense, with some knowledge of the bibliography of the subject, would again happen to be in concurrence. During the same period, and after my return to America, I was led to procure, also, whatever related to the duties of those in the high concerns of the nation. So that the collection . . . extends more particularly to whatever belongs to the American statesman (September 21, *L&B, XIV*, 191–192).

The last sentence was intended, of course, to emphasize the appropriateness of the library for the Congress of the United States. The penultimate sentence summarizes very modestly the enormous labor and care that went into his collecting between 1789 and 1814. Miss E. Millicent Sowerby's recent invaluable *Catalogue of the Library of Thomas Jefferson* supplies detailed and interesting information from his correspondence and book orders covering these years.[6] Booksellers all over America and western Europe supplied his demands. Professional dealers and publishers like John Stockdale and James Lackington in London, Armand Koenig of 'Strassburg,' Dufour of Amsterdam, Mathew Carey of Philadelphia, and Samuel Pleasants of Richmond, among several dozen others, sought books for him. But he also called upon friends, men like Joseph Hopkinson in Philadelphia, to secure copies of significant items.

According to the *Catalogue* published in 1815 after this collection became the Library of Congress, it contained approximately 3,200 items in about 6,500 volumes. Miss Sowerby, using both the 1815 *Catalogue* and an earlier manuscript rough-draft catalogue and counting in a somewhat different way, actually numbers 4,931 items, books and pamphlets, in her published list of those received by Congress.[7] Because so many of the items have disappeared, she was unable to check effectively the earlier count of number of volumes.

Even before the wagonloads of this library began their slow journey toward Washington, Jefferson had begun collecting a third library, intended "to amuse" him in his old age. Again he resorted to professional agents like Carey and Dufief in Philadelphia, and he accepted the offers of friends abroad like David B. Warden, Richard Rush, and George Ticknor to procure for him convenient editions of the classics. A fa-

6. E. Millicent Sowerby, *Catalogue of the Library of Thomas Jefferson* (5 vols.; Washington, D.C., 1952–59). Miss Sowerby also identified editions and imprints whenever possible. Until her work appeared such a survey as this would have been impossible.

7. Sowerby, *Catalogue*, gives individual item numbers to pamphlets gathered by Jefferson into bound groups. This accounts for much of the difference between her 4,931 items and the 3,200 items listed by George Watterston, the Librarian of Congress, in *The Catalogue of the Library of the United States* (Washington, D.C., 1815).

vorite agent, George Milligan of Georgetown, D.C., continued to bind and procure books for him.[8] Individual admirers continued to contribute copies of their own writings. A sales catalogue of this collection, published in 1829, indicates that by 1826 it contained between 900 and 1,000 items.[9] Miss Sowerby recently completed a descriptive catalogue based on this list. Meanwhile the short titles of the printed sales list may be fairly easily, though sometimes tentatively, identified.

The last Jefferson library, the one assembled for the University of Virginia, contained over 3,000 items in more than 7,000 volumes. Jefferson drew up its catalogue, persuaded friends like Madison and Ticknor to assist him, and in 1824 sent abroad an agent, Francis Gilmer, who was to procure both professors and books.[10] Particularly rich in science, this collection is least rich in Virginiana, though it contains some twenty-eight items in seventy-odd volumes, principally history and law, most of which duplicate the Virginiana items in one of Jefferson's personal libraries.

As some of the above quotations from his letters indicate, Jefferson was at the same time an incidental and a deliberate collector of Virginiana. Some items were thrust upon him. Others were simply constituent elements of his Americana assemblages. But he went to the trouble himself to secure many books about his "country" primarily for the sake of preserving them, as good collectors have often done.

8. William H. Peden, "Some Notes Concerning Thomas Jefferson's Libraries," *William and Mary Quarterly*, Ser. 3, I (1944), 265–72; see also Sowerby, *Catalogue, passim*.

9. Peden, "Some Notes," 268; and *A Catalogue of the Extensive and Valuable Library of the Late President Jefferson* (Washington, D.C., 1829).

10. William H. Peden (ed.), *1828 Catalogue of the Library of the University of Virginia* (Charlottesville, 1945); and R. B. Davis, *Francis Walker Gilmer: Life and Learning in Jefferson's Virginia* (Richmond, 1939).

Almost two dozen of the printed Virginiana were authors' presentation copies, ranging from medical treatises to law reports. Scattered items came into his possession from various fellow Virginians: his brother-in-law Dabney Carr; the Tory William and Mary Professor Samuel Henley; several members of the Corbin family; his physician George Gilmer; Lunsford Lomax; Philip Ludwell; his friend John Page; his kinsmen Beverley and Edmund Randolph and John Randolph of Roanoke; his son-in-law Thomas Mann Randolph; and Robert Beverley. Probably Jefferson's wife contributed seventeen books from the library of her father John Wayles, and twenty-one from her first husband's brother Bathurst Skelton.[11] Over a span of several years, Jefferson obtained some ten volumes from the famous collection of William Byrd of Westover,[12] and sixteen bearing the autograph of his second son-in-law John Wayles Eppes. George Wythe bequeathed his library to his former student. Though only about thirty-one volumes from it now survive in the Library of Congress,[13] some of the extant legal items are quite valuable. From the administrators of the estate of Richard Bland (1710–1776) Jefferson purchased whole segments of a library, including a number of seventeenth- and eighteenth-century manuscript records. Perhaps his most valuable purchase, from any point of view, was that of his kinsman Peyton Randolph's library, "bookcases and all as they stood."[14] Much

11. Dumas Malone, "The Wayles Family," in *Jefferson the Virginian* (Boston, 1948), 433.

12. Sowerby, *Catalogue*, V, Index; and Edwin Wolf II, "The Disposal of the Library of William Byrd of Westover," *Proceedings of the American Antiquarian Society*, LXVIII (1958), 19–106.

13. Sowerby, *Catalogue*, I, xiii; V, Index. Miss Sowerby estimates that less than one-third of the items sold by Jefferson to Congress survive. Two-thirds were probably destroyed in the fire of December 24, 1851.

14. Jefferson to W. W. Hening, September 3, 1820, quoted in Sowerby, *Catalogue*, II, 241.

of this collection had come to Peyton from his father, the distinguished Sir John. More than fifty items survive from it today, including several priceless and unique volumes of early Virginia laws and records in manuscript. To add to these Bland and Randolph manuscripts, Jefferson's friend Page gave him a volume of unpublished laws which had once belonged to his grandfather Mathew Page.

Jefferson's famous cataloguing system, based upon the divisions of learning made by Francis Bacon, did not allow him to place all his Virginia materials together, though within subclasses they often do appear side by side. Jefferson sent his manuscript catalogue, with its three major divisions of History, Philosophy, and Fine Arts, to the Librarian of Congress, George Watterston, who used it with slight modifications when he published the 1815 *Catalogue of the Library of the United States,* a list of the books as they were received from Jefferson. Miss Sowerby in her five-volume *Catalogue* followed the same system, listing in Volume One all of the History, in Volumes Two, Three, and part of Four the Philosophy, and in the remainder of Four and Five the Fine Arts and "[Polygraphical] Authors who have written on various branches."

In order to indicate clearly the nature, quality, range, and significance of the Virginiana items, it is necessary to depart somewhat from this awkward system of classification and group the material primarily according to format, allowing it to fall into natural subdivisions. Therefore printed books and pamphlets with either Virginia as subject, Virginians as authors, or Virginia imprints will be considered first. These will be followed by an account of Jefferson's Virginia newspapers. Then his remarkable collection of Virginia manuscripts will be surveyed, and their use and means of preservation discussed. Unless otherwise indicated, references will be to his 1815 library, his greatest collection, for in it were most of his

significant acquisitions. Within the format classifications suggested above, individual items will usually be discussed in the
order in which they appear in the 1815 and 1952 (Sowerby)
catalogues.[15]

I. *Printed Books and Pamphlets*

A. WITH VIRGINIA AS SUBJECT AND/OR VIRGINIANS AS AU-
THORS: In his *Notes on the State of Virginia* Jefferson emphasized the importance of the study of the past: "History,
by apprizing [young men] of the past, will enable them to
judge of the future; it will avail them of the experience of
other times and other nations; it will qualify them as judges
of the actions and designs of men; it will enable them to know
ambition under every guise it may assume, and knowing it,
to defeat its views" (*L&B*, II, 207). In many other places he
emphasized History's significance.[16] It was one of the major
classifications for his library, as noted above. Under it he included subdivisions of Civil and Natural; under Civil, Civil
Proper and Ecclesiastical; under Civil Proper, Ancient and
Modern; under Modern, Foreign, British, and American.
Under American History, Sowerby lists ninety-two items (not
counting newspapers, which have an informal subclass of
their own). Of these only fifteen, including a dozen books,
two pamphlets, and a manuscript volume, were strictly Virginiana; but that was far more than he had on any other
state. Among the books of Virginiana were John Smith's
Generall Historie (1632); Keith's *History of the British Plan-*

15. See outline of Jefferson's classification system as printed in Watterston's *Catalogue* of 1815 and in Sowerby, *Catalogue*, I; The outline is
reproduced on p. 203.
16. See, for example, Thomas Jefferson to J. D. Burk, February 21,
1803, in Sowerby, *Catalogue*, I, 212; Jefferson to John Carey, November 10, 1796, in Sowerby, *Catalogue*, I, 239; and Jefferson to S. H. Smith,
September 21, 1814, in Lipscomb and Bergh (eds.), *Writings of Jefferson*,
XIV, 191.

tations in America . . . *Part I Containing the History of Virginia* (1738); William Stith's *The History of the First Discovery and Settlement of Virginia* [1747]; John Daly Burk's *History of Virginia* (1804, 1805); William Robertson's *History of America, Books IX and X* (1799), and Robert Beverley's *Histoire de la Virginie* (1707, the French edition). With the exception of Robertson, all these works are today considered valuable. Several George Washington items were present, including the *Journal* (1754), *Official Letters to the American Congress* (1795), Marshall's *Life* (1804, 1805, 1807; Jefferson was an original subscriber), Weems' *Life* (1808), and *Ramsay's Life* (1807). In addition there were Henry Lee's *Memoirs of the War in the Southern Department* (1812) and several interesting pamphlets by Edmund Jenings and Lewis Littlepage.

Before he died in 1826, Jefferson was able to replace some of the items which had gone to Congress. Again he had Keith's *History* (the same 1738 edition), Marshall's *Washington*, and several other Washington items including the *Letters*. He added the new Girardin supplement to John Daly Burk's *History,* William Wirt's *Sketches of the Life and Character of Patrick Henry* (1817) and Lee's *Memoirs of R. H. Lee* (1825), along with a number of historical pamphlets incompletely identified in the 1829 sales list.

Under the second division of History, Natural, Jefferson included Physics, Natural History Proper, and Occupations of Men. Under Physics were Natural Philosophy, Agriculture, Chemistry, Surgery, and Medicine. Jefferson seems not to have done much deliberate collecting under the last five subheadings, although his letters show considerable interest in most of the topics discussed. Many of the items which might be designated as Virginiana are so because their authors were Virginians. Medical theses and essays from Edin-

OKS may be classed according to the faculties of the mind employed on them: these are—

I. MEMORY.   II. REASON.   III. IMAGINATION.

Which are applied respectively to—

I. HISTORY.   II. PHILOSOPHY.   III. FINE ARTS.

I. HISTORY

				Chapt.
il	Civil Proper	Antient	Antient History	1
		Modern	Foreign	2
			British	3
			American	4
	Ecclesiastical		Ecclesiastical	5
tural	Physics		Natural Philosophy	6
			Agriculture	7
			Chemistry	8
			Surgery	9
			Medicine	10
	Nat. Hist. Proper	Animals	Anatomy	11
			Zoology	12
		Vegetables	Botany	13
		Minerals	Mineralogy	14
	Occupations of Man		Technical Arts	15

II. PHILOSOPHY

					Chapt.
ral	Ethics			Moral Philosophy / L. of Nature & Nations	16
	Jurisprudence	Religious		Religion	17
		Municipal	Domestic	Equity	18
				Common Law	19
				Law Merchant	20
				Law Maritime	21
				Law Ecclesiastical	22
			Foreign	Foreign Law	23
		Œconomical		Politics / Commerce	24
thematical	Pure			Arithmetic	25
				Geometry	26
	Physico-Mathematical			Mechanics / Statics / Dynamics / Pneumatics / Phonics / Optics	27
				Astronomy	28
				Geography	29

III. FINE ARTS

		Chapt.
Architecture	Architecture	30
Gardening	Gardening	
Painting	Painting	31
Sculpture	Sculpture	
Music	Music	32
Poetry	Epic	33
	Romance	34
	Pastorals / Odes / Elegies	35
	Didactic	36
	Tragedy	37
	Comedy	38
	Dialogue / Epistles	39
Oratory	Logic / Rhetoric / Orations	40
Criticism	Theory	41
	Bibliography	42
	Languages	43
thors who have written on various branches	Polygraphical	44

burgh to Philadelphia, by James McClurg, Theodorick Bland, William Tazewell, William Stokes, and Thomas and James Ewell discuss a variety of topics from yellow fever to the human bile to "asphyxia." Then there is John Rouelle's *Complete Treatise on the Mineral Waters of Virginia* (1792). Other books and pamphlets on agriculture (in this case both subject and author were frequently Virginian) were probably closer to Jefferson's personal interests. Here one finds John A. Binns' *Treatise on Practical Farming* (1803), Jacquelin Ambler's *Treatise on the Culture of Lucerne* (1800?), G. W. P. Custis' *Address . . . on the Importance of Encouraging Agriculture and Domestic Manufactures* (1808), John Randolph's *Treatise on Gardening* (1793), and John Taylor's famous *Arator* (1813).

Under Natural History Proper appear other Virginians' books or pamphlets on surgery, the laws and property of matter, and *The Noble and Useful Animal the Horse* (Petersburg, 1811). Quite valuable among the botanical books is the Gronovius-Clayton *Flora Virginica* (1762), though it is not a first edition. And under the Technical Arts (*i.e.,* "The Occupations of Men") there is Quesnay de Beaurepaire's interesting *Memoire* (1788) concerning the proposed Academy of the Sciences and Fine Arts for Richmond. James Rumsey's *Explanation of the Steam Engine* (1788) and William Tatham's prospectus for a Dismal Swamp Canal (1808) indicate that all of Jefferson's contemporary fellow citizens were not farmers, politicians, lawyers, or physicians.

In the years after 1814 Jefferson continued to receive medical treatises from the Ewells and replaced his editions of Binns, Randolph, Taylor, and Gronovius-Clayton. James Madison sent his own *Address* on agriculture (probably the one he delivered before the Agricultural Society of Albemarle). His letters show that in these last years Jefferson was more than ever the farmer.

Under his second major division of Philosophy Jefferson had the headings Moral and Mathematical. Under Moral were Ethics and Jurisprudence; under Jurisprudence, Religious, Municipal, and Œconomical. Under Municipal were Domestic and Foreign; under Domestic were Equity, Common Law, Law Merchant, and Law Ecclesiastical. Under Œconomical were Politics and Commerce. Virginians contributed something in each of these classes. Joshua Peel, from Bedford County, dedicated to Jefferson his *Truth and Reason: or, A Fair Investigation of many of those things which keep them in the shade delivered in a course of Theological Lectures* (1805). Virginia-born Quaker Warner Mifflin contributed to the Ethics of Nature and Nations *A Serious Expostulation with Members of the House of Representatives of the United States* [1793]. Mason Locke Weems, David Rice, Barnaby Nixon, Richard Watson, and an anonymous Anglican clergyman sent him sermons, letters, and addresses dated from 1797 through 1806, all placed in the Religious classification.

Under the various Law classifications Jefferson listed a large number of Virginia items. Perhaps the most valuable of the items, the manuscript volumes, will be discussed later. But Jefferson was equally proud of his printed laws. In 1803 he wrote John Daly Burk: "I possess a tolerably compleat set of the printed laws of Virginia. this being the only set in existence, (for they are lost from the offices) and being now resorted to from all parts of the state as the only resource for laws not to be found in the late publications, I have been obliged to decline letting the volumes go out of my possession further than Milton or Charlottesville, because the loss of a volume would be irreparable. . . ." (February 21, Sowerby, I, 212).

Jefferson owned John Purvis' *A Complete Collection of all the Laws of Virginia now in Force* (ca. 1684); *A Collection of the Acts of Assembly* (1733); the *Revisal* of 1661/2–1748; the *Acts of Assembly* (1661/2–1678); the Chancellor's *Collection of Acts and Ordinances* (1783); an eight-volume "collection of all the printed laws of Virginia" which included Purvis; the *Revisals* of 1733, 1748, and 1768; the "Fugitive Sheets of printed laws" of 1734–1772, and 1775–1783; and the *Revisals* of 1783 and 1794. He also possessed William Waller Hening's *Statutes at Large* (1809, 1810, 1812). Among other items are his copy as committeeman of the *Report of the Committee of Revisors appointed by the General Assembly of Virginia . . . in* [1776] (1784); *Draughts of Such Bills, as Have Been Prepared by the Committee Appointed under the Act, Intituled. . . .* (1792); Edmund Randolph's *Abridgement of the Public Permanent Laws of Virginia* (1796); *A Collection of all Such Acts of the General Assembly of Virginia, of a Public and Permanent Nature, as are now in force* (1803); William Beverley's *Abridgement* (1728); John Mercer's *Exact Abridgement* (1737) and another edition of the same (1759); two accounts of the Burr trial (1807, 1808); George Webb's *The Office and Authority of a Justice of the Peace* (1736); Hening's *The New Virginia Justice* (1795); George Hay's *Essay on the Liberty of the Press* (1803), Bushrod Washington's *Reports* (1798–1799); Daniel Call's *Reports* (1801); William Tatham's *Report of a Case* (1794); and Hening and Munford's *Reports* (1808, 1809). The Common Law section of Virginiana is rounded off with a copy of *The Charter, Transfer, and Statutes, of the College of William and Mary* (1758). And the whole Law section concludes with a James Madison pamphlet on neutral trade (1805); Jefferson's own *Report of the Secretary of State, on the Privileges and Restrictions on the Commerce of the United States in Foreign Countries* . . . 1793 (1806); and *An Abridgement of the Laws in Force and Use in His Majesty's Plantations; (viz.) of Virginia.* . . . (1704). To these may be added some of the books received from George Wythe, including Wythe's *Decisions of Cases in Virginia, by the High Court of Chancery* . . . (1795) and a set of six pamphlet *Reports* (*ca.* 1796?) of cases with annotations in Wythe's hand.

After 1814, Jefferson managed to duplicate a number of these works, notably: Wythe's *Chancery Decisions,* Hening's *New Virginia Justice,* Washington's *Reports,* Mercer's *Abridgement* of 1759, and a number of *Acts of Assembly.* And according to the 1829 catalogue (see items 562–583) he added *Revised Codes* and *Reports* of the *Session Acts* of the 1814–1825 period, as well as Munford's *General Index to the Virginia Law Authorities* (1819).

Under the subdivision of Politics, Jefferson sent to Congress his largest number of printed items pertaining to Virginia. Of a little over thirteen hundred items from all nations, about one hundred are by Virginians, frequently on Virginia topics. In these books and pamphlets one may trace among other things the history of Democratic-Republican and Jeffersonian politics over a quarter of a century, from Jefferson's years in Paris to those of his retirement from public life. In this group are his own *Act for Establishing Religious Freedom* (an English-French edition of about 1786); *A Summary View of the Rights of British America* (a unique copy with manuscript notes by the author, *ca.* 1774); *An Appendix to the Notes of Virginia Relative to the Murder of Logan's Family* [1800]; the *Speech of* . . . *delivered at his Instalment, March 4, 1801* [*First Inaugural Address*] (1801); *A*

Test of the Religious Principles of Mr. Jefferson; Extracted (Verbatim) from His Writings (1800); *Discorsi del Signore Tommaso Jefferson delli Stati Uniti di America fatti tradurre e pubblicare dall' Illustrissimo Signore Leandro Cathcart* (Livorno, 1804); *The Proceedings of the Government of the United States, in maintaining the Public Right to the Beach of the Missisipi, and adjacent to New-Orleans* . . . (1812, two copies); and *Message from the President of the United States, Communicating Discoveries Made in Exploring the Missouri . . . by Captains Lewis and Clark* . . . (1806). And there is an interesting edition of Destutt de Tracy's *Commentary and Review of Montesquieu's Spirit of Laws* (Philadelphia, 1811), for which Jefferson wrote the preface.

The first president is also well represented in *George Washington to the People of the United States, Announcing his Retirement from Public Life* (1800); *A Message of the President of the United States to Congress relative to France and Great-Britain* [1793]; and *Letters from George Washington to Several of His Friends* . . . 1776 (ca. 1795; Washington declared the 1778 edition of this spurious). And it is not remarkable that Jefferson's close friend James Madison is even better represented by *The Federalist* (1788; on the flyleaf Jefferson has identified the numbers by Madison); *Letters of Helvidius: Written in Reply to Pacificus, on the President's Proclamation of Neutrality* [1796]; *Political Observations* (1795; Jefferson identifies this as Madison's); *A Memoir, Containing an Examination of the British Doctrine, Which Subjects to Capture a Neutral Trade, Not Open in Time of Peace* (1806); *All Impressments Unlawful and Inadmissible* (1806); *Letters from the Secretary of State to Messrs. Monroe and Pinkney* (1808); and *Extract from a Letter from the Secretary of State to Mr. Monroe, Relative to the Impress-*

ments (1806). James Monroe, naturally, is also represented: *Some Observations on the Constitution &c.* (1788; Jefferson attributed this to Monroe); *The Governor's Letter, of the 6th of December, 1802, to the Speaker of the House of Delegates of Virginia* (1802); *A View of the Conduct of the Executive in the Foreign Affairs of the United States, as Connected with the Mission to the French Republic during the Years 1794, 5, and 6* (1798); and *Correspondence in Relation to the British Treaty of Peace* (1808).

Many Virginia followers of Jefferson's party from its beginnings to the War of 1812, as well as a few anti-Jeffersonians, are represented among the political books and pamphlets. St. George Tucker's *Dissertation on Slavery: with a Proposal for the Gradual Abolition of It, in the State of Virginia* (1796) and his *Reflections on the Policy and Necessity of Encouraging the Commerce of the Citizens of the United States of America* (1785) are significant essays by the William and Mary professor. Jefferson's Albemarle neighbor, the Italian Philip Mazzei, is represented by two essays, one in French and one in Italian (1788 and 1803); English physician James Currie, and Scottish economist Patrick Colquhoun, both of whom lived in Virginia for some years, are represented by one treatise each (1793 and 1788 respectively). Included here are essays by prominent citizens such as Fulwar Skipwith (1806), Richard Henry Lee (1787), Arthur Lee (1774), Robert Carter Nicholas (1774), Carter Braxton (1776), William Tatham (1791), John Taylor (1794), Edmund Randolph (1795, 1796), John Page (1796), W. C. Nicholas (1799?), Benjamin Watkins Leigh (two in 1811), Richard Evers Lee (1800), John Daly Burk (1803), Philip Grymes (1803), William Branch Giles (1808), and John Thomson (1804). Other native Virginians whose reputations were acquired outside the state, men such as William Henry Harrison (1807) and Henry Clay (1813), are also represented.

There are two essays by Jefferson's eccentric neighbor, the orator and schoolmaster James Ogilvie (1798, 1802); several pseudonymous pieces published under names like Virginius and Oliver Fairplay, biased either for or against Jefferson; and several contributions to the Logan controversy. There are Virginia essays on systems of banking (1811), militia (1813), the Navy (1808), and the Burr Trial (1807). Here may be found the notorious James Thomson Callender's *The Prospect before Us* (1800).[17] Here is the only known copy of a 1769 edition of John Dickinson and Arthur Lee's *The Farmer's and Monitor's Letters, to the Inhabitants of the British Colonies*. Altogether these items form an amusing and entertaining as well as significant representation of early American politics.

Naturally, it was difficult if not usually impossible, to replace these frequently topical books and pamphlets after 1814. But Jefferson did manage to secure a new copy of Hay's essay on the liberty of the press, and a new 1818 edition of *The Federalist* as well as an additional older one. Old friends sent him their current political writings, and this section of the 1829 catalogue lists a now valuable collection of essays and books by people such as John Taylor of Caroline, who sent *Construction Construed, and Constitutions Vindicated* (1820) and *New Views of the Constitution of the United States* (1823); Francis Gilmer, who contributed his *Vindication of the Laws . . . against Usury from the Objections of*

17. This is one of the two books in Jefferson's library called objectionable in the debate in Congress as to whether to buy his collection. The book has a Richmond imprint and may be called Virginiana whether Callender's brief "residence" within the state entitles him to be called a Virginian or not.

Jeremy Bentham and the Edinburgh Reviewers (1820); and David B. Warden, whose book *On the Origin, Nature, Progress and Influence of Consular Establishments* (1813) must have interested the old statesman at Monticello a great deal. Jefferson also received in this period printed copies of a series of State Papers covering the 1793–1820 period. Almost all these seem to have been gifts. There is little or no evidence of conscious collecting of this kind of Virginiana during these last dozen years.

The second principal subdivision of the classification Philosophy was Mathematical, and under Mathematical were included the various types of Mathematics, Physico-Mathematics, Astronomy, and Geography. Under Pure-Mathematics and Astronomy one finds no Virginiana in the collection completed in 1814, and under Physico-Mathematics only Jefferson's own *Notes on the Establishment of a Money Unit, and of Coinage for the United States* [ca. 1785] and *Report of the Secretary of State, on the Subject of Establishing a Uniformity in the Weights, Measures and Coins of the United States* (1790). It is not until we come to Geography that there is Virginiana again. Here are a group of sixteenth- and seventeenth-century books that might perhaps have been included with History earlier. A magnificent set of DeBry's *The Great or American Voyages*, Parts I to XI, in Latin (1590–1619); Richard Hakluyt's *Principal Navigations* (1589, the Richard Bland library copy); Edward Williams' *Virginia: More especially the South part thereof, Richly and truly valued* (1650); Robert Johnson's *Nova Britannia* (1609); and William Bullock's *Virginia Impartially Examined* (1649) are in themselves realizations of a book collector's dream. Here under Geography he also includes a rare tract by his friend William Tatham, *Address to the Shareholders and Others Interested in the Canals of Virginia*

(1794); and the two-volume 1814 edition of Lewis and Clark's *History of the Expedition under the Command of Captains Lewis and Clark*. Also he lists here a first edition of his *Notes on the State of Virginia* (Paris, 1785); *Appendix to the Notes on Virginia* (1800; there was another copy earlier in the *Catalogue*); and *Message from the President of the United States, Transmitting a Roll of the Persons Having Office or Employment under the United States* (1802).

Jefferson had a good collection under the third and final major classification, Fine Arts, but it is hardly surprising that very little of it is Virginian in subject or author. What little there is is hardly indicative of his aesthetic tastes, for most of the items were presentation copies from authors, such as Thomas Northmore's *Washington, or Liberty Restored: a Poem in Ten Books* (1809). Judith Lomax's *The Notes of an American Lyre* (1813) was dedicated to Jefferson, who subscribed for twelve copies, presumably out of friendship for the author's father Thomas Lomax. A more interesting volume of verse is St. George Tucker's (identified as the author by Jefferson himself) *The Probationary Odes of Jonathan Pindar, Esq.* (1796). After 1814, Jefferson received one more volume of native poetry, Mrs. Alfred W. Elwes'[?] *Potomac Muse* (1825).

Under Logic in the Fine Arts division were Rhetoric and Oratory. Here one finds Jean François Coste's oration given at Williamsburg in 1782 in Latin (1783), and James Lyons' medical dissertation, in Latin, on the cholera (1785). Here also are a volume of eulogiums on Washington (probably 1802); an oration (1808) by Ferdinando Fairfax; Thomas E. Birch's anthology (containing an ode to Jefferson); *The Virginian Orator: being a Variety of Original and Selected Poems, Orations and Dramatic Scenes; to improve the American Youth in the Ornamental and Useful Art of Eloquence and Gesture* (1808); a copy of William Wirt's volume of essays, *The Rainbow, First Series* (1804); and (all that was ever published of) James Lyon's *National Magazine: or, A Political, Historical, Biographical, and Literary Repository, for June 1, 1799* (1799). Only one such item of Fine Arts-Virginiana does the 1814–1826 library contain, a copy of George Tucker's *Essays on Various Subjects of Taste, Morals, and National Policy* (1822), probably presented by the author in 1825 when he came to Charlottesville as first chairman of the faculty of the University of Virginia.

B. VIRGINIA IMPRINTS. The bibliographer may be even more interested in Jefferson's Virginia imprints than in his Virginia subjects and authors. These imprints can be determined accurately only for his greatest library, that already catalogued by Miss Sowerby. But even these few reveal a great deal about printers and publishers in early Virginia. The many Richmond, Williamsburg, and Petersburg impressions indicate more or less sustained publishing activity in those places, and the smaller numbers for Abingdon, Alexandria, Charlottesville, Fincastle, Fredericksburg, Martinsburg (now West Virginia), Norfolk, Shepherd's-Town (now West Virginia), and Staunton are significant in various ways.[18]

Joshua Peel's *Truth and Reason* [1805], though written by a resident of Bedford County, was taken to a printer named David Amen, of Fincastle in neighboring Botetourt, for publication. It might not be too hard to guess why Richard Watson, bishop of Landaff's *Christian Panoply*, a series of letters addressed to Thomas Paine, was published by P. Rootes & C.

18. One should keep in mind that all the books once in Jefferson's library do not survive today, though many of them do. In the instances when Miss Sowerby had only the title as printed in the *Catalogue*, she exercised considerable effort and ingenuity in determining other bibliographical data.

Blagrove of Shepherd's-Town for the Presbyterian Synod of
Virginia in 1797. William Thomson, an Abingdon lawyer,
got the *Holston Intelligencer* in his place of residence to print
his *Compendious View of the Trial of Aaron Burr . . .
Together with Biographical Sketches of Several Eminent
Characters* (1807), a volume Jefferson professed to have read
with great satisfaction. Martinsburg is represented by a Protestant Episcopal sermon, published by John Alberts. James
Lyon, and later John McArthur, published the *Political Mirror*
under a Staunton imprint. John Dunlap and James Hayes in
Charlottesville published two official volumes of state *Acts*
and *Journals* for 1781. Fredericksburg appears on the dateline
of two newspapers, *The Genius of Liberty*, G. Carter and
others 1798–1800, and *The Virginia Herald and Fredericksburg & Falmouth Advertiser*, Timothy Green 1795–1796. In
Norfolk, besides newspapers like the *American Gazette*, William Davis 1795–1796, there had been printed William
Tatham's *View of the Proposed Grand Junction Canal*
(1808), presumably by the author; Daniel Bedinger's *Letter
. . . to Robert Smith* (1808), A. C. Gordon & Co.; and
Arrowsmith and Lewis' *New and Elegant Atlas* (1804),
Bonsal, Conrad, and Co. (this last also published at a number
of other places). Sir Robert Wilson's *History of the British
Expedition to Egypt* (1803) and Benjamin Rush's *An Inquiry into the various Sources of the usual Forms of Summer
& Autumnal Fever in the United States . . .* (1805) likewise have Norfolk imprints along with those of other cities.
Alexandria, though a part of the District of Columbia rather
than of Virginia during much of this period, may also be considered. This city's printing activity is evident in a number
of pamphlets such as James Ogilvie's *Cursory Reflections on
Government, Philosophy and Education* (1802), J. & J. De
Westcott; James Workman's *Political Essays, Relative to the*

War of the French Revolution (1801), Cottom and Stewart; Richard Dinmore's *A Long Talk, Delivered before the Tammany Society of Alexandria* (1804), the Expositor Office; August B. Woodward's *Consideration on the Government of the Territory of Columbia* (1802), S. Snowden & Co., and G. W. P. Custis' *Address to the People of the United States* (1808), also Snowden.

Jefferson's thirty-five Williamsburg imprints, in several instances multivolumed with different printers within the series, range in time from 1733 to 1781 and include a number of the official records of the colony and state. The first printer, William Parks, is represented in eleven items such as *Journals of the House of Burgesses* (1740–1748); *A Collection of All the Acts of Assembly, Now in Force* (1733, the first collection of Virginia laws published in Virginia); Biscoe's *The Merchant's Magazine* (1743); Stith's *History* (1747); *Treaty Held with the Indians of the Six Nations at Lancaster* (1744); Mercer's *Abridgement* (1737); Webb's *Justice of the Peace* (1736); the *Virginia Gazette* (1741–1750); interesting English books on fencing and the smallsword (1734); a sermon on death (1744); and a treatise on the Lord's Supper (1740). William Hunter's press is represented in four imprints, including some of the official papers and the *Virginia Gazette*, 1751–1778. John Dixon and Alexander Purdie appear in combination twice, Dixon and Thomas Nicolson together four times, Purdie alone about ten times. William Rind's name on his *Virginia Gazette* and official papers appears alone at least three times, with Purdie and Dixon once. Rind also printed the rare edition of *The Farmer's and Monitor's Letters* (1769, referred to above). His widow, Clementina Rind, published Jefferson's *Summary View* in 1774; and John Pinkney printed Francis Hopkinson's *A Pretty Story* "for Clementina Rind's Children" the same year.

Petersburg is represented by eight imprints, three of which are also Norfolk imprints: the Sir Thomas Wilson, Benjamin Rush, and Arrowsmith and Lewis (map) items referred to above. But John Daly Burk, a resident of the little city, published there in 1804 and 1805 the three volumes of his *History of Virginia,* printed for the author by Dickson & Pescud, and in 1803 *An Oration,* T. Field. Here appeared Richard Mason's *The Gentleman's Pocket Companion* (1811), John Jackson; [James Monroe's] *Some Observations on the Constitution* (1788), Hunter and Prentis; and *Debates and Other Proceedings of the Convention of Virginia* [1788, 1789], Hunter and Prentis, and Prentis.

Richmond is represented in more than sixty items, ranging in time from 1780/1, when the official printers Dixon and Nicolson moved to the new capital from Williamsburg, to items published in 1813. Again the largest single group is the official state publications, more than two dozen, works such as *Acts Passed . . . A Collection of Such Acts . . . ,* *Debates* and *Journals* of the Senate and House of Delegates, and *Reports* of the Supreme Court of Appeals. The official printers include Nicolson alone, Dixon and Nicolson, Dixon and Holt, Nicolson and Prentis, J. Dunlap and James Hayes, Augustine Davis, Pleasants and Pace, Pleasants alone, Meriwether Jones, and various combinations of these men. The same firms also printed semiofficial and private books and newspapers. Pleasants published several newspapers, including the *Virginia Gazette* (1795); the *Virginia Argus* (1797) and its successors (Jefferson's copies 1797–1803, 1804–1808, 1809–1813, etc.); and the *Richmond and Manchester Advertiser* (1795–1796). He also printed the volumes of Hening's *Statutes at Large* (1809, 1810, 1812) and belletristic items such as Birch's *The Virginia Orator* (1808) and Lomax's *The Notes of an American Lyre* (1813). Thomas Ritchie printed the famous Richmond *Enquirer* and items like

Sidney Smith's *Letters on the Subject of the Catholics* (1809), "from the Office of the Enquirer;" and his firm of Ritchie and Worsley published Wirt's *Rainbow* essays (1804). Thomas Nicolson printed a number of things other than the official records: agricultural pamphlets such as Ambler's *Treatise on the Culture of Lucerne* (1800?) and John Randolph's *Treatise on Gardening* (1793), and semiofficial books like Hening's *The New Virginia Justice* (1795). Seaton Grantland's imprint appears on *Sketches of the History of France . . . By an American* (1806) and Barnaby Nixon's *A Serious Address to the Rulers of America in General, and the State of Virginia in Particular . . .* (1806). John Dixon supplemented his official printing with two newspapers, the *Virginia Gazette and Richmond Chronicle* (1795) and *Richmond Chronicle* (1795–1796), neither apparently very successful. Jones and Dixon as a firm published another James Ogilvie essay, *A Speech . . . in Essex County* (1798), and Jones alone printed Richard Evers Lee's *Letters* (1800) and James Monroe's *Governor's Letter* (1802, perhaps semiofficial). Dixon and Holt printed St. George Tucker's *Reflections* on commerce (1795). Augustine Davis supplemented his official publishing with such works as *Decius' Letters on the Opposition to the New Constitution in Virginia* (1789). *The National Magazine* (1799–1800) was printed "by and for the Editor," James Lyon, who also lived and worked elsewhere. Other Richmond imprints bear the names of printer-publishers Manson and John O'Lynch. Jefferson's library alone would indicate that for the quarter of a century between the Revolution and the War of 1812 the new little village-town-capital of Richmond was a fairly busy publishing center.

C. RARE BOOKS AND PAMPHLETS. The fact that only a fraction of the library which went to Congress in 1814 survives makes it impossible to assess at all precisely the rare-book value of Jefferson's greatest library. But the items which do remain, added to others which may be identified, indicate that the Americana or Virginiana collector today would place a high valuation upon it. First perhaps one should take a glance at the association and dedication copies.

There were hundreds of presentation copies in the library without Virginia or even American relationship. Sowerby's index lists all of the presentation copies together (V, 385–391). Among those of Virginia origin in some sense are Mason L. Weems' *Washington* (1808) and *The True Patriot* (1802); medical essays by Edmund Jennings, William Stokes, William Tazewell, and the two Ewells (see below); Thomas Northmore's *Washington* (1809); Colvin's *Historical Letters* (1812) and his *Letter to the Honorable John Randolph* (n.d.); and Birch's *The Virginian Orator*. Sowerby also lists all the dedication copies (V, 329). Dedicated to Jefferson, though of course his copy does not always survive, are, among others, Burk's *History of Virginia,* James Ewell's *Medical Companion* (1807), Thomas Ewell's *Plain Discourses* (1806), Lomax's *Notes of an American Lyre,* Joshua Peel's *Truth and Reason,* and Stokes' *De Asphyxia* (1793). The list of books in which Jefferson is mentioned (Sowerby, V, 329–331) runs into the hundreds.

Already pointed out in connection with their listing under author, subject, or imprint above were a number of interesting association copies. Other association copies, with manuscript additions of value, are Sir John Randolph's commonplace book bound with *A Brief Method of Law* (1680); Jefferson's own *Summary View* (1774) with several notes by the author; and the two volumes of the 1788 *Federalist* with Madison's contributions noted in Jefferson's handwriting. This last book is of interest also as the copy once belonging to

Mrs. Alexander Hamilton, received by Jefferson through his good friend her sister Mrs. Angelica Church.

Other items now or once present are scarce editions or apparently unique copies (as far as present location is concerned). No copy is known to exist of the 1793 edition of John Randolph's *Treatise on Gardening* which Jefferson once owned, and the only copy Miss Sowerby was able to locate of the Dickinson-Lee *Farmer's and Monitor's Letters* is Jefferson's. Rare Virginia pamphlets, many of them not included in most Virginia bibliographies, are Peel's *Truth and Reason* (1805) and Sherlock's *A Practical Discourse Concerning Death* (1744). *Hakluyt's Principall Navigations* (1589), Johnson's *Nova Britannia* (1609), and Bullock's *Virginia Impartially Examined* are first editions of considerable value. Williams' *Virginia* (1650) and DeBry's *Voyages* (1590–1619), the latter not quite complete, are also rare. The first editions Jefferson owned of the histories of Virginia by Smith (1632, first issue), Keith (1738), Stith (1747), and Burk (1804, 1805) bring high prices today. And the first editions of Marshall's *Washington* (1804, 1805, 1807), Jefferson's own *Notes on the State of Virginia* (Paris, 1785), and Lewis and Clark's *History of the Expedition. . . .* (1814) are prized items. There are scores of others.

As noted above, Jefferson was well aware that his most valuable printed items were his copies of the Virginia laws and legislative journals. He knew that he had the most nearly complete collection of them in existence. They were equally useful to lawyer, historian, and statesman.

II. Newspapers

Though the irresponsible attacks made on him, especially during the election campaigns of 1800 and 1804, soured Jefferson as to the usefulness or veracity of newspapers, he did preserve a considerable number of them in bound files. They are included in the 1815 *Catalogue* under American History (items 535–602), each item representing one or more volumes. Among them were journals published in fifteen American cities outside Virginia and in one foreign capital. But by far the largest number, consisting of approximately eighteen items,[19] are from Virginia.

Originally he owned many more. In a letter to John D. Burk of June 1, 1803, he mentions his collection of newspapers which Burk had asked to borrow. They dated "from 1741. downwards. the vols. preceding 1752. shall be sent with the other [sic] to Richmond to be used by you either there or at Petersburg according to your convenience. these also [as well as printed laws] being the only collection probably in existence, I purchased & cherish it with a view to public utility. it is answering one of it's principal objects when I put it into your hands . . ." (Sowerby, I, 213).

It is well that Burk used them profitably, for Jefferson never recovered his newspapers, and they have disappeared from view. A later letter (October 29, 1810) from Thomas to his kinsman George Jefferson mentions that the collection included "3 volumes of Virginia Gazette from 1741 to 1760." The writer adds the interesting information that he purchased these volumes from "Parson Wiley's executors before the revolution, and paid their original cost for them which I think was £30. for the whole collection down to his death" (Sowerby, I, 213).

19. This is following Miss Sowerby's listing, which is necessarily inconclusive, since no known volume of Jefferson's newspapers survives and the detailed listing, as pointed out below, has to be guessed at from a later Library of Congress listing. One may add that the designation of eighteen out of sixty-eight items as Virginiana seems reasonably accurate by this later (1831) catalogue.

The Library of Congress does not possess a single bound volume of newspapers from the 1815 library, at least not in recognizable form. But the manuscript and printed catalogues indicate that he had twelve volumes folio and one volume quarto of "Virginia gazettes." These included in whole or in part Parks's *Virginia Gazette*, 1741–1750; Hunter *et al*, *Virginia Gazette*, 1751–1778; Rind's *Virginia Gazette*, 1766–1776; Purdie *et al*, *Virginia Gazette*, 1775–1780; all Williamsburg; and Dixon and Nicolson's *Virginia Gazette*, 1779–1781, Williamsburg and Richmond. Another manuscript catalogue entry, "Gazettes. 1795–7, d° 1797" [or in the 1815 printed *Catalogue*: "Miscellaneous Gazettes, 1795–1800, 4 vols."] seems hopelessly obscure until one looks with Sowerby at the 1831 Library of Congress catalogue, which breaks this down and lists in two places a number of out-of-state items as well as the *Political Mirror*, 1800–1802, Staunton; the *Genius of Liberty*, 1798–1800, Fredericksburg; the *Enquirer*, 1809–1814, the *Virginia Argus*, 1797, the *Virginia Argus and Virginia Enquirer*, 1804–1808, 5 vols., the *Virginia Argus and Virginia Examiner*, 1797–1803, 1809–1813, 7 vols., the *Virginia Gazette*, June, 1795, the *Virginia Gazette and Richmond Chronicle*, 1795, the *Richmond Chronicle*, 1795–1796, the *Richmond and Manchester Advertiser*, 1795–1796, all Richmond; the *American Gazette*, 1795–1796, Norfolk; and the *Virginia Herald and Fredericksburg and Falmouth Advertiser*, 1795–1796, Fredericksburg.[20] Not long before he died, Jefferson named one of these Virginia journals as his favorite in a letter to his old friend William Short: "but at the age of 80. I seek quiet and abjure contention. I read but a single newspaper, Ritchie's Enquirer, the best that is published or

20. Publishers of most of these papers are named in the discussion of imprints just above. For others, see Sowerby, *Catalogue*, I, 267–85.

ever has been published in America. you should read it also to keep yourself au fait of your own state; for we still claim you as belonging to us" (September 8, 1823, Sowerby, I, 279).

Although Jefferson may have overestimated the uniqueness of his collection of Virginia newspapers, much would be given today for his eighteenth- and early nineteenth-century files. The Cappon and Duff microfilmed edition of the *Virginia Gazette* of Williamsburg, for example, might be far more complete than it is. In most cases today files of the other newspapers are incomplete or fragmentary.[21] Jefferson never made any claim for inclusiveness or completeness for his own collection, but quite obviously it was at least on a par with his printed laws in terms of historical value.

III. Manuscripts

Jefferson's collection of manuscript materials relating to the history of the colony and state grew as steadily and intelligently as his printed collections. From young manhood he was on the alert for unpublished materials. He was so well-known by 1816 as an authority on Virginia manuscripts that the American Philosophical Society appealed to him for information when it wanted to identify the author of an unpublished "History of the Dividing Line between Virginia and North Carolina" which it had recently discovered among its papers. Jefferson did not fail the Society; he reported promptly that it was probably "Dr. Byrd's" and suggested that members of the Westover family be consulted. In doing so he

21. See C. S. Brigham, *Bibliography of American Newspapers, 1690–1820* (Worcester, Mass., 1947); William Clayton-Torrence, *Trial Bibliography of Colonial Virginia* (Richmond, 1908–1910); Henry S. Parsons, *Eighteenth Century Newspapers in the Library of Congress* (Washington, D.C., 1936).

gave evidence that he knew of a considerable number of Virginia private papers still at large.[22]

Jefferson's own Virginia manuscripts came to him in a variety of ways, all of them indicative of his awareness of the need to preserve records of the state's history. They consist of twenty-one items, some comprised of several bound volumes each; seventeen or eighteen of these items went to the Library of Congress in 1815 and the remainder in 1829. Of the total number, only three are not legal, legislative, judicial, or miscellaneous records of the colony. That he considered these official relics of time worth considerable care is indicated in a letter to his old law teacher, George Wythe, who wished to borrow the manuscript as well as the printed laws in Jefferson's library. Jefferson declined to send the manuscripts with the excuse that they were not pertinent to the study Wythe was making, and that they were too fragile anyway. Some, said Jefferson, would fall to powder at the touch:

These I preserve by wrapping and sewing them in oil cloth, so that neither air nor moisture can have access to them. Very early in my researches into the laws of Virginia, I observed that many of them were already lost, and many more at the point of being lost, as existing only in single copies in the hands of careful or curious individuals, on whose death they would probably be used for waste paper. I set myself therefore to work, to collect all which were then existing, in order that when the day should come when the public should advert to the magnitude of their loss in these precious monuments of their property, and our history, a part of their regret might be spared by information that a portion had been saved from the wreck, which is worthy of their

22. See Jefferson to P. S. Duponceau, January 22, 1816, in Lipscomb and Bergh (eds.), *Writings of Jefferson*, XIX, 232–33; and Maude H. Woodfin, "Thomas Jefferson and William Byrd's Manuscript Histories of the Dividing Line," *William and Mary Quarterly*, Ser. 3, I (1944), 363–73.

attention and preservation. In searching after these remains, I spared neither time, trouble, nor expense; and am of opinion that scarcely a law escaped me, which was in being as late as the year 1790 in the middle or southern parts of the State. In the northern parts, perhaps something might be found. . . . But recurring to what we actually possess, the question is, what means will be most effectual for preserving these remains from future loss? (January 16, 1796, *L&B*, IX, 319–320).

His answer is that everything should be printed and distributed "How many of the precious works of antiquity were lost while they were preserved only in manuscript!"

He demonstrated this belief in publication in his handling of the most valuable of the non-official manuscripts which came into his hands. In 1803 Rufus King sent for Jefferson's perusal an account of Bacon's Rebellion which he had picked up abroad, and which differed from the published accounts.[23] In 1804 Jefferson returned the manuscript to King with a letter saying he had taken the liberty of making a copy of it. The copy was being placed in the hands of a person who was writing a history of Virginia. He promised King that he would try to trace the author, who in 1705 had signed only the initials "T. M.", "among the antient MSS. I possess at Monticello." The copy seems to have gone to George Wythe, who turned it over to the editor of the Richmond *Enquirer* for publication. It was printed in that paper on September 1, 5, 8, 1804. The *Enquirer* states that the printed account is an exact copy of the original sent by the President of the United States for the express purpose of publication.

The copy now in the Jefferson papers in the Library of Congress seems to be that returned by Jefferson to King. It clearly dates from around 1705, but if it is the original it has

23. See Sowerby, *Catalogue*, I, 165, for an account of the King-Jefferson correspondence on the matter.

lost its covers and other marks of identification. It appears in the 1815 printed *Catalogue* but not in Jefferson's rough-copy manuscript catalogue. How and why it stayed in or came back to the Jefferson library is puzzling. This work, T[homas] M[athew]'s "The Beginning Progress and Conclusion of Bacon's Rebellion in Virginia in the years 1675 & 1676," is of course one of the major documents of this era in colonial history.

The other non-official papers are not nearly so valuable. One, Sir John Randolph's manuscript commonplace-[legal]-book bound with *A Brief Method of the Law* (1680) and written partly by Benjamin Harrison and partly by Randolph, has been noted. Another commonplace book of legal materials precedes it (Sowerby, II, 225). The other non-official manuscript is bound with the non-Virginia manuscript of Paul Alliot's *Reflections historiques et politiques sur la Louysiane* (*ca.* 1803), and is called "Extracts from a letter written by a Gentleman who had explored Kentucky to his Friend in the lower part of Virginia relative to that Country—Bedford in Virginia." Covering only two leaves, it was labeled laconically by Jefferson "Western country."

Of the official or semiofficial items, the six containing records from 1606 to the dissolution of the Virginia Company are described in detail in Susan Myra Kingsbury's *Records of the Virginia Company of London.* She points out that they came to the Library of Congress in two different groups, in 1815 (with the library) and in 1829 (when they were bought at the auction). Those which came in 1815 are themselves in four groups: (1) "Laws and Orders concluded on by the General Assembly March the 5th. 1623";[24] (2) "Jour-

---

24. Sowerby, *Catalogue,* II, 236. See also Susan Myra Kingsbury, *Records of the Virginia Company of London* (4 vols.; Washington, D.C., 1906, 1933, 1935), I, 41–52.

nal of the Council and Assembly 1616–1634";[25] (3) "Miscellaneous Records, 1606–1692"; (4) "Miscellaneous Papers, 1606–1683, Instructions. . . ."[26] The 1829 acquisitions were: (1) the "Records of the Virginia Company" in two volumes folio, and (2) the "Old Records of Virginia," in four volumes folio (1829 catalogue item 122).

All those acquired in 1829 are unique copies or contemporary transcripts of incalculable value. The "Miscellaneous Papers, 1606–1683" is a seventeenth-century transcript. The "Laws" of 1623 and the "Miscellaneous Records, 1606–1683" are transcripts of the earlier eighteenth-century attested by R. Hickman, clerk of the general court in 1722. Jefferson himself gives the best account of the provenance of the 1829 volumes in a letter to Hugh P. Taylor, October 4, 1823. The letter states that the first two volumes are accounted for in the preface to Stith's *History of Virginia;* that they are the records of the Company copied under the eye of the Earl of Southampton; and that they were bought at the sale of the Earl's library by William Byrd, who lent them to Richard Bland, in whose library they reposed when Jefferson bought it.[27] The other four volumes, Jefferson goes on to say, he supposes were original office records borrowed by Sir John Randolph for a projected history of Virginia and never returned. They remained in the library Jefferson bought from Peyton Randolph's executors. Though Kingsbury and Sow-

25. For an assemblage made by Mrs. Vincent Eaton from recently discovered manuscripts in the Library of Congress with the same dates, 1616–34, see Sowerby, *Catalogue,* II, 238–39. Miss Sowerby entitles these "Commissions and Proclamations." Unless the rediscovered Sowerby item and Miss Kingsbury's second item are the same, the two authorities' descriptions of the manuscripts do not agree.

26. Miss Sowerby gives 1606–1692 as the dates here.

27. Kingsbury (ed.), *Records,* I, 43, 44; and Lipscomb and Bergh (eds.), *Writings of Jefferson,* XV, 471–74 (the latter gives the year as 1823, the former as 1825).

erby do not agree with this information in certain details, they do, in general, support it.

Of the items from the 1815 *Catalogue* listed in Kingsbury, the three volumes containing transcripts of the Virginia records are unique. The "Laws and Orders" of 1623 bears an endorsement in Jefferson's hand to the effect that it was found among the manuscript papers of Sir John Randolph and given by his son Peyton to Jefferson. It is an early eighteenth-century transcript attested by Hickman. The "Miscellaneous Records, 1606–1692" is a seventeenth-century copy bought from the Bland library. The "Miscellaneous Papers" is another eighteenth-century copy attested by Hickman and once belonging to Bland (Sowerby, II, 244). As noted above, the "Journal of the Council and Assembly, 1616–1634" as listed by Kingsbury (I, 42n) is probably the rediscovered "Commissions and Proclamations, 1616–1634."[28] If so, it came from the library of Peyton Randolph.

Most of the other official manuscript gatherings, ignored by Kingsbury because they did not affect the story of the Virginia Company of London, came to Jefferson, as did those already discussed, from various other libraries. Manuscript copies of John Mercer's "Abridgement of the Public Acts" and "An Abridgement of the Common Law" have no known provenance beyond Jefferson's library. The first is an eighteenth-century, the second a seventeenth-century manuscript. Sir John Randoph's "Opinions of Learned Counsel" (the second half of his autograph) is in seventeenth- and eighteenth-century hands. It bears the names of Sir John and Peyton Randolph on the flyleaf, and certainly came from their library (Sowerby, II, 224). The "Journal of Council and Assembly, 1642–1662," the "Edmund Randolph copy," was on

28. See note 25 above, and Sowerby, *Catalogue,* II, 238.

loan from Jefferson to Edmund for many years, lost, recovered, and finally sent by Hening to the Library of Congress (Sowerby, II, 240). It also had once belonged to Sir John and Peyton Randolph. "Legislative Records, 1652–1660," in Jefferson's own autograph, was copied from the Mercer manuscript used by Hening (Sowerby, II, 242). Jefferson stated that he found the "Laws, 1662–1702" ready to be used for waste paper in Lorton's tavern in Charles City county. The Clerk of the Court, Debnam, gave it and "Laws. 1705" to Jefferson without hesitation (Sowerby, II, 242–243). "Laws. 1662–1697" came from the Randolphs' library (Sowerby, II, 242). The "Acts of Assembly. 1705–1711" was given to Jefferson by his old friend John Page. It had belonged to the latter's grandfather, Matthew Page, who had in 1705 been one of the commissioners for a revisal of the laws. An edition of Purvis' *A Complete Collection of All the Laws* (ca. 1684) contains a manuscript continuation of some interest. Jefferson says the volume was given to his father-in-law, Mr. Wayles, by the late Colonel William Byrd [III] (Sowerby, II, 245). "The Virginia Court Book, 1622–1629" has been taken apart and rebound so that its provenance is difficult to determine (Sowerby, II, 352). In the 1828 sales list (no. 565) appears one more manuscript, a copy of the "Revised Code, 1779."

That Jefferson acquired any of the manuscripts listed in 1829 after 1814 is improbable. Though it seems unlikely that he consciously held back anything when he sent his library to Washington (he complained in 1815 to Hening that he had never intended selling his Virginia law items to Congress but had been obliged under the terms to do so), we do know that he did not include a very few things and that some things "missing" or on loan but represented in the *Catalogue* never got to Washington. Whatever the cause, the Library of Congress did in 1829 add these companion volumes to its collection.

IV. The "Usefulness" of Jefferson's Collection

From the quotations given above it is clear that Jefferson had posterity more in mind when he acquired Virginiana than he did when gathering more general materials. These manuscripts, newspapers, pamphlets, and books would probably not, he felt, be preserved at all, and certainly not together so that they might be used, unless he undertook the task. He was almost surely right. There had been in past generations men like William Byrd II and Sir John Randolph who might be numbered among the careful or the curious, but even they seem to have been haphazard collectors as far as matters pertaining to the Old Dominion were concerned.

Jefferson had no illusions about the immortality of libraries in private hands. He was too well-acquainted with the fine old collections of his Virginia predecessors for that. And he sent documents of *national* significance, when they came to him, (such as certain Lewis and Clark materials), to the American Philosophical Society library as a way of ensuring their survival. Perhaps he took some satisfaction in the anticipation that the things he sent to the Library of Congress would be carefully preserved.

But, as he says in his correspondence several times, he never intended for the Virginia manuscript and printed laws and other records to go to Washington. Though in 1814 the University of Virginia was not so near physical realization as in 1823–1824, it is probable that even in 1814 Jefferson had it in mind as a repository for his Virginia materials. Certainly it was the destination he planned for the volumes of the proceedings of the Virginia Company of London and the other miscellaneous early records, for he informed Hugh Taylor in 1823 that he "would deposit them in the library of the University" (October 4, *L&B*, XV, 472). His testamentary gift of the whole of his last library to the University was never realized because of the financial conditions of his estate when he died. It had to be sold at auction.

Even during his lifetime, Jefferson put his Virginiana to good use. Young neighbors or relatives like Francis Gilmer and Peter and Dabney Carr came to browse or study in his library. One of the tasks he urged upon them was the acquisition of an extensive knowledge of their own "country." Their letters give evidence that they acquired something. Dabney Carr became a judge and an authority on Virginia law. Gilmer not only was elected first professor of law in the infant University of Virginia but instigated the first American printing of one of the books he probably first saw in Jefferson's library, Captain John Smith's *Historie*.[29] Gilmer's letters harp on the theme that Virginia must fulfill the promise of her past. A book which remains one of the most significant items of pure Virginiana, Jefferson's own *Notes on the State of Virginia*, was composed in part while he was surrounded by his beloved books at Monticello.[30] The famous bibliography of Virginia history at the end of Query XXIII could hardly have been compiled without his own volumes.

Still essential for any student of Virginia is John Daly Burk's three-volume *History of Virginia* (1804, 1805). As already noted, Jefferson lent Burk an invaluable file of Virginia newspapers which Burk never returned, but which he used most effectively. In dedicating the comprehensive study to the

29. R. B. Davis, "The First American Edition of Captain John Smith's *True Travels* and *General Historie*," *Virginia Magazine of History and Biography*, XLVIII (1939), 97–108.

30. William H. Peden (ed.), *Notes on the State of Virginia* (Chapel Hill, 1955), xii–xiv.

man who had supplied so much of its primary material, Burk said that "The History of Virginia, by a sort of national right, claims you as its guardian and patron."[31]

Without the manuscript and printed laws described above, William Waller Hening could not have compiled his monumental *The Statutes at Large; being a Collection of all the Laws of Virginia, from the First Session of the Legislature, in the year 1619* (1809, 1810, 1812). In the preface, Hening traces the history of Jefferson's connection with the publication, beginning in 1795 when George Wythe approached his former student as to the use of his materials for such a work. After much correspondence Jefferson in June, 1808, sent Hening eight units of "Manuscripts of the laws," which the owner systematically listed.[32] These items included the Peyton Randolph, the Bland, the John Page, and Charles City-derived manuscripts described above. Later Jefferson lent him other laws, manuscript and printed. Hening collated these manuscripts with other surviving copies when possible, but often had to use them as his only source.

In the twentieth century most of Jefferson's Virginia *manuscripts*, especially, have been reproduced with scholarly introductions or used as bases for critical and historical studies of the periods they represent. H. R. McIlwaine printed "The Virginia Court Book, 1622–1629" (Sowerby, II, 352–353) in his edition of *Minutes of the Council and General Court of Virginia, 1616–1676* (Richmond, 1924). Susan Myra Kingsbury, in the four volumes of *The Virginia Company of London* (Washington, D.C., 1906, 1933, 1935) describes the Jefferson manuscripts and reproduces all the old records per-

---

31. See Sowerby, *Catalogue*, I, 212–14; and Lipscomb and Bergh (eds.), *Writings of Jefferson, passim*, for Jefferson-Burk correspondence.
32. Sowerby, *Catalogue*, II, 258; see II, 255–61 for Sowerby's full discussion of Jefferson's part in Hening's *Statutes*.

taining to the years she covers (1606–1624); her work is used by students of the period everywhere in the English-speaking world. Historians like Charles M. Andrews and Wesley F. Craven, among others, have studied Jefferson's Virginiana, in the original or in later printed forms, in preparing their own distinguished interpretations of colonial history. The scholars who have concentrated especially on Virginia history (to whom manuscripts such as Mathew's "Bacon's Rebellion" are of particular interest) and have employed Jefferson's materials, from Thomas Jefferson Wertenbaker to the most modest of genealogists or local historians, run at least into the scores.

Thomas Jefferson, one recalls, measured almost everything by the degree of its *usefulness* to mankind. His definition of *usefulness* was an inclusive one, embracing the production of intellectual and aesthetic pleasure as well as of material comfort. If he could come back and observe the ways in which his collections of materials relating to Virginia have been put to use, there is every evidence that he would be well satisfied.

The Virginia Novel
Before Swallow Barn

[Early Virginia library inventories reveal that citizens of the Old Dominion have, ever since the late seventeenth century, devoured novels—a literary genre neither particularly pious nor purposeful. Throughout the colonial period, their tastes in fiction were very much those of the rest of the English-speaking world—including a relish for the French romance, Defoe, Smollett, and Fielding. Not unnaturally, their favorites seem to have been Smollett and Fielding at a time when their New England neighbors preferred Richardson, though many persons in both regions read all these writers.

With the advent of the historical and sentimental novel, from eighteenth-century British lady writers through the more robust Sir Walter Scott, Virginians (and southerners generally) made the fictional combination of historical setting-action and sentimental characters their favorite light reading. One must admit that most of the rest of the world did too.

But the combination of their own history with the hedonistic enjoyment of the tale *per se*, brought forth what may still be considered a sub-genre in fiction, the Virginia novel. It is a subdivision of the historical novel and of the plantation novel. It was occasionally written by visitors to Virginia, but usually by Virginians. Frankly nostalgic (for most authors realized that Virginia's great age was already passing), it was a distinguishable literary entity several years before John

Pendleton Kennedy published what has usually been considered both the first Virginia and the first plantation novel.]

THAT CERTAIN nineteenth-century fiction may be described as lying within a rather loose genre known as the "Virginia novel" is generally agreed upon, implicitly and explicitly, by almost all literary historians and critics of the past fifty years. Loose as the designation may be, it carries a much more restricted connotation than other such delimiting phrases used for convenience in discussing American fiction. The "Western novel" and the "New England novel," for example, as terms convey much less definite impressions than does "Virginia novel." Every casual reader of our national fiction is at least vaguely aware that a "Virginia novel" is a work set either amid the great scenes and events of the state's political and martial history or within the confines of a Virginia antebellum plantation. It need not have been written by a native of the state; and merely having a setting within the Old Dominion's borders, be it city, town, or small farm, does not make a book into a "Virginia novel." Ellen Glasgow's work may constitute, as she so firmly insisted, a social history of Virginia over two generations; but those novels she included in her unified group are not really "Virginia novels" in the traditional sense, for they present no great figures or events, and they are not set upon a great slave-operated estate.

Yet readers and critics who agree with and employ the term "Virginia novel" (usually without quotation marks, which I shall discard in most instances hereafter) are quite often vague about more detailed qualities of the genre, and only a few have given it a definite chronological beginning and common elements of characterization, theme, and style. Some literary historians have discussed the Virginia novel as a mere minor branch of the American historical novel, largely derived from Sir Walter Scott and James Fenimore Cooper, and coming into being some time after Cooper's early work was complete. Others see the Virginia novel as the beginning of the "Plantation novel," a term often embracing any and all fiction with an agrarian setting anywhere in the antebellum South. Thus Francis P. Gaines, in *The Southern Plantation* (1925), sees John P. Kennedy's *Swallow Barn* (1832) as the beginning of the "Plantation novel" tradition and at the same time the first "Virginia novel," though he mentions the names of a few earlier works that share some of the qualities Kennedy's book possesses. Most other critics, including the ablest writer on the subject, Jay B. Hubbell, have agreed generally as to the primacy of *Swallow Barn* and 1832, though Hubbell has discussed the details of some earlier novels.[1] The novelist-historian who did most to popularize the plantation and Virginia history in his fiction, John Esten Cooke, observed as early as 1883 in his *Virginia*,[2] however, that the genre may be said to have begun with William A. Caruthers' *The Cavaliers of Virginia* (1835) and *Knights of the Horse-Shoe* (1841), "excellent romances in the style of Scott." Alexander Cowie[3] suggested that George Tucker's *The Valley of Shenandoah* (1824) was probably the "first Virginian novel," but even Cowie is much more interested in the work of Kennedy and Caruthers. Arthur Hobson Quinn[4] ignores anything earlier than *Swallow Barn*. Carl Van Doren,[5] without naming names or terms, simply observes that

1. Jay B. Hubbell, in several essays, and in his *Virginia Life in Fiction* (Dallas, 1922), *The South in American Literature* (Durham, N.C., 1954), and *Southern Life in Fiction* (Athens, Ga., 1960).
2. John Esten Cooke, *Virginia* (Boston, 1883), 295.
3. Alexander Cowie, *Rise of the American Novel* (New York, 1948), 277.
4. Arthur Hobson Quinn, *American Fiction* (New York, 1936).
5. Carl Van Doren, *The American Novel* (Rev. ed.; New York, 1940), 45.

Virginia "without many native novels, began to undergo, in the hands of almost every romancer who dealt with either the settlement or the Revolution, an idealization which made it seem the most romantic of American states."

With *Swallow Barn* in 1832 and *The Cavaliers of Virginia* three years later, there had emerged a Virginia novel leaning in one of two directions. This novel was romantic in general tone but often strongly realistic in detail, presenting stereotypes of a particular kind of lady and gentleman and young belle and beau, and including "originals" and slaves (the last often comic or minstrel-show types). Frequently it was realistic in the same sense that Scott's novels were, its reality springing from a mass of detail and from a sort of Scottish common-sense philosophical conception of idealized actuality. From Caruthers through Cooke and Thomas Nelson Page to the early Ellen Glasgow and Mary Johnston, it celebrated various dramatic and significant moments in state history, which was also national history. Its character stereotypes developed further into symbols of Virginia life and southern life. Its heirs in local-color romance, in fictional common-sense realism and ideality, and even in the social-problem novel are to be met with even in our own time.

The assertion of this chapter is that there was a Virginia novel almost a full generation before *Swallow Barn*; or rather that there were some four or five really significant Virginia novels in the thirty years before Kennedy published his loosely joined series of sketches of Virginia life. And these earlier novels, taken together, actually anticipate or at least adumbrate almost every quality the historical-event and plantation-setting variants of the genre ever developed. Although all the later Virginia novels were not written by Virginians, all these early examples were produced by natives or residents. Actually, Van Doren's statement that Virginia was "without many native novels" cannot be accepted for this early period. Besides the five qualified novels to be discussed here, several other fictions by Virginians were well known and reasonably widely read. As early as 1797 Virginian Samuel Relf (b. 1776) had written a sentimental novel of Philadelphia family life, *Infidelity,* which has a definite place in the domestication of the type in America. The notorious traveler and gossip Anne Royall, who considered herself a Virginian through long residence, had published in 1827 *The Tennessean,* a wretchedly constructed melodramatic tale of Southwestern life. Also in 1827 George Tucker, whose earlier novel is discussed below, published *A Voyage to the Moon,* a prose satire concerned with contemporary American social and political problems, which included a recognizable portrait of Thomas Jefferson. Tucker's work is a significant contribution to a then popular form but does not fall within the genre here to be discussed. Then in 1828 an anonymous author (probably Miss A. M. Lorraine) dedicated *Donald Adair: A Novel by a Young Lady of Virginia*[6] "To the Young Ladies of Virginia." Covering a period from 1753 to the Revolution, it contains references to Patrick Henry and James Fenimore Cooper, and includes George Washington as a character; but its setting is not clearly Virginian.

The earliest writer who presented a real Virginia setting in the novel was the Englishman John Davis (1774–1854), who spent many of the years between 1798 and 1817 at Occoquan on the Potomac, and in Richmond, Petersburg, and Washington. Schoolmaster, private tutor, poet, journalist, world-traveler, and prolific novelist, he touched Virginia life in every one of these capacities. As a writer, he is best remembered for his popularization of the Pocahontas-John Smith

6. *Donald Adair: A Novel by a Young Lady of Virginia* (2 vols.; Richmond, 1828).

legend.[7] "It was in the tall forests of Virginia, before the door of my plantation log-hut, that, contemplating the moon, and listening to the mock-bird, I first conceived the project of writing this story," Davis reveals in the preface to one version of the tale.[8] Drawing the nucleus of the story from William Robertson's *History of the Discovery and Settlement of America,* Smith's own accounts, and perhaps other histories, Davis gives his first version in *The Farmer of New Jersey* (1800), a two-page tale-within-a-tale which depicts Smith's rescue as he was about to be burned at the stake. In his *Travels of Four Years and a Half in the United States of America* (1803), Davis retells the story in much greater detail and with more effectiveness, this time getting straight the kind of execution to which Smith had been condemned. In 1805 appeared his novelette, *Captain Smith and Princess Pocahontas,* and later in that year a full-length novel on the same subject, *The First Settlers of Virginia.*[9] Both novel and novelette were reprinted, the former in 1806 and the latter in 1817, 1818, and 1837. The shorter form is the more attractive, for *The First Settlers* is overloaded with historical detail inserted in all manner of awkward ways. In the Pocahontas accounts, as in other works, Davis indicates his literary origins in Ossian and the sentimentalists generally, as well as in the Scottish philosophical ideas of beauty, sublimity, and reality.

Perhaps its celebration of a mythic-historical episode in Virginia history is alone enough to qualify *The First Settlers*

7. See Jay B. Hubbell, "The Smith-Pocahontas Story in Literature," *Virginia Magazine of History and Biography,* LXV (1957), 285.

8. John Davis, *Captain Smith and Princess Pocahontas* (Philadelphia, 1817).

9. The 1805 *Captain Smith* was published in Philadelphia, *The First Settlers* in New York. Later editions have New York, Philadelphia, and Richmond imprints.

of Virginia as the beginning of the Virginia novel genre. But this book includes also some other elements reappearing in later Virginia fiction. Though Davis relies heavily on the historians and Smith's own account for his main facts and some details, he also presents in his scene paintings and attempted mood creations many aspects of life in the Chesapeake Bay area. He was fascinated by Virginia birds. The mockingbird, especially, he sentimentally celebrates again and again; but the dove, redbird, catbird, and whip-poor-will, also with eerie or mournful calls, contribute to the Ossian-like moods of his characters. The Virginia cypress and oak, the pine and the laurel, the black snake and the squirrel, he employs as background for Rolfe's midnight vigil or the Indian maiden's lonely sighs for her lover. The conclusion is a primitivistic lament for the lost race of red men. All these materials have been used by later novelists at one time or another.

More significant are the characterization of Captain Smith and his red princess, characterizations far more suggestive of the later fictional Virginia gentleman and plantation belle than of the historical duo they purport to describe. Granted their debt to the sentimental characters of the eighteenth-century English novel, they still suggest their American descendants as well as their British progenitors. The redoubtable Captain, for example, is thus epitomized as the practitioner of the Horatian mean that the "first gentlemen of Virginia" held as their ideal:

The person of Smith was tall, graceful and manly. His visage was striking. He had an eye to commend, to threaten, or soothe. His aspect bespoke a man ready to face his man, yet capable of moderation; a character comprehending both firmness and refinement; blending taste with energy, and while ready to hit, yet able to forbear. It was a countenance that indicated a mind not easy to be deceived, and ever disposed more to suspicion than credulity. His vigorous, active figure qualified him eminently for the exercises of the field. It resembled more the graceful manliness of the Belvidere Apollo than the robust structure of the Farnese Hercules.[10]

Pocahontas is Virginia belle as well as sentimental female and noble savage:

This tender girl was the daughter of the Indian monarch. She was of a delicate form, but admirably proportioned. Her fine dark eyes beamed forth that moral sense, which imparts a magic to every look, and constitutes expression. There was a dash of melancholy in her countenance more interesting than smiles. It denoted a vacancy of heart; the want of some object on which to fix her affections. There was a delicious redness in her cherub lips. . . . Her long black hair . . . bowed in luxuriant tresses down her comely back and neck, half concealing the polish and symmetry, the rise and fall, of the bosom just beginning to fill.[11]

Another element of later Virginia and plantation fiction was introduced by Davis in his *Travels* and in novels which actually were not set in the state. This was the often oppressed Negro servant or slave. Strongly anti-slavery in feeling, Davis told lurid tales of miscegenation and the mistreatment of slaves in several of his works. But some years before Scott's Caleb Balderstone as faithful and resourceful servant or Cooper's varied Negro characters, Davis depicted the faithful Negro servant speaking in dialect. In *The Farmer of New Jersey* (1800), Orpheus and Old Dady speak of "Mosser" and "Missee." In *Walter Kennedy, an American Tale* (1808), "Captain Jack, alias Quashee," anticipates the minstrel-show stereotype of the Negro of later Virginia romances. Like several other Davis Negroes, Quashee can sing to the accompaniment of his "banger" (banjo). One of the singer's favorites is his "Seditious Ode" voicing Davis' feeling

10. John Davis, *The First Settlers of Virginia* (New York, 1806), 37.
11. *Ibid.*, 38.

about slavery, though the stanza quoted may seem an ironic attack on anti-slavery attitudes. It attempts fairly successfully the sort of dialect to be used often later:

> Our massa Jefferson he say,
>   Dat all mans free alike are born;
> Den tell me, why should Quashee stay,
> To tend de cow and hoe de corn?
> Huzza for massa Jefferson[12]

Thus several years before Scott's *Waverley,* and many more before Cooper's use of Virginia elements in *The Spy* (1821) and *The Two Admirals* (1842), John Davis had written two fictional versions of the most dramatic episode in Virginia's early history and in them had drawn a Virginia gentleman and Virginia belle. Elsewhere he had introduced the dialect-speaking Negro slave who was also a comic minstrel. Many of Scott's novels and some of Cooper's early work were to appear before the next Virginia novel in 1824, but Davis had between 1800 and 1806 already employed several of the characteristic features of the form. The reprints of *Captain Smith and Princess Pocahontas* in 1817 and 1818 may have served to keep some of these features fresh in the American mind.

Two Virginia novels appeared in 1824. One of them, the anonymous *Tales of an American Landlord; Containing Sketches of Life South of the Potomac,*[13] has been almost totally ignored in this century. Yet on its appearance it was hailed as a serious rival of Scott's work, and it includes several features of the later Virginia novel.

---

12. There are seven more stanzas. John Davis, *Walter Kennedy: An American Tale* (London, 1808), 20–21.
13. *Tales of an American Landlord: Containing Sketches of Life South of the Potomac* (2 vols.; New York, 1824).

On August 27, 1824, the well-known essayist and United States Attorney General William Wirt wrote[14] to his friend Judge Dabney Carr that he had just read that morning in the *National Intelligencer* "an extract from a Virginia novel, yet unpublished. I think it excellent." Wirt went on to inquire as to its authorship, and mentioned that he himself had for some time been contemplating just such "a historical novel, *flagrante bello*, of the revolution." The newspaper of that date includes under the caption "An American Novel, or Tale," an excerpt from *Tales of an American Landlord* concerned with Lafayette, "now [1824] the Nation's Guest," and pronounces this passage equal in interest to anything of parallel length which had appeared from the British "Great Unknown."

Although the few literary historians who have commented at all on this book have dismissed it as a sort of Methodist tract, it is far more and far different from this. It does present: an old Methodist preacher, John Fell; one hellfire sermon containing the phrase "suspended over the pit of destruction by a single hair,"[15] reminiscent of Jonathan Edwards; and a young aristocratic hero in disguise as a Methodist preacher. Though these elements are themselves historically indigenous to a Virginia setting, they by no means dominate the book. As its title suggests, *Tales of an American Landlord* owes something to Sir Walter Scott in structure, for it is a frame story encompassing three long tales and a number of shorter ones. The major characters—Colonel Berkley and his son the incognito hero, Mrs. Sparkle and her two daughters, and Mr. Percy the Byronic hero-villain—accompanied by literally dozens of lesser figures, move from one Virginia tavern to another

14. William Wirt to Dabney Carr, August 27, 1824, in William Wirt Papers, Virginia State Library, Richmond.
15. *Tales of an American Landlord*, I, 65–66.

(recall the title), making short stops at private houses in between. The novel is crowded with characters who go in and out and often do not return—innkeepers, robbers, Methodists, Quakers, Episcopal clergy, sentimental young females, etc. The author mentions[16] the fictional qualities of Fanny Burney, Jane Porter, and Maria Regina [or Regina Maria] Roche. The novel is also reminiscent of Fielding, among others.

The time of the frame story action is the early 1790s, when Washington is president of the United States. Appropriate characters relate incidents of Indian captivity and torture and of Quaker patience and inner conflict during the Revolution. Three fairly long poems are quoted at proper moments: "Columbia's Farewell to General La Fayette On His Return to France at the Close of the Revolutionary War"; "The Genius of America, Inscribed to His Excellency General Washington. On His Return to Mount Vernon, in December, 1783"; and "Sonnet to General Washington, President of the United States of America." Although the old Methodist John Fell is presented most sympathetically, and the Quakers are depicted as genuinely good people, it is perhaps significant that neither a Methodist nor a Quaker, but an Episcopal clergyman, Mr. Marmaduke Scott (a sort of Devereux Jarratt) converts old Ben Lock, the jailer, who afterwards lives an exemplary life. One should note that the character of the local parish rector, often resembling the Reverend Mr. Scott, was to become, after *Swallow Barn,* a familiar figure in the later Virginia novel.

Actually the Washington newspaper, by excerpting one brief dramatic scene, presented the novel at its best. As already suggested, it contains too many characters and too many episodes; it also employs too frequently Gothic claptrap and

16. *Ibid.*, 143.

sentimental disguise. On the other hand, the rhetoric is relatively restrained and the language, though stilted, is not actually stiff. Though the events of the main action might have happened in England as well as in America, such things as the plantation-settings of the Northern Neck and Piedmont, the Quakers in the Revolution in Virginia, the stockade and Indian massacre on the western frontier of the state, the names of Colonel Berkley and Colonel Hopewell and the county estates Rosemount, Hopewell Hall, Norborne Lodge, Berkley Park, and Marlevale, are convincingly domesticated in the Old Dominion. The two colonels may be, in a sense, transplanted Squire Westerns, but they are also the more than faint beginnings of fictional Virginia and Southern colonels. Even the Negro servant is here, though "good mammy Nellie" (II, 184–185) speaks more like the less literate white than did Davis' Quashee. Old Sambo and Jenny (also in II) make only brief appearances and are not described in enough detail to establish them as types or original characters. But they are present, and even their names will later become stereotypes.

Altogether, *Tales of an American Landlord* is a not uninteresting novel. Its depiction of mores and manners from several levels of Virginia society, its combination of historical and plantation scenes and settings, and its county colonels and faithful Negroes suggest that it anticipated *Swallow Barn* and even Cooke's *Surry of Eagle's-Nest* (1866) in some specific as well as general features.

The second novel of the year 1824, George Tucker's *The Valley of Shenandoah; or Memoirs of the Graysons*,[17] has in recent years received a little more attention, though not all it

17. George Tucker, *The Valley of Shenandoah; or Memoirs of the Graysons* (2 vols.; New York, 1824).

deserves. Its author, whose reputation today is based primarily on his work as a political economist and biographer of Jefferson, composed this, the best-known of his three novels (one is still in manuscript), between his years as a practicing attorney and member of Congress and his appointment to a professorship at the newly opened University of Virginia. On January 1, 1825,[18] Tucker wrote to Joseph C. Cabell, who had approached him on the subject of the professorship, that he wanted more time before deciding:

> I have for more than a year conceived the project & indulge the hope that I might pursue the business of authorship as a profitable calling—I have (but this is a secret) actually essayed the public favor in a novel just published in New York and should I meet with any thing like the success which has attended Cooper, I should think my prospects of profit much greater than any professorship could hold out—He has made about $5000 by each of his novels—and the Valley of Shenandoah, my new work was written in two months—The situation to which you invite me would almost put a stop to my efforts as an author.

Thus Cooper's alleged financial successes in his very earliest novels impelled this Bermuda-born Virginian to try his hand. Tucker's book was a conscious attempt to portray actual Virginia life in fiction. The plot, in which seduced heroine, avenging brother, and Lovelace-like seducer are disposed of in the best Richardsonian manner, traces the decline of a Virginia family because of the inherent weaknesses of the society they represent. The father of the tragic heroine had been a real Southern colonel, "Colonel Grayson, a meritorious officer of the 'continental line,' in the war of the revolution."[19]

18. George Tucker to Joseph C. Cabell, January 1, 1825 (misdated 1824), in Cabell Deposit, University of Virginia, Charlottesville.
19. Tucker, *The Valley of Shenandoah*, I, i.

His widow, forty years old, well-read, a good housekeeper, is the first of a long line of gracious plantation mistresses. Her daughter Louisa, though more like Clarissa than Scarlett O'Hara, shows in vivacity and grace some of the qualities of the later more developed plantation belle. Her brother Edward, somewhat saturnine and "misanthropical," who dies in the attempt to avenge his sister's lost honor, is in pride, generosity, and nobility of heart the ancestor of all later young plantation heroes. James Gildon, the New Yorker-seducer, is more weak than dastardly, as are other figures of sentimental romance; he is not so highly individualized as the Graysons are.

Though the pages of *The Valley of Shenandoah* are not so cluttered with characters as were those of *Tales of an American Landlord*, there are a score of fairly significant minor *dramatis personae,* who, in a remarkable number of instances, were clearly drawn from close personal observation. There are three plantation colonels who are convincingly individualized: Major (the rank didn't matter for some years yet) Fawkner, easygoing father of plantation-belle Matilda, and the two Tidewater officers, Colonel Mason and Colonel Barton. Colonel Grayson's attorney Barbawl and Dr. Cutaway, both Matilda's suitors, and the attorneys Trueheart and Worricourt, despite their eighteenth-century tag names, remind the reader at once of certain recognizable Virginia types drawn later by Kennedy in *Swallow Barn,* and actually earlier anticipated in William Wirt's gatherings of essays, *Letters of the British Spy* (1803), *The Rainbow* (1804), and *The Old Bachelor* (1814). Equally localized are the amusingly drawn portraits[20] of the two rival Winchester physicians, one educated at Edinburgh, the other at Philadelphia, the one a

20. *Ibid.,* II, 149–50.

disciple of Cullen, the other an admirer of Brown. These all belong more or less to the upper classes, most of them being Episcopalians or deists. For society here is feudalistic, as it was to remain in the later Virginia novel. But both Tucker and the anonymous author of *Tales of an American Landlord* depart from the orthodox Virginia novel tradition in their interest in and depiction of middle and lower-middle class persons. In *The Valley of Shenandoah* the middle class, often Presbyterian and Scottish, are as accurately drawn as the upper-class figures: *e.g.,* Frederick Steenor, who went to "Lexington College" (now Washington and Lee), and his attractive but rather ironically presented love Susan Tidball, whose social status may be at least another half-step down the ladder. Jacob Scryder, the German wagoner, and M'Culloch, the free-spoken mountaineer, were types often to be met with in the Valley of Virginia. Primus, the faithful slave-servant, and Granny Mott, who has an aristocratic pride in her social position as an eighty-four-year-old slave, are quite realistic, for they have not yet become stereotypes. Another side of Tucker's realistic presentation of slavery is the Grayson auction, at which dire necessity forces the family to dispose of their slaves.[21]

Local color is everywhere: the Fredericksburg races; the lovely old college town of Williamsburg in 1796, including its literary circle, politics, and student love affairs; Richmond, the new metropolis; the taverns of Colchester and Dumfries; Harper's Ferry much as it was in Jefferson's famous romantic description. Lesser details of deer hunting, morning mint juleps, pieced bedquilts, and fine old furniture give further touches of verisimilitude. The snapshot glance at a family in the act of moving from Westmoreland County near the

21. *Ibid.,* 203.

Chesapeake to Kentucky, and the analysis of the "pioneer feeling" and other reasons for the move, are the work of a keen observer, conscious of economic and psychological factors in the march of civilization.

Unlike most settings of the plantation novel now or later, the principal agrarian scene here is beyond the Blue Ridge in the Great Valley, though the author does follow his characters to Tidewater and contrasts the eastern and western forms of Virginia life. He points out the mixture of Scotch-Irish and "Dutch" in the Shenandoah Valley and describes and analyzes each group. The Germans are "the dray horses of society,"[22] the Scotch-Irish, their opposites, imaginative, bold, and daring.[23] Slavery is presented in a remarkably realistic fashion, as suggested above, but the general tone is unfavorable toward it. Tucker knows and distinguishes between Cohees and Tuckahoes.[24] East and west, it is a society in flux, and the author tries to make sure his reader is aware of the evolution which is going on.

The soon-to-become-familiar description of the plantation mansion is for the first time here present. This first time it is a double portrait, for Tucker describes both a Valley and a Tidewater country house, though with not quite the detail Kennedy later lavishes upon the simple old domicile of Swallow Barn. The Valley home of the Graysons in its materials suggests the region:

The house itself was a modest mansion of rough blue limestone, in the form of the letter L, having three rooms on one floor. Below, were a passage, drawing-room, dining room, chamber, and a large closet which had been used as a dressing room, and was now the lodging room of Louisa—the three rooms above were bedchambers. A large kitchen garden was on the east of the

22. *Ibid.*, I, 49 ff. 23. *Ibid.*, 54 ff. 24. *Ibid.*, 40.

house, containing a succession of falls as the ground sloped to a little rivulet, which was formed by a limestone spring, not half a mile from the house. But the most beautiful part of the view was the river, presenting always to the eye, except after a heavy rain, a smooth surface and a limpid stream when near and a broad sheet of mirror when seen at a distance, in which the mountains, with its woods all crimson and gold; its jutting cliffs and patches of cleared land, were doubled to the eye, and inverted in their position.[25]

The Stafford County house of Colonel Barton was quite different, yet typical, as the author suggests, of all the Northern Neck. Like the limestone house of the Valley, it gives the impression of unostentatious simplicity: "The house was of brick, and consisted of a wide passage through the middle, with two rooms on each side, both above and below stairs. There was, besides, a smaller building near the main one, in which there were two lodging rooms that were occasionally occupied by young gentlemen and other visitors."[26]

Tucker's personal ideas as to the weaknesses of the Virginia economic system are blended remarkably into his love plot. For the tragedy of Gildon and Louisa is the direct result of the involved financial position of her family, itself in turn the result of wasteful wearing out of arable lands and of reckless speculations, both matters very much in the minds of Virginians in the 1820s. Another theme to which space is devoted and which is close to Tucker's heart is the political opposition of "federalists" to "democrats,"[27] for Tucker, though later he gradually became quite conservative, was at this time a strong Jeffersonian.

Tucker's novel, then, presents no great historical character, no notable political or martial event. It has a local-color setting suggestive of Scott's or Cooper's, of Virginia life as it was

25. *Ibid.,* 17.   26. *Ibid.,* II, 21.
27. *Ibid.,* 148, for example.

about 1796. It was much more realistic in the problems it depicted, if not in detail, than anything Cooper had written up to that time, so realistic that it injured Virginia pride.[28] It is a problem-and-thesis novel, yet it was written with the avowed intention of making its author a good income by faithful depiction of Virginia life. Though Professor Hubbell suggests that it "had no part in the building of the romantic plantation tradition,"[29] its careful and sympathetic descriptions of rural mansions, barbecues, and hunting, its strongly emphasized Virginia gentlemen, as well as the fact that Virginians read it,[30] would suggest that it marked a stage in the development of the Virginia plantation tradition, whether or not it specifically influenced later writing.

Almost as ignored in the twentieth century as *Tales of an American Landlord* is James Ewell Heath's *Edge-Hill, or, The Family of the Fitzroyals.*[31] Much more romantic in tone than *Swallow Barn,* it combines stirring events with a plantation setting, and quite clearly anticipates William Alexander Caruthers, John Esten Cooke, and Thomas Nelson Page. Avowedly indebted to Scott[32] and obviously also to Cooper, it is individual in the details of setting, in some aspects of characterization, and in its presentation of the Negro and his dialect.

In outline it is a typical sentimental novel. It begins with the return to Edge-Hill of its master, Charles Fitzroyal, with his new second wife, formerly the Widow Dashwood. Old

28. See M. M. Robinson to William Short, April 14, 1825, in Short Papers, Manuscript Division, Library of Congress.
29. Hubbell, *The South in American Literature,* 252.
30. See Robinson to Short, April 14, 1825, in Short Papers.
31. James Ewell Heath, *Edge-Hill, or, The Family of the Fitzroyals* (2 vols.; Richmond, Va., 1828).
32. Heath, *Edge-Hill,* II, 205.

Fitzroyal, determined to marry his son Charles to his new stepdaughter, plays the heavy parental role tolerated only in this type of novel. The son, in love with the beautiful but persecuted Ruth Elmore, joins the Continental Army against the wishes of his Tory father. Ruth is the near-victim of several malicious plots, including an abduction and attempted seduction. After many vicissitudes, young Fitzroyal is forgiven, Ruth is rescued so that she may marry him, and the sweetmeats and sugarplums are distributed in lavish fashion to all save Albert Monteagle, the former Widow Dashwood, and her daughter Cornelia.

In style Heath's book is stumbling and uneven. Homely colloquialisms in dialogue, words like "swivet" and "racket," frequently lend an air of reality. But in other places the rhetoric is strained and overdone. For example, when the heroine Ruth is tending a favorite rosebush in the presence of Cornelia: "Mordecai at the King's gate, was not more odious to the repining Haman, than the unoffending Ruth whilst rearing the blooming shrub, was to her resentful rival."[33]

Harriet Wilton, Ruth's "sprightly friend"; Albert Monteagle, Byronic hero-villain; and historical figures such as Benedict Arnold, Tarleton, and Lafayette are recognizable counterparts of characters in Richardson, Scott, or Cooper. But more original (though already suggested in the earlier *Tales of an American Landlord* and later developed in *Swallow Barn*) here is an American clergyman of a rural parish, in this case the Reverend Mr. Rubrick, who lives on the glebe near Edge-Hill. Rather caustically he is described as orthodox, moral, but really deficient in any "perception of divine truth."[34] Here again also is a sympathetically drawn Southern plantation master, Harriet's father, Major Wilton (again not yet a colonel). Here is an anticipation of the middle-aged

33. *Ibid.*, 5.   34. *Ibid.*, I, 46.

bachelor frequently met with in the later novel (*cf. Swallow Barn*), in this case the lawyer-tutor Claude Kilwarden, who speaks a strong Scots dialect. And here are Negro gardeners and house servants and attempted dialect. The last is often merely ungrammatical English, but in such expressions as "a little arter dark," it represents sound and idiom rather accurately.

Perhaps the most dramatic character in the novel is a Negro version of Cooper's Harvey Birch in *The Spy*. James, young Fitzroyal's body servant, saves his master's life on the battlefield, plans and executes an unsuccessful stratagem to kill Benedict Arnold (now a British officer), and spies on the British successfully for Lafayette. In the last paragraph of the novel, when Lafayette in 1824 (on his return visit to America) recognizes his old sable companion in arms and espionage, James' testimonial letter from Lafayette (*cf.* Harvey Birch's from Washington) as to hitherto unrecognized services is quoted in full. Thus James is the faithful Negro retainer raised to heroic proportions. He does not occupy enough space in the narrative, however, to become the memorable figure Birch is.

It is perhaps in its regional setting, the estate bordering on the James River in 1781, that *Edge-Hill* marks the greatest step forward toward the work of John Esten Cooke and Thomas Nelson Page. For the aura or halo these principal popularizers of the Virginia novel threw over mansion and garden, a sentimental light not evident in either the earlier *Valley of Shenandoah* or slightly later *Swallow Barn,* is here considerably developed. Mellowed traditions, hallowed past, and Cavalier ancestors are all implied or expressed, for instance, in the description of Edge-Hill itself:

The mansion was situated on the northern bank of the James, or more properly the Powhatan, the name by which, according to that romantic adventurer Captain Smith, "this fair and delightful river" was first known. It was a large commodious brick building, constructed of materials principally brought from *home*, as England was familiarly called, and although it might have been inferior to more modern structures in elegance of design, it could hardly be surpassed for durability and convenience. Its front, or northern side, overlooked a spacious lawn, which was shadowed by some of the finest forest trees of lower Virginia; and in the rear, extending in terraces to the river bank, lay the garden, which abounded in delicious fruit and beautiful shrubbery, and was accomodated with summer houses and pavilions, in various positions. The out-houses and offices, disposed at convenient distances, occupied the flanks of the edifice, and beyond these the green clover paddocks, and fields of early wheat and corn, announced the owner's opulence, and presented a refreshing picture of rural beauty. The whole landscape, moreover, seemed mellowed by the hand of time, and amidst all the freshness of the vernal season, objects would here and there catch the attention, bearing a significant relation to long past days. The low gothic windows, and mouldered aspect of the walls—the high and thick set hedges of box which bordered the walks, and the majestic height of the oak, elm and poplar, which threw their venerable boughs over the front lawn, referred to a distant period when the mansion of Edge-Hill . . . was first erected. More than a century had elapsed since Sir Rupert Fitzroyal, a loyal cavalier and gentleman of wealth and family, disheartened by the tragic fate of the elder Charles, migrated to Virginia, and became proprietor of the estate. By him it was named in commemoration of the scene of one of those hard-fought battles between the English royalists and republicans, in which he himself bore arms, and was dangerously wounded; and from him, through three or four intermediate descendants, it was ultimately derived by the present occupant.[35]

Yet for all the halo cast over lost things in this and other descriptions in the novel, if the author had ever heard the term "idealized realism" applied to his work, he would cer-

35. *Ibid.*, 6–7.

tainly have insisted that of the two words, it was *realism*, as fidelity to fact, which should be emphasized. In 1835, in writing the ablest contemporary review of Caruthers' *The Cavaliers of Virginia*, Heath took the later novelist sharply to task,[36] and in painstaking detail, for carelessness with facts about historical characters, places, and events. But Heath also remarked upon the lack of finish, of roundness, in Caruthers' portraits. It is perhaps what he calls *roundness,* or finish, which brings the *idealization* to the *actuality* and forms the mellow light around it.

Heath, earlier a country gentleman and Virginia legislator and later editor of the *Southern Literary Messenger* and a playwright, was in 1841 called by Poe[37] almost the only person of any literary distinction still residing in Richmond. George Tucker ranked *Edge-Hill* with the novels of Cooper, Kennedy, and Robert Montgomery Bird. Yet because of its obvious weaknesses of plot and sentimental characterization, *Edge-Hill* has been forgotten even by those who still read *Swallow Barn* or *The Cavaliers of Virginia.*

Thus there were novels between 1805 and 1828, set in Virginia and written by Virginians, which contained in one place or another every major quality or element embodied in the later conceptions of Kennedy, Caruthers, Cooke, Page, and Johnston. By 1828 the gallant gentleman who followed the Horatian mean already administered some broad-acred fictional plantation. His gracious wife, well read and pious, yet gay, presided over a country mansion. Young sons and daughters, fresher replicas of the master and mistress, carried

36. James Ewell Heath, review of William A. Caruthers' *The Cavaliers of Virginia,* in *Southern Literary Messenger,* I (1835), 385–86.
37. James A. Harrison (ed.), *The Complete Works of Edgar Allan Poe* (17 vols.; New York, 1902), XV, 241.

on their affairs of honor, love, rescue, and war. Local "origi-nals," lawyers and clergy, added zest and humor in convivial fireside conversation. Perhaps the most sympathetic and laudatory portrait ever drawn of the faithful Negro servant, James of Edge-Hill, had already been completed. And already painted in full colors was Virginia's greatest colonial hero, Captain John Smith, a figure mentioned again and again even in the Virginia novels in which he does not appear as a living character. Sketched into backgrounds, and sometimes coming front and center, were Washington and Lafayette. Accompanied by Jefferson, Stonewall Jackson, and Robert E. Lee, these three still live in fiction. Smith's story, for example, occupies forty-odd pages in the first edition of *Swallow Barn;* and whole novels by John Esten Cooke and George Eggle-ston, among many others, include his or his fair rescuer's name in the title.

One must grant that George Tucker's *The Valley of Shen-andoah* is not quite a full-fledged Virginia novel, for the nos-talgic atmosphere which usually accompanied glorious deeds or plantation life is not its main tone. Only in the twentieth century, when the critical spirit had again meshed with the creative, could novelists like Ellen Glasgow in *Barren Ground* or Willa Cather in *Sapphira and the Slave Girl* see Virginia life in its full irony and paradox as Tucker had, and one may argue that even they never quite overcame a certain senti-mental myopia. Like them, Tucker probed and analyzed *con amore.*

John Davis and the author of *Tales of an American Land-lord* also saw that all was not right in the Virginia world they depicted. Slavery and Indian brutality and white men's broken pledges marred this lovely Eden. James Ewell Heath, a little farther away in time from the eighteenth century and conscious of the South's growing need to defend its peculiar institutions, is in 1828 as nostalgic, as sentimental over a past Virginia heroic age as Thomas Nelson Page would ever be.

In 1817, when he wrote his *Sketches of the Life and Character of Patrick Henry,* William Wirt had felt that the glory of Virginia was passing. By the 1820s most literate Virginians knew that the crest of their wave had passed. Here and there, in that decade before *Swallow Barn,* men attempted to preserve in fiction the memory of that high tide. For the rest of the century others followed their example. All of them together created a sort of American dream in reverse, or in retrospect.

⌒(XII)⌒

The Valley of Virginia in Early American Literature

[From the first landing in 1607 to the present, Virginians have shown a developing appreciation of the physical beauties of their region.* The Great Valley is one of its majestic geographical areas which has aroused aesthetic appreciation from the time of Governor Spotswood's expedition in 1716 to our own day. From a Huguenot's travel journal to Ellen Glasgow's and Willa Cather's novels, attempts have been made to express its glories in literature.

Much of the descriptive writing of Virginia, as this essay suggests, is mediocre. But Thomas Jefferson, John Pendleton Kennedy, George Tucker, Philip Pendleton Cooke, and William A. Caruthers, with a few other early commentators, have caught facets of Virginia's beauty in adequate terms. And the novelists, especially, have also presented phases of life in the Valley.

The settlement of the Shenandoah may represent a distinct second stage in the colony-state's development, when German and Scotch-Irish folk mingled with the Anglo-Saxons of Tidewater and Piedmont to develop a Virginia-with-a-difference. But it is actually a small difference, albeit a refreshing one, for it brought new blood into an old culture when the infusion was needed.]

* This essay was originally delivered as the James Madison Lecture at Madison College Founder's Day, March 12, 1971.

TODAY THE American creative artist with brush or pen, if he is inclined to find subject and inspiration in our natural wonders, is likely to turn to the relatively newly found—to us Anglo-Americans—the Grand Canyon, the giant sequoias, the Yosemite, or the Grand Tetons. A few years back he might have depicted the Great Plains and the Rockies, a little earlier than that Niagara Falls. Then still further back was the Hudson River school of painters, who corresponded in the sublimity and sentimentality of their landscapes to Bryant, Cooper, and a host of lesser writers. In the United States, as elsewhere, artistic expression has generally conformed to the aesthetic fashions of the particular age in which it was produced.

One of the earliest subjects of our descriptive art and our storytelling, for a variety of reasons, has been the Great Valley of Virginia or the Shenandoah (for convenience's sake I use the terms interchangeably). It has been one of the most persistent American art subjects, for its expression endured from 1669 to at least 1940. In the seventeenth century, Virginia Secretary of State Ludwell described it to royal authorities in London from early explorers' reports. The explorer-traders themselves, such as Henry Batts, Abraham Wood, and most appropriately the German Dr. Lederer, recorded their view of small portions of it; Dr. Lederer's account contained the observation that from the top of the Blue Ridge he "had a beautiful prospect of the *Atlantick*-Ocean washing the *Virginian*-shore."[1]

But there is a constant quality which endures in descriptions of the Great Valley. It is to be seen today in the critical-creative, nostalgic emotions recollected and depicted in tranquillity by two great women novelists. The Valley's own

1. See Douglas Rights and William P. Cumming (eds.), *The Discoveries of John Lederer* (Charlottesville, 1958, *passim*. The book was originally edited by Sir William Talbot, Bart.

daughter, Willa Cather, displays this quality in *Sapphira and the Slave Girl* (1940), with its fusion of mountain streams and racial and social groups from recollections of her early childhood (Miss Cather and her family moved to Nebraska in her girlhood). Closer in feeling, perhaps because of frequent visits throughout her life, are the descriptions of a granddaughter of the Valley, Ellen Glasgow, whose *Vein of Iron* incorporates even a human quality of the region in its title. In this novel she ponders the section in which her paternal ancestors were born and bred. Shut-in Valley and the Fincastle family may remind knowledgeable readers at once of Botetourt and its county seat. But it is the physical land itself which helps to set the mood and theme of the novel from the first page. For example, the heroine's interior monologue begins thus:

The hills shook themselves like ponies and rushed headlong among the mountains. The Blue Ridge and the Alleghenies toppled over and tumbled far down into the Valley of Virginia. . . . The child lay on the flat rock and watched the road that climbed through the small valleys within the Great Valley.
God's Mountain, Father said, was the oversoul of Appalachian Virginia. Whenever she gazed at it alone for a long time, the heavenly blue seemed to flood into her heart and rise there in a peak. That must have been the first thing God created, and blue she supposed, was the oldest color in the world.[2]

Two and a half centuries elapsed between Lederer and these novelist children of the Valley. If there were space, my subject would be "The Valley of Virginia *and* Early American Literature," showing how racial and religious groups, cultural societies, printers, schools, and teachers had their part in developing writing in and of the Valley. As it is, these elements can only be touched upon incidentally.

2. Ellen Glasgow, *Vein of Iron* (New York, 1935), 3, 15.

After Lederer, the next important literary document, penned as a journal in 1716 but not published until 1853, was the work of a young French Huguenot, John Fontaine, who in the former year had accompanied Virginia Governor Alexander Spotswood on what has been called the most famous cookout—for men only—in American colonial history. Spotswood, who knew that to survive British America must push to the west and stake out its claim to lands on which the French were already encroaching, got together a group of young gentlemen, yeoman farmers, and wilderness scouts for what one would consider today a short march over a gap (here Swift Run) and down to the Shenandoah. In August, 1716, heavily laden with refreshments (especially alcoholic), his party climbed the Blue Ridge. Fontaine, member of a family since famous in Virginia and Valley history, describes the activity, including the strenuous climb on the first iron-shod horses in Virginia, the celebrative volleys from the muskets, and the toasts drunk. At the very top they drank King George's health, then descended into the valley, named the Shenandoah the Euphrates (which, one recalls, was one boundary of the Garden of Eden), had a good dinner, and fired volley after volley. Between firings they drank toasts, first in champagne, then burgundy, then claret, then Virginia red and white wine, then whiskey, then two sorts of rum, canary, punch, cider, and water! It may well have been the first form of the Virginia Reel they executed as they climbed eastward again through Swift Run Gap.

As far as we know, Spotswood's contemporaries saw the expedition celebrated in only two accounts: the historical summary in the Reverend Hugh Jones's *The Present State of Virginia, and the College* (1724),[3] which tells of the fabled

3. Hugh Jones, *The Present State of Virginia, and the College,* ed. R. L. Morton (Chapel Hill, 1956).

golden horseshoes presented by the governor to members of the expedition and the foundation of the Transmontane Order; and the Arthur Blackamore-George Seagood poem "Mr. Blackamore's *Expeditio Ultramontana, render'd into English Verse*" (printed in the *Maryland Gazette* in 1729 but written originally in Latin in 1717).[4] Neither work was of great importance, save that they give a historical basis for what became a legend even before Fontaine's journal was known in 1853.

The period of primary settlement of the Valley, 1728–1782, produced principally travel and captivity accounts, most by outsiders who were seeing America's wonders, but some by German, Scotch-Irish, Dutch, Welsh, and eastern Virginians who came to settle there. The writers included several surveyors, the most famous being Peter Jefferson, Joshua Fry, John Lewis, and George Washington,[5] and they traveled anywhere from short distances to the whole extent of the Valley —Harper's Ferry to modern Roanoke. They rode on horseback or in sturdy carriages which sometimes were jolted to pieces, or they simply walked. Britishers Andrew Burnaby in 1759–1760, Harry Toulmin in 1793, and Thomas Anburey in 1780, German soldier Johann Conrad Dohla in 1781, and the French Marquis de Chastellux[6] are among many who have left their records of observations, from simple journals to elaborate travel accounts.

4. See reference above to Earl G. Swem's edition, Chap. VIII, n. 9.
5. See John W. Wayland (ed.), *The Fairfax Line: Thomas Lewis's Journal of 1746* (New Market, Va., 1925), *passim;* and any edition of Washington's Journal, and the Fry-Jefferson Map of 1754 (a major item of American cartography).
6. See Thomas Anburey, *Travels in America* (2 vols.; Boston, 1923); Johann Conrad Dohla (or "Doehla," according to trans. Robert J. Tilden), "The Doehla Journal," *William and Mary Quarterly,* XXII (July, 1942), 229–274; and the Marquis de Chastellux, *Travels in North America in the Years 1780, 1781 and 1782,* ed. Howard C. Rice, Jr. (Chapel Hill, 1963). There are several other travel accounts written before 1789.

But it was Thomas Jefferson's *Notes on the State of Virginia,* begun about 1780 and printed in France, England, and America in 1785–1787, which made known to all the western world the glories of the Shenandoah Valley—the Blue Ridge, the Peaks of Otter, Harper's Ferry, the Natural Bridge. After its publication almost every traveler, observer, poet, or novelist who described its wonders referred or deferred to Jefferson's accounts. The most famous passage in the book describing scenes from nature is the sentimental pre-romantic description, ironically, by the greatest American son of the Enlightenment and of Reason: "The passage of the Patowmac through the Blue ridge is perhaps one of the most stupendous scenes in nature. You stand on a very high point of land. On your right comes up the Shenandoah, having ranged along the foot of the mountain an hundred miles to seek a vent. On your left approaches the Patowmac in quest of a passage also. In the moment of their junction they rush together against the mountain, rend it asunder, and pass off into the sea. . . . This scene is worth a voyage across the Atlantic. . . ."⁷ And a little further on he rhapsodizes in his delineation of the *"Natural bridge,* the most sublime of Nature's works. . . . It is impossible for the emotions, arising from the sublime, to be felt beyond what they are here: so beautiful an arch, so elevated, so light, and springing . . . the rapture of the Spectator is really indiscribable!" These phrases on the bridge (which happened to be on Jefferson's own land) were borrowed by the inveterate critic Henry Adams when he attempted to paint in words the glory of Chartres cathedral a full century later. In the new republic after 1789 the march of observers contained all sorts of people, from various European nobility to that fascinating sometime resident of the Valley Anne Royall the

7. Thomas Jefferson, *Notes on the State of Virginia,* ed. William Peden (Chapel Hill, 1955), 19, 24–25.

journalist, to Charles Johnston, the proprietor of Botetourt Springs (now the site of Hollins College), who in 1827 published a graphic and philosophcial account of his Indian captivity in the 1790s. There was Francis W. Gilmer, a Winchester lawyer whose scientific essay explaining the formation of the Natural Bridge is still accepted as the correct one; or Major Francis Bailey, gambler, bigamist, speculator, alcoholic, duelist, unsavory politician, who almost got himself hanged.[8] Most of these commentators are of course complimentary to the land, though not always to its inhabitants.

Meanwhile, especially between 1800 and 1840, the rapidly growing Valley towns, from Shepherdstown and Martinsburg to Lexington, were developing schools, a major college, seminaries for young ladies (the two most famous being in Lexington and Harrisonburg), printing presses, and socio-intellectual clubs. The prime purpose of the printers was to produce newspapers, of course, but the Henkel Press at New Market became famous for its German-language books on religion, music, or primary education.[9] And Laurenz Wartmann[10] and several others in Harrisonburg, Staunton, and Lexington produced what are today collector's items on music, poetry, and religion. In Harrisonburg alone appeared a well-known anti-slavery sermon by George Bourne (1813); Daniel Bryan's epic *The Mountain Muse* (1813) and his *Oration on Female Education* (1816), delivered several times at Valley schools for young ladies; Conrad Speece's *Mountaineer . . . Essays* (1818, 1820); Anasias Davidson's *Kentucky Harmony* (1815, 1825); James P. Carrell's *Songs of Sion*

8. For details about most of these people, see R. B. Davis, *Intellectual Life in Jefferson's Virginia, 1790–1830* (Chapel Hill, 1964).

9. Lester Cappon and Ira V. Brown, *New Market, Virginia, Imprints 1806–1876, A Checklist* (Charlottesville, 1942).

10. For information about Wartmann, see John W. Wayland, *Twenty-Five Chapters on the Shenandoah Valley* (Strasburg, Va., 1957), 261.

(5th ed., 1826); and Joseph Funk's *Choral-Music* (1816). Many of these, especially the music books, were reprinted throughout the century. In Winchester was published in 1814 a strong Methodist sermon against political slander, with the picturesque title "The Fiery-Flying Serpent Slander, and the Brazen Serpent Charity, Delineated," by the Reverend Richard Ferguson. And Lexington for a brief period in 1821 had a genuine literary magazine, *The Mountain Laurel,* including essays, verse, and fiction. Curiously enough, though the Valley was still a semifrontier, it possessed in some abundance what is usually found only in longer-settled communities—the really essential ingredient for encouraging the potential writer—the printing press.

The "Frugal Fare Club" was founded in Winchester about 1812. A sort of intellectual social group, it numbered among its participating members Henry St. George Tucker (later congressman and writer on legal questions), Francis Gilmer, Jefferson's nephew Dabney Carr (who while in Winchester contributed to William Wirt's famous collection of essays *The Old Bachelor*), and a dozen others who later made names for themselves as governors, judges, or civil servants in the new Southwest and West.[11] They wrote, sang individually and collectively, and imbibed in moderation. A much longer-lived club (*ca.* 1800–1891) was the town-and-gown Franklin Society and Library Company in Lexington, of which Henry Ruffner, William Alexander Caruthers, and later Matthew Fontaine Maury, Robert E. Lee, and Stonewall Jackson were illustrious members—at least three of them writers of prominence. Both Ruffner and Caruthers, for example, used materials in the Franklin Society Library, said to be the largest

11. See "Dabney Carr," *Southern Literary Messenger,* IV (February, 1838), 65–70; and R. B. Davis, *Francis Walker Gilmer: Life and Learning in Jefferson's Virginia* (Richmond, 1939), 93–119.

book collection west of the Blue Ridge, in composing their own works.[12] The Valley's one major institution of higher learning of the period, Washington College in Lexington, was a mighty force in local regional and general southern education, despite a later eminent alumnus' sour comment that when he entered (about 1808) it was "a college super-intended by lazy and ignorant Presbyterian preachers, and filled with dirty boys of low manners and morals."[13] The principal Presbyterian preacher-in-charge during the period, Henry Ruffner, pastor, teacher, money raiser, active abolition-ist, theological and educational essayist, and short story writer and novelist, among several other things, was anything but "lazy and ignorant." During this generation, in many respects the age of James Madison, the whole Valley was very much alive intellectually. And, incidentally, the little fourth Presi-dent received some of the strongest support and sympathy for his far-seeing and liberal policies from its inhabitants and their congressional representatives.

Poets celebrating the Valley, some native and some out-siders, after the 1717 verses on Spotswood already mentioned, probably began pushing the pen again a full generation later. Their lines are stiff, sentimental, and often just bad; but their subjects have inherent color and some interest. Britishers An-drew Burnaby and John Davis, Quaker Virginian Samuel Janney, the lady "Potomac Muse" [Judith Wormeley], and

12. For accounts of the Franklin Society, see Charles W. Turner, "The Franklin Society, 1800–1891," *Virginia Magazine of History and Biog-raphy,* LVIII (1958), 432–47; Curtis C. Davis, *Chronicler of the Cava-liers: A Life of the Virginia Novelist Dr. Caruthers* (Richmond, Va., 1953), *passim;* and Ollinger Crenshaw, *General Lee's College: The Rise and Growth of Washington and Lee University* (New York, 1969), 74–75.

13. William C. Preston, *Reminiscences,* ed. Minnie C. Yarborough (Chapel Hill, 1933). Preston was later a South Carolina state governor, U.S. Senator, and university president.

266 % Literature and Society in Early Virginia

Hanover county Presbyterian minister Samuel Davies produced verses still at least occasionally remembered. Davies described the French-Indian barbarities in the 1750s; the two Britishers wrote of the mountains themselves, Harper's Ferry, the Potomac, or the Natural Bridge. John Kearsley Mitchell, Poe's friend and physician in Philadelphia and the father of a major novelist who was also an early psychiatrist, wrote fairly good verses on "My Native Vale" (he was born in Shepherdstown). Janney's verses on "Jefferson's Rock" at Harper's Ferry are almost a paraphrase of the Jefferson *Notes:*

> From this huge rock o'er the adjacent lands,
>   How grand the scenes that round us rise to view;
> So vast the prospect hence the eye commands,
>   The name of Jefferson is justly due.
> While on the south the Shenandoah laves,
>   The mountain's base, o'erhung with tufted woods
> Down from the west, Potomac's rolling waves
>   Impetuous rush to meet their kindred floods.

But the rollicking verses of St. Leger Landon Carter on "The Girl of Harper's Ferry" are quite different.

> Ah! tell me not of the heights sublime
>   The rocks of Harper's Ferry
> Of mountains rent in the lapse of time—
>   They're very sublime—oh very!
> I'm thinking more of the glowing cheek
>   Of a lovely girl and merry,
> Who climb'd with me to yon highest peak—
>   The girl of Harper's Ferry![14]

14. See also Andrew Burnaby's description of Valley and river in his *Juvenile Poems* (London, 1790), Elegy 7, pp. 14–15 (composed 1759–60); Samuel Janney used Valley subjects in several of *The Last of the Lenapé and Other Poems* (Philadelphia, 1839), 72–76; Conrad Speece had a poem printed in F. V. N. Painter (ed.), *Poets of Virginia* (Richmond, 1907), 95; Hiram Haines published his verse in *Mountain Buds and Blossoms, Wove in a Rustic Garland* (Petersburg, Va., 1825), 47 ff.;

The Natural Bridge, which as a geological marvel appealed to early nineteenth-century Americans as much as the Grand Canyon has appealed to us in our century, was a major subject for writers of many kinds. Francis Gilmer's scientific essay; Chastellux's quasiscientific interpretation; Ruffner's full-chapter prose description in his *Judith Bensaddi;* and the verses of Yale graduate Virginian William Maxwell, historian Samuel Kercheval (in hymn form in 1816 and 1836), and British pedagogue-novelist John Davis are all worth noting. Davis' verses, which seem the best of the poetry, were printed first in the Philadelphia *Port-Folio* and then in a volume with his epic *The American Mariners* (1822). The first and last stanzas of the epic show his kinship in period, imagery, and general aesthetics with Philip Freneau, and afford a faint reflection of at least two of Poe's poems, but the themes of corroding time and red Indian primitivism are treated with a certain individuality:

> When Fancy left her native skies
>   To visit earth, before unseen,
> She bad the swelling fabric rise
>   In this sequester'd, sylvan scene.
>
> . . . .
>
> And here, perhaps, the Indian stood,
>   With hands upheld, and eye amaz'd
> As, sudden, from the devious wood,
>   He first upon the fabric gazed.
>
> See Tadmor's domes, and halls of state,
>   In undistinguished ruin lie;
> See Rome's proud columns yield to fate

John Kearsley Mitchell's verses were published as *Indecision: A Tale of the Far West, and Other Poems* (Philadelphia, 1839), 208 ff.; St. Leger Carter's as *Nugae, by Nugator, or, Pieces in Prose and Verse* (Baltimore, 1844), 63–64. Among other celebrants of the Valley in verse or prose before 1840 are the Duke of Saxe-Weimar, and George Tucker (see below).

268 ※ *Literature and Society in Early Virginia*

And claim the pensive pilgrim's sigh.
But while consuming Time impairs
The monuments of human art,
This pile unfading grandeur wears,
Eternal in its every part.[15]

Two other kinds of Valley verse are quite different. The native ballad, as opposed to the traditional British product surviving also in the Valley, is probably best represented in the stanzas on Joe Clark, an early resident of Rockbridge County whose fame has spread at least as far as Oklahoma. Of the innumerable verses on his attributes, one or two will probably be sufficiently indicative:

Old Joe Clark set out to preach.
He preached all over the plain
The highest text he ever took
Was high, low, Jack, and game.

or

Old Joe Clark had a mule
His name was Morgan Brown
Every tooth in that mule's head
Was sixteen inches round.[16]

At the other extreme in grandiloquent dignity is Daniel Bryan's *The Mountain Muse: Comprising the Adventures of Daniel Boone,* published in 1813 in Harrisonburg by a relative of the immortal pioneer. It is no worse, and sometimes better, than Joel Barlow's more celebrated American epic of a few years before, *The Columbiad.* Boone never becomes a real or even a genuinely heroic figure, but there are interesting ideas and idealism. Bryan indicates in this heroic poem

---

15. For a discussion of this and other works, see Davis, *Intellectual Life.*

16. See B. A. Botkin, *A Treasury of American Folklore* (New York, 1944), 814–18.

of the New West his own enormous interest in education and
contemporary philosophical and aesthetic theory:

> To Locke and Reid they gave the ingenious skill
> T'unfold the labyrinthian web of mind;
> To teach us how the variegated weft
> In different parts, peculiar tints assumes;
> How light runs into shade, and shade to light
> Until in mingled hues, the changeful whole
> A beauteous intellectual landscape forms.[17]

In another poem bound with *The Mountain Muse,* Bryan
makes a versified plea for the desirability of female education
(he is more specific on the subject in prose). He almost uses
the term "co-ed":

> Shall not Virginia's lovely Daughters share
> Coequal fame with Freedom's worthiest Fair?
> They shall. . . .

The laureate of actual life in the Shenandoah was Poe's
friend Philip Pendleton Cooke of the Winchester region, the
brother of a later novelist. Cooke, who died young, was a
gifted prose fictionist as well as lyricist, and an active, out-
door-loving, hunting and riding son of his native clime.
Among his better and more characteristic poems is "Life in
the Autumn Woods." Two stanzas suggest this character-
istically southern subject and mood,

> Summer has gone!
> And fruitful autumn has advanced so far,
> That there is warmth not heat in the broad sun
> And you may look with steadfast gaze upon
> The ardours of his car;

17. Daniel Bryan, *The Mountain Muse: Comprising the Adventures of
Daniel Boone* (Harrisonburg, Virginia, 1813), Book I, ll. 87–93, 197.

> The stealthy frosts, whom his spent looks embolden,
>   Are making the green leaves golden.
>
> . . . .
>
>   I love the woods
> In this best season of the liberal year;
> I love to haunt their whispering solitudes,
> And give myself to melancholy moods,
>   With no intruder near;
> And find strange lessons, as I sit and ponder,
>   In every natural wonder.

All this is prelude for his descriptions of the delights of various kinds of hunting. Cooke was a meditative hedonist.

The best verse of the period is probably a lyric embedded in a novel by Dr. Henry Ruffner of Washington College. The haunting refrain of "Sally of the Valley" is suggestive of the Graveyard School and of Poe; according to the author, it was based on a ballad:

> Once I wandered through a valley,
>   Where waters flow;
> There I saw the lovely Sally;
>   'Long time ago.'

and in conclusion:

> By the rock beneath the mountain,—
>   Saw willow grow
> O'er a grave beside the fountain,
>   'Long time ago.'[18]

But the Valley novel, in content or theme and usually in authorship, is the most significant literary form produced in the period. Of the nine major examples, one is anonymous; another is of obscure authorship; two each were written by three well-known inhabitants of the Shenandoah region or

18. Henry Ruffner, *Judith Bensaddi, Southern Literary Messenger,* V (October, 1839) 481.

frequent visitors there; and the ninth was by a major Virginia intellectual who had merely observed the region for a time. The anonymous *Tales of an American Landlord* (1824), reminiscent of Sir Walter Scott, has some Valley character types and scenes, as does Miss A. M. Lorraine's *Donald Adair: A Novel By a Young Lady of Virginia* (1828), though the latter goes back to 1753 for its setting and action. The Reverend Dr. Henry Ruffner's double novel, *Judith Bensaddi* (1828 and 1839), and its sequel *Seclusaval* (1839) appeared only in periodical form[19] and both have more or less international and interracial themes, but the Valley is everywhere in them, from the narrator-hero's home town of Lexington to his finally acquired estate of "Seclusaval." Descriptions of the Natural Bridge, House Mountain, and other rugged scenery occupy whole chapters. The story deserves reprinting for itself and for this abundant local color. For the author-narrator, the Great Valley is "the loveliest land on the face of the earth" to which he can and does come home again, unlike Thomas Wolfe.

The other two pairs of novels are better known, and all four appeared in book form. Marylander John Pendleton Kennedy, congressman and secretary of the navy, had many kinsmen in the Valley and spent much of his time there. In his 1832 *Swallow Barn,* a loosely unified series of scenes in Tidewater Virginia, he borrowed from his Valley experiences in describing the low-country Virginia mansion, modeled his hero Frank Meriwether on a Valley Pendleton uncle, and introduced a German Valley type in the character Hafen

19. *Judith Bensaddi* appeared in abbreviated form in the Philadelphia *Souvenir* of 1820; the later enlarged tale and its sequel were run in the *Southern Literary Messenger,* V (October, 1839). See Curtis C. Davis, "*Judith Bensaddi* and the Reverend Doctor Henry Ruffner," *Publications of the American Jewish Historical Society,* XXXIX (December, 1949), Pt. 2, pp. 115–42. Ruffner's story is said to be based on fact.

Blok. In the 1835 *Horse-Shoe Robinson,* a tale of the Revolution, Kennedy wrote a better story with more complex characters. Most of the action, including the Battle of Lookout Mountain, took place farther south, but the "Dove Cote" plantation, the "South Garden in western Virginia," and the Blue Ridge, which form the background-setting again and again, are clearly Valley-derived.

The Shenandoah Valley's native son William Alexander Caruthers (1802–1846) has in recent years had all three of his major works reprinted, and was the subject two decades ago of an excellent biography.[20] Lexington-born, educated at Washington College and the University of Pennsylvania, Caruthers divided his adult life and medical practice between Lexington and Savannah, Georgia, his wife's home. His first novel, *The Kentuckian in New York. Or, the Adventures of Three Southerners* appeared in 1834.[21] The Kentuckian, a sort of blue-grass Horse-Shoe Robinson, is well-drawn and amusing enough in both speech and manners. But much of the regional scene, which is more the upper Valley than it is New York, is created around the three young southern gentlemen, one a Virginian named Beverly Randolph, who furnish the action and love-plots of the novel. A graphic description of Harper's Ferry, the economic question of slave labor in the Valley (here the Virginians are antislavery), and the enduring mountains are themes and setting. Already Caruthers shows himself an intensely patriotic Virginian pondering (like his contemporary William Wirt) her declining place in the American scene. In doing so he distinguishes the state's major regions: "Poor, exhausted, eastern Virginia! she is in

20. Curtis C. Davis, *Chronicler of the Cavaliers.*
21. William Alexander Caruthers, *The Kentuckian in New York. Or, the Adventures of Three Southerners* (2 vols.; New York, 1834). See Curtis C. Davis, *Chronicler of the Cavaliers,* Chapter VI.

her dotage. . . . but with all her weakness, with all the imbecilities of premature age upon her, I love her still." (II, 194).

Caruthers' second novel[22] had nothing to do with the Valley, but his third, last, and best, published in magazine form and then as a book by an obscure Alabama printer, is in a sense entirely about the Valley—the *Knights of the Golden Horse-Shoe: A Traditionary Tale of the Cocked-Hat Gentry*.[23] The subject is colonial Governor Spotswood's first great expedition to reconnoiter, or discover, the Valley of Virginia, and the chivalric order mentioned above. A good many liberties are taken with the facts of history, but despite a conventional sentimental plot Spotswood emerges as a great and patriotic figure, with a vision of what the West would become in the development of English America.

The blue peaks loom high, and the Governor's rhetoric is rotund, yet even now rather impressive: "I ardently desire to see before I die, the western half of this great glorious, and gigantic picture—In the language of our red brethren, I long to travel toward the setting sun . . ." The great project is initiated, and Caruthers brings the leaders to their first view of the Shenandoah Valley as he himself may first have looked *down* upon it—*by moonlight*. After an arduous climb the little band reaches a prominence which affords a view:

It was a bleak and barren spot, made up wholly of huge fragments of rock, piled up one upon another, as if in some far remote

22. William Alexander Caruthers, *The Cavaliers of Virginia: Or the Recluse of Jamestown* (New York, 1835).

23. William Alexander Caruthers, *Knights of the Golden Horse-Shoe: A Traditionary Tale of the Cocked-Hat Gentry*, ed. Curtis C. Davis (Chapel Hill, 1970). The book was originally published in the *Magnolia: Or Southern Monthly* in 1841, and in book form by a man named Yancey in Wetumpka, Alabama. The title sometimes omits the word "Golden."

age, they had been cast thus by a violent convulsion of nature. It was fortunate, however, that it was thus barren of vegetation, for what an uninterrupted view it gave of what has since been called the Valley of Virginia! . . . The vale beneath looked like a great sea of vegetation in the moon-light, rising and falling in undulating and picturesque lines, as far as the eye could read towards the north-east and south-west; but their vision was interrupted on the opposite side by the Alleghenies. . . . There lay the valley of Virginia, that garden spot of the earth, in its first freshness and purity, as it came from the hands of its maker. . . .[24]

So much for sublimity, romantic tradition, and a view of an American promised land as a native son imagined it must have been when the first white man looked upon it! Any of us who have climbed a peak on either side and looked into the now cultivated floor of the Valley must still gain much of the effect Caruthers imagines for his explorer.

The last novel to be considered even bears the title *The Valley of Shenandoah* and appeared in 1824. Its author, George Tucker, was later a University of Virginia professor in five areas, including literature and economics; he had already been a congressman, essayist, and poet, and was to live to achieve eminence in half a dozen other fields. In the Valley he had been merely a visitor. Though he wrote another novel Poe may have employed as a model for two short stories, it is *The Valley of Shenandoah* which has been more frequently evaluated and has been reprinted within the past few months. The sentimentality is here in spots, but the book also anticipates *Swallow Barn* in characters and setting as a plantation novel—up to a certain point. It is much more a problem piece than any earlier discussed, for Tucker faces squarely the problems of an obviously decaying Virginia, in economy and in character. It is also a panoramic picture of

24. Caruthers, *Knights*, 122, 229.

Virginia life in all its levels of society—especially as represented in the Valley—and in three of its major geographic and cultural regions. Even the principal families with whom Tucker sympathizes have like most eastern or English-descended Virginians, "always been remarkable for spending their incomes before they made them, and for rating them very extravagantly."[25] He seems prejudiced against Valley Germans and in favor of Valley Scotch-Irish, and finds the two elements exact opposites in everything. Though he sees the Germans as thrifty and moral, they are but "the dray-horses of society." The more mettlesome Scotch-Irish, though often inclined to be improvident and drunken, have the courage, imagination, and endurance to build the new empire in the West. As we have seen, he was simply ignorant of the remarkable German culture of certain towns of the upper Valley.

Though the story moves all about Virginia and even to New York, it centers in the Valley, from Chapter I's description of the mansion of the Graysons on the banks of the Shenandoah. In other pages he describes typical Northern Neck or extreme eastern Tidewater mansions, but in "Beachwood," anyone who has visited the region will recognize the Shenandoah architecture and its peculiar appropriateness in its surroundings (much the same quotation appears in XI above):

The house itself was a modest mansion of rough blue limestone, in the form of the letter L, having three rooms on one floor. Below, were a passage, drawing-room, dining room, chamber, and a large closet which had been used as a dressing room. . . . [so on with terraced gardens and limestone springs]. . . . But the most beautiful part of the view was the river, presenting always

25. George Tucker, *The Valley of Shenandoah* (Chapel Hill, 1970), I, 119.

to the eye, except after a heavy rain, a smooth surface and a limpid stream when near and a broad sheet or mirror when seen at
a distance, in which the mountains, with its woods all crimson
and gold; its jutting cliffs and patches of cleared land, were doubled to the eye, and inverted in their position.[26]

Slavery, court scenes, agricultural economy are realistically
presented. Tucker concludes the novel by referring to "this
true but melancholy history . . . [of what] prevailed [a few
years ago] in Virginia and especially in that part of it called
the Valley of Shenandoah."[27] All the real tragedy, even the
murder and seduction, is directly or indirectly the result of
the mismanagement by Virginians of their naturally productive estates—of their carelessness and over-optimism in
money matters. Here in part is Tucker the economist speaking, but he does not preach or lecture—he demonstrates. If
one agrees with Hawthorne that the novel (as opposed to the
romance) is a form of composition "presumed to aim at a very
minute fidelity not merely to the possible, but to the probable
and ordinary course of man's experience," *The Valley of
Shenandoah* may be, as a recent editor points out, one of the
very few *novels* written in the South in the nineteenth century. And today we look back on this intense presentation of
the Valley of Virginia as a southern, or perhaps frontier,
microcosm as a most significant work.

Thus in the age of James Madison, from 1800 to 1840, the
Great Valley was the scene and subject of writing of many
kinds. Undoubtedly its physical features were a major attraction. That they have not been entirely superseded in the
twentieth century by the more rugged beauties of the Great
West is borne out by Lowell Thomas, the famed radio news
announcer and world traveler of a generation ago, who, when

26. *Ibid.*, 17.   27. *Ibid.*, II, 320.

describing the land between the two great mountain ranges, called it "the American vale of Kashmir,"[28] to be appreciated fully only by him who has seen it. In the earlier nineteenth century scores of writers attempted to give to men outside some idea of the spirit and form of the region. Their best work stands with the genuine literature of America.

28. As reported to me personally in 1935–36 by a Valley newspaper editor who had entertained Thomas when he visited the Valley.

Homer in Homespun:
A Southern Iliad

[William Munford's blank-verse translation of Homer is the
last literary expression we shall consider of a characteristic
Virginia quality first evident in George Sandys in 1621–1625
—a love of the Greek and Latin classics and an ability to use
and enjoy them in many ways. Munford and Sandys also
represent another southern and Virginia tradition, the combination of legal training and practice with literary creativity.
For both Sandys' Ovid and Munford's Homer are creative
translations in that the verse ranges beyond mechanical word-
for-word rephrasing in English.

As Sandys snatched time from night and repose at Jamestown in order to complete his translation in heroic couplets,
Munford employed his routine hours of attendance as official
reporter for the Virginia Supreme Court of Appeals in translating his author into blank verse. Unlike Sandys, Munford
had a large family to support, and his literary labor was spread
out over most of a lifetime of earning his bread and butter as
a legal specialist.

Love for and knowledge of the classics was by no means an
exclusive property of early Virginia among the American
provinces. But as Richard M. Gummere has shown in two
recent books (*The American Colonial Mind and the Classical
Tradition* [1963] and *Seven Wise Men of Colonial America*
[1967]), a remarkable number of major minds of the early

Old Dominion wrote, studied, and expressed themselves in classical terms and classical precedent. Munford enjoyed classical verse and, realizing that a knowledge of Greek and Latin was declining, decided to render at least the spirit of the ancient poetry in the language of his own time and in what is still the most impressive of English meters.]

IN 1846 THE regional complacency of northern literary critics was somewhat disturbed. From out of the South, much to their surprise, came a translation of Homer! The very attempt seemed something new for America. The quality of the poetry and the accuracy of the scholarship, however, induced or compelled favorable comment, and the New England journalists were as generous as the southern.

The publication was most unusual. The work was a complete translation of the *Iliad,* and the author was a Virginian and a Richmonder. The very magnitude of the mental labor thus displayed was out of the ordinary, but the circumstances of publication were stranger still; for the translator, William Munford, had been dead for twenty-one years when this first edition appeared.[1]

Despite all this the reviewer in the *Southern Literary Messenger* took its appearance quite calmly. Though he had been a personal friend of Munford's and had known of this translation for at least thirty years, his equanimity is not thus to be explained. Like other educated southerners, he understood that such a book was a somewhat extended, though not extraordinary, product of a classic tradition as old as the South itself. He knew that from the early seventeenth century to his own day the planter had been as vitally interested in Greek and Latin as in politics, and had spent more time with the latter partly because it was more lucrative.

1. A part of this translation was published in September, 1835.

Today, when the knowledge of the sectional backgrounds of America is common to us all, the classic quality in the literary life of the *antebellum* South is entirely familiar. In the main, of course, classicism was a way of thinking and talking. In writing it usually appeared, if at all, in the form of pseudo-Addisonian essays or jocular epigrams.

There was, however, a relatively purer classicism dealing more directly with the glories of Athens and Rome. Frequently it was marked by attempts to translate or adapt the ancients into good English verse or prose. And since it was an offshoot of the general attitude of the planter who liked to imagine himself a scholar as well as a gentleman, the attempt at translation is fairly persistent. Brief or long, semiserious or grave, these exercises became a minor tradition.

Particularly may this be said of Virginia, where the precedent was established by one of the Jamestown colonists, George Sandys. Exceptional in quality and design as his magnificent work is, it is indicative of the enduring affection for the classics. A century later William Byrd read and imitated his Homer and Horace. In later generations Thomas Jefferson and particularly William Wirt, in the most peaceful or troubled of times, would quote the Latin or Greek, or translate, or parody, in any company or in any circumstance. Wirt, for example, sent the Supreme Court of Appeals of Virginia into gales of laughter by his punning Latin quatrain of the lawyer George Hay on the horns of a dilemma, and brought it back to admiring silence in his long sonorous and rolling hexameters from the *Æneid*. And others might be picked at random who were even more intensely interested in translation itself.

When the two English scholars, George Long and Thomas Hewett Key, subsequently recognized as among the major classicists of the nineteenth century, came as members of the first faculty of the University of Virginia, they found in such gentlemen as Thomas Mann Randolph and Francis Walker Gilmer[2] amateurs who possessed what was to them an amazing knowledge of both Greek and Latin. In fact, it was in great part the amazing erudition Gilmer had displayed in England which induced the two Cambridge fellows to venture into the unknown America.

Thus the reviewer—and Virginians generally—accepted Munford's blank verse translation with considerable interest and no surprise. Munford was simply a fellow citizen who had turned his tastes and his learning to more account, and had shown more energy, than was usual. The interest was the same they would have given any other writer who showed talent or originality. His learning was more or less taken for granted.

Since Munford's life affords as good an illustration as his work of the educated Virginian's attitude toward literature and the classics, the two should be considered jointly. Like so many of his contemporaries, he was trained for the law and gave the major portion of his time to his profession. His time spent with literature must have been stolen from his leisure hours as Sandys' had been, for the very quantity of his accomplishment is no small one.

The only son of the dramatist Colonel Robert Munford, William received his education in the Grammar School and College of William and Mary. Impoverished by his father's early death, the boy was able to complete his education through the kindness of George Wythe, then a professor at the college. From Wythe, as Munford shows in his letters, he gained an abiding love of the classics as well as a genuine

2. See R. B. Davis, *Francis Walker Gilmer: Life and Learning in Jefferson's Virginia* (Richmond, Va., 1939).

understanding of the law. He lived in the house of the great jurist, and was so closely connected with the Wythe family that in later years he was requested by the governor of the state to compose the official eulogy on the death of his mentor.

At the age of twenty-one Munford completed his legal training, and almost immediately entered politics. By 1797 he was representing his native county of Mecklenburg in the legislature, and in 1802 he was elected to the state senate. In the latter year he made an enduring place for himself in the history of representative government by addressing a circular letter to his constituents urging the extension of the franchise to all white freemen. Only the accomplishment of his aim ended the agitation thus begun.

In 1806 he became a member of the Virginia Council of State and thereafter made his home in Richmond. During the last sixteen years of his life (1809–1825) he served as Clerk of the House of Delegates. First with Hening, and then alone, he reported the decisions of the Supreme Court of Appeals. A faithful and active Episcopalian, he served for many years as an official of the Diocese of Virginia.

One of the reviewers of the Homer summarized the translator's life thus: "the scholar and poet subsided into a professional drudge; and a name, which seemed destined to stand high among the literary men of Virginia, is now known to the reading public only as it stands in the title page of ten volumes of the Judgments of the Court of Appeals."

It is hard to believe, however, that Munford saw this implied tragedy or even considerable drudgery in the situation, for he gave every indication that he loved the law. During his whole life the two interests existed side by side with little evidence of conflict.

In 1798, while serving his first term in the legislature, Munford published *Poems and Compositions in Prose on*

Several Occasions, with the modest line *Not free from faults, nor yet too vain to mend,* beneath the title. The author confessed in his preface that some of the contents were written as early as his sixteenth year. He published them for three reasons: that they might afford entertainment and improvement; that they might procure some reputation for the writer; and that they might fill his not overburdened purse.

The subjects of the *juvenilia* throw light on the tastes of both author and age. *Gen. St. Clair's Defeat,* three *Odes* of Horace translated, five selections from *Ossian* versified, *An Elegy on the Death of Mrs. Cocke,* and a blank-verse tragedy of *Almoran and Hamet* are typical. The ballad stanza of *Chevy Chase,* the heroic couplet, and alternate rhyme of varying measures are the principal forms employed. The quality of imagery and language is unexceptional, and of course highly derivative. There is external evidence that Munford did not himself take this work very seriously.

Though by the time this little book was published its author was immersed in the duties of his profession, he kept open two outlets for his literary energies. Both became as natural a part of his daily life as dining or reporting.

In fact, the first of them was frequently a part of his dining. He proved his kinship with earlier and contemporary Virginia gentlemen, and with the later John Banister Tabb, by his love of issuing or accepting social invitations in doggerel or epigrammatic verse. He was also a prolific coiner of English or Latin epigrams for his own court speeches or for memorial uses, such as one inscribed on a tablet in the courthouse in Mecklenburg.

For thirty or more years, however, the steady occupation of his leisure hours was the translation of Homer. Whenever the Supreme Court of Appeals or the legislature was not in session, even at times when they were, he rendered his poet's lines into English. Much of his work he repeated aloud to test the rhythm. His son George Wythe Munford many years later told an amusing story of the Negro house boy "Beverley" who was discovered repeating with sonorous emphasis some of the lines he had just heard his master composing—

"No man can send me hence
To Pluto's hall before the appointed time;
And surely none of all the human race,
Base or e'en brave, has ever shunn'd his fate."

And Munford's appointed time came, strangely enough, a month or two after he had completed his translation and written his preface. Though two decades passed before publication, the preface is almost as valuable as the poem, for in it he explained his aims in translation, an explanation exhibiting sound judgment and some critical acumen.

His first sentence, stating simply that he undertook the task because of his admiration for the "unparalleled beauty and sublimity of the original," may be taken at face value. In rendering the epic into English he endeavored throughout to avoid affectation, to shun the obscure and obsolete, and to resort as seldom as possible to Greek or Latin idiom. He attempted to follow Homer's flights without swelling into bombast, and to render the plainer passages with simple dignity.

"My opinion of the duty of a translator," Munford explains, "is that he ought uniformly to express the meaning and spirit of his author with fidelity, in such language as is sanctioned by the use of the best writers and speakers of his own time and country; not to render word for word, with servile accuracy, especially in cases where, from diversity of idioms, the effect would be awkward and unpleasant. . . ."

Munford scrupulously avoided Elizabethan archaisms. Blank verse was employed because he considered it best suited to Homer's fancy and passion; he denied imitation of Milton or any other writer. His aims were simplicity and fidelity: "Pope has equipped him (Homer) in the fashionable garb of a modern fine gentleman; Cowper displays him, like his own Ulysses, in 'rags unseemly,' or in the uncouth garb of a savage. Surely, then, there is room for an effort to introduce him to the acquaintance of my countrymen in the simple yet graceful and venerable garb of his own heroic times."

In the same month of July, 1846, in which the *Southern Literary Messenger* criticized Munford's work, two other extended reviews appeared. Both were favorable, and each was typical of scholarly attitudes in the place of its authorship. Professor C. C. Felton of Harvard, writing in the *North American Review,* expressed the mixture of surprise and pleasure mentioned at the beginning of this article. George F. Holmes in the Charleston *Southern Quarterly Review* adopted a bristling Southern patriotic attitude and awarded the translation perhaps more superlatives than it deserves. All in all, the *Messenger* criticism is the best balanced of the three, though the magazine was published in Munford's own city and the reviewer, Edward W. Johnston, was the translator's friend. He pointed out excellencies and defects wherever he felt that they existed, and he found many of the former and several of the latter.

Undoubtedly there are many passages of real beauty in Munford. His figures, though somewhat derivative, are pleasing: Greece, "the land of lovely dames," or "loud-sounding Ocean's stormy waves." His lines in Book VI, 626 ff., describing the farewell of Hector to his son, are frequently pointed out as a product of true poetic inspiration. In them Munford shows deeper feeling than Pope or Cowper, and a clarity of expression certainly lacking in the latter.

His "lists" of chieftains, ships, or deities are rendered pleasingly, and many of his descriptions compare favorably with those of Chapman and Pope, as his lines (I, 616–626):

> and when the sun
> Descended to the sea, and darkness came
> They, near the cables of their vessel, slept.
> Soon as the rosy-finger'd queen appear'd,
> Aurora, lovely daughter of the dawn,
> Towards the camp of Greece they took their way
> And friendly Phœbus gave propitious gales.
> They rais'd the mast, and stretch'd the snowy sheet
> To catch the breeze which filled the swelling sail.
> Around the keel the darken'd waters roar,
> As swift the vessel flies . . .

Even the rendering into English of the father of poets, the literary labor of a lifetime, had not been taken too seriously, however, by this simple Virginia gentleman. For this *Iliad* was more of a love than a labor, more of a recreation than a task. And because of this the reader may feel through all the length of the poem something of Munford's own delight in the men and the gods who had fought far on the ringing plains of windy Troy.

⌒⟨XIV⟩⌒

The Early American Lawyer and the Profession of Letters

[This essay is concerned with three of the best minds of the first national period—men representing Massachusetts, South Carolina, and Virginia—and it shows, perhaps incidentally, why New England got a head start on the South in producing belletristic literature. Economic considerations played a part in this imbalance, as well as differing conceptions of the legal profession as a means to eminence and to art. Ticknor gave up the law, partly because he could afford to do so financially, and partly because Boston was ready to encourage purely professional men of letters as Charleston and Richmond were not.

Legaré and Gilmer were realists; both wanted to write, but they were frank in admitting that they could not devote themselves wholly to the art. Also they saw in the law something Ticknor did not—perhaps a rationalization—that legal practice in a Ciceronian sense might be an art. Both southerners possessed literary abilities, as their scant publications bear witness. But they were personally ambitious for eminence in their society, and they saw the law as the way to that eminence.

Southerners were not the only Americans to combine literature and law, or to subordinate the former to the latter. The intellectual climate of their region and their era probably directed this decision. Yet they and other young southern lawyers did produce belletristic literature, of which historians are just now becoming conscious.]

THOMAS JEFFERSON, writing as late as 1825 to a member of Parliament, observed:[1] "Literature is not yet a distinct profession with us. Now and then a strong mind arises, and at its intervals of leisure from business, emits a flash of light. But the first object of young societies is bread and covering; science[2] is but secondary and subsequent." William Wirt, whom Jefferson probably considered one of these strong minds, had nearly a quarter of a century earlier indicated[3] his own and the general conception of the proper outlet for superior ability: "Men of talents in this country . . . have been generally bred to the profession of law; and indeed, throughout the United States, I have met with few persons of exalted intellect, whose powers have been directed to any other pursuit. The bar, in America is the road to honour. . . ." And, he might have added, to fortune.

But some years before Jefferson made his observation, many of his young countrymen—who might in another age and clime have been poets, novelists, or critics, and yet who were trained as lawyers—were beginning to question the wisdom of their choice of a career, or to weigh its advantages, or to rebel and desert the bar for the strange new realm of letters. Their course of thought and action was naturally as much a result of their regional and economic environment as of their mental bent. Their thinking on the subject affords, therefore,

1. Thomas Jefferson to the Honorable J. Evelyn Denison, M.P., November 9, 1825, in H. A. Washington (ed.), *The Writings of Thomas Jefferson* (9 vols., Washington, D.C., 1854), VII, 418.
2. The word *science* is used here, of course, as Jefferson and his contemporaries usually employed it, to mean *knowledge*.
3. William Wirt, *Letters of the British Spy* (10th ed.; New York, 1832), "Letter VIII," 206.

a key to the whole situation of intellectual endeavor in the first quarter of the nineteenth century in America. It also provides a significant commentary on and anticipation of the reasons why, in the next generation or two, a Longfellow[4] or a Henry James, Jr., in the North could turn decisively from law to letters, while a John Pendleton Kennedy,[5] or even the later John Esten Cooke or Thomas Nelson Page, in the South, never would or could entirely relinquish the legal profession.

In a consideration of this matter, three young lawyers of the year 1815, personal friends, represent their respective states and regions most effectively. George Ticknor, born in 1791 of a wealthy and learned Boston family, had by 1815 practiced law for a brief period quite successfully.[6] Francis Walker Gilmer, born in 1790 as the youngest son of Jefferson's friend and neighbor Dr. George Gilmer, had in 1815 recently completed a four-year legal apprenticeship[7] under William Wirt and was just beginning to distinguish himself. Hugh Swinton Legaré of Charleston, born in 1797, had been graduated in 1814 at the head of his class at the South Carolina College and was in 1815 making up his mind as to what profession he should pursue.[8]

The three had become acquainted in various ways. In

4. Longfellow, of course, never did more than consider the law (though he considered it quite seriously) as the obvious means of making a living.

5. See Vernon L. Parrington, *The Romantic Revolution in America,* Vol. II of *Main Currents in American Thought* (New York, 1927–30), 56, on Kennedy: "He was a man of letters rather than a lawyer, and if he had eschewed politics and law and stuck to his pen our literature would have been greatly in his debt. Few Americans of his day were so generously gifted."

6. George S. Hillard et al., *Life, Letters, and Journals of George Ticknor* (2 vols., Boston, 1876), I, 22–23.

7. R. B. Davis, *Francis Walker Gilmer: Life and Learning in Jefferson's Virginia* (Richmond, 1939), 75–92.

8. Linda Rhea, *Hugh Swinton Legaré: A Charleston Intellectual* (Chapel Hill, 1934), 42–44.

January, 1815, Ticknor, making a tour "at the South" before sailing for Europe, was being entertained in Philadelphia.[9] At the same time Gilmer, with letters of introduction from Jefferson, and accompanied by his friend the Abbé Joseph Corréa da Serra, Portuguese minister to the United States, was also being introduced to Philadelphia society, literary and otherwise.[10] As Ticknor shows in his letters,[11] the two spent many hours together. When Ticknor returned to Massachusetts, in enclosing some notes on Virginia provincialisms to John Pickering, he observed[12] that they were assembled by "the most intelligent *young* man, I saw during an absence of three months at the South."

Later in 1815 Gilmer, again with the Abbé Corréa, made a long botanical excursion[13] into Georgia and South Carolina. In Charleston, according to a notebook he kept during the journey, he met several young men interested in intellectual

9. Hillard, *Ticknor*, I, 16–17.

10. R. B. Davis, *Gilmer*, 78–81. For Jefferson's letter to Gilmer concerning the proposed journey, see R. B. Davis (ed.), *Correspondence of Thomas Jefferson and Francis Walker Gilmer, 1814–1826* (Columbia, S.C., 1946), 33. Jefferson wrote a letter of introduction to Dr. Caspar Wistar. Among other interesting and valuable acquaintances Gilmer made during this journey were John Vaughan, secretary of the American Philosophical Society, and a fellow Virginian John Randolph of Roanoke. Gilmer kept up a correspondence with both these men for some years.

11. *E.g.*, George Ticknor to Francis Walker Gilmer, May 31, 1816, in William P. Trent, *English Culture in Virginia* (Baltimore, 1889), 133.

12. See Allen Walker Read, "The Collections for Pickering's 'Vocabulary,'" *American Speech* XXII (1947), 280–82. Professor Read reproduces Gilmer's enclosure, which indicates that Gilmer had promised Ticknor such a list. That Ticknor underlines *young* probably indicates that he was thinking of Gilmer, by whom he had been much more impressed (cf. Hillard, *Ticknor*, I, 34–38).

13. For accounts of this journey, see R. B. Davis, "Forgotten Scientists in Georgia and South Carolina," *Georgia Historical Quarterly*, XXVII (1943), 271–84; and R. B. Davis "An Early Virginia Scientist's Botanical Observations in the South," *Virginia Journal of Science*, III (1942), 132–39.

matters. Among them he lists Hugh S. Legaré.[14] Though both Legaré and Ticknor wrote to Gilmer several times during the 1815–1818 period, there is no indication that the South Carolinian and the New Englander knew each other until 1818–1819, when they met at the University of Edinburgh.[15] Thereafter they were warm friends. Gilmer died prematurely in 1826. Legaré died in Ticknor's arms in Boston in 1843. Ticknor lived on until 1871.

The three are representative of the finest intellectual attainments of their generation. Ticknor's distinguished career as critic, scholar, and teacher needs no commentary. Gilmer, called by Jefferson "the best educated subject we have raised since the Revolution,"[16] was elected first professor of law at the University of Virginia and was sent by Jefferson to England in 1824 to collect the first faculty for that infant institution. Before his death at the age of thirty-six his scientific and general essays had attracted considerable attention, and he had become a very successful lawyer. Legaré, editor of the *Southern Review*, 1828–1832, and attorney general and acting secretary of state under Tyler, was one of the really well-educated men of his time.

Ticknor's decision to abandon the law for a literary and

14. The list appears in R. B. Davis, "Forgotten Scientists," 278. Gilmer lists them simply as "Young men of Charleston."

15. See Rhea, *Legaré*, 55; and Hillard, *Ticknor*, I, 278. Miss Rhea's reference (note 22) is here somewhat confusing, for it was not Ticknor but Mrs. Grant (see Hillard, *Ticknor*, I, 278) who wrote to America of William Campbell Preston and Legaré. Miss Rhea also is mistaken in the statement that "Ticknor made the mistake of saying that Preston came from Virginia." He did come from Virginia (see the *Dictionary of American Biography*, s. v., Preston, William Campbell), though he had been educated with Legaré at the South Carolina College. That Gilmer had anything to do with introducing Ticknor and Legaré to each other appears very doubtful.

16. Thomas Jefferson to Richard Rush, April 26, 1824, in R. B. Davis, *Gilmer*, 200.

scholarly career came early in his life, and apparently easily. His father was a rich man. Ticknor's biographer states[17] that the young man made his decision before he sailed for Europe in 1815, but Ticknor's letters to Gilmer indicate that the decision was not final until he had surveyed the potentialities of European scholarship. When he sailed in April he hoped[18] to see Gilmer in Europe, and he thought they might indulge their love of classical learning and at the same time prepare themselves for the profession they had both already adopted. A year later, however, Ticknor announced[19] to his friend that his own plans were definitely changed:

[I] could learn nothing of you, until day before yesterday, when your very welcome letter came to tell me all I had hoped to hear except that you had renounced your intention[20] of coming to Europe. In this respect you have changed your plans; and as you intend to be a lawyer, I rather think you have done wisely. I too have changed my plans, I have renounced the law altogether, and determined to prolong my stay in Europe, that I may do something towards making myself a scholar, and perhaps you will smile, when I add that my determining motive to this decision, of which I have long thought, was the admirable means and facilities and inducements to study offered by a German university. But however you may smile on the other side of the Atlantic, you would if you were on this, do just as I have done. My inclination is entirely and exclusively to literature—the only question with me, therefore, was, where I could best fit myself to pursue *haud passibus aequis* its future progress & improvement. . . .[21]

17. Hillard, *Ticknor*, I, 24–25.
18. Ticknor to Gilmer, April 2, 1815, in R. B. Davis, *Gilmer*, 82.
19. Ticknor to Gilmer, May 31, 1816, in Trent, *English Culture*, 131–34. Later letters of Ticknor to Gilmer appear in the same volume, 134–41. The originals are now in the Gilmer Collection, Alderman Library, University of Virginia, Charlottesville.
20. Gilmer and the Abbé Corréa had planned a mysterious, and fortune-making, journey to Europe (see Trent, *English Culture,* 38).
21. Ticknor here goes into an interesting discussion of the relative states of English, French, and German scholarship.

You may perhaps smile at all this, my dear Gilmer, and think that my reasons for spending over a year and a half in Göttingen are as bad as the revolution itself. If we live twenty years, however, & then meet one another, you will be prepared to tell me I have done right. . . .

Gilmer's opposite decision was partially an economic one, for he had to make his own living.[22] Perhaps the Southern tradition of the law as the gentleman's profession influenced him, too. At any rate, he gave some of his own reasoning in his choice to his young nephew Thomas Walker Gilmer,[23] who had himself decided to become a lawyer. Apparently Gilmer was under no illusions regarding the state of literary culture in America.

In a country where intelligence is so generally & so equally diffused, where political power is so infinitely divided and distributed, where Government goes on rather by the inherent principles of its own motion, than the accidental impulse of particular men, it would be absurd to expect a Solon or a Lychurgus [*sic*] to teach us new principles of civilization and Law. As to distinction in literature or science, the obstacles are full as great. We have neither the Libraries, nor the learned associations, nor the munificent patronage under whose genial influence the arts & learning of Europe have spread their branches over the world. . . .

Be not discouraged by these considerations. Tho' some paths of ambition be closed upon us, there are enough, & glorious ones still open. The United States have been the first country to place the restful professions above all the arts of peace or war. . . .

22. His small legacy from his father's estate had not even paid for all of his education at the College of William and Mary (see R. B. Davis, *Gilmer*, 83).

23. Gilmer to Thomas Walker Gilmer, April 8, 1817, in R. B. Davis, *Gilmer*, 105–106. It is interesting to note that Thomas Walker Gilmer served with his uncle's friend Legaré in President Tyler's cabinet (see the *Dictionary of American Biography*, s. v., Gilmer, Thomas Walker).

It is in these hitherto unpublished letters[24] written by Legaré to Gilmer, however, that one gets the most interesting and significant discussion of both Legaré's and Gilmer's ideas as to the relation of law and letters in the young republic. In them Legaré is quite clearly arguing with himself and for and against Gilmer's opinions on the subject. As a young man just entering upon his career, he shows some deference to the slightly older Gilmer, who has already won his spurs. And the letters are perhaps equally valuable in their evidence of profound classical learning and seriousness of purpose on the part of these two young southerners of the late Jeffersonian period.

What Ticknor or Gilmer or Legaré meant by "the literary life" is obviously not exactly what the next American generation meant by the expression. It is, as Legaré implies, a Ciceronian conception. It seems far from the journalistically flavored career of Poe or of the still later Bret Harte, yet both men would probably have approved of it as a concept, at least; and Poe might have said that this was precisely his ideal of the life of the man of letters. That it came from a lawyer rather than from a professional writer would have given the idea more rather than less weight in Poe's mind, for he considered that the ablest writers of his day existed among those who owed their first allegiance to the bar.[25]

Boston (Mas) 24th Aug. 1816.

Dear Gilmer:

My stay in Baltimore where I landed after my voyage from Charleston was so short that I had not time to let you know I

24. A portion of an October 1, 1816 letter has been published in R. B. Davis, *Gilmer*, 111–12. The three letters are part of the Gilmer Collection, Alderman Library, University of Virginia, Charlottesville, through whose courtesy they are reprinted here.

25. See Margaret Alterton, *The Origins of Poe's Critical Theory* (Iowa City, 1925), 46–67; and Edgar Allan Poe to F. W. Thomas, in James A. Harrison (ed.), *The Complete Works of Edgar Allan Poe* (New York, 1902), XVII, 132.

was taking a northern excursion this summer & flattered myself with the hope of seeing you in Virga on my return. As it has become very doubtful however whether I shall travel back by land or water, & if I do not see you this time, God knows when we shall meet again, I shall not make you an apology for provoking you to a few moments conversation in this way.

Since our parting[26] in South Carolina (which I need not assure you was with a great deal of regret on one side) I have had information of you thro' yr. friends[27] in that state. All accounts of you gave me the greatest satisfaction, except one which hinted of your bad health.[28] For God's sake take care of that one thing needful to all others. I speak from my own bitter experience[29] on this subject—for I have felt for some time past & am afraid will always feel the effects of my imprudence in the manner of conducting my studies. I have spent seven of the ten months which have gone by since I saw you, in the country—where I have been almost altogether cut off from all sorts of company & pleasure.

26. In his notebook of his excursion through Georgia and South Carolina in 1815, Gilmer notes that he left Charleston on November 8 (see R. B. Davis, "Forgotten Scientists," 279).

27. Gilmer lists [Robert Y.] Hayne, William Crafts, and Frederick Grimké (along with Legaré) as the "Young men of Charleston" in his notebook. He probably knew also William C. Preston, later governor and U.S. senator from South Carolina, and president of the South Carolina College. Preston was a Virginian who had been Legaré's college friend and who later made Gilmer's own native county, Albemarle, his summer home. Gilmer's friendship with James Ogilvie (see R. B. Davis, "James Ogilvie, an Early American Teacher of Rhetoric," *Quarterly Journal of Speech,* XXVII [1942], 289–97), who had many South Carolina connections, may also have aided Gilmer in making friends in the state during the 1815 tour.

28. Gilmer early showed evidences of pulmonary or other physical weaknesses (see R. B. Davis, *Gilmer,* 58, 95–96, 103).

29. See Rhea, *Legaré,* 2–4. Following an inoculation for smallpox when he was four years old, Legaré suffered "complications," and probably developed some form of infantile paralysis, with the result that for eight or nine years he scarcely grew in height. Later, his body developed powerfully above the waist but remained shrunken in its lower extremities. This illness, his biographer notes, changed his whole life; thereafter contact with outdoor life was denied him and books were his delight. Aside from this early illness, however, Legaré's biographer notes no later illness or chronic ill-health which might have handicapped him during his adult years. Legaré's feeling that he had "over-studied," at the cost of his physical health, is probably correct, however.

You know how few temptations there are to a man who is engaged in the pursuits I allude to, to leave his chamber. Certain it is, they were very scarce in the rustic neighborhood:[30] & my business at home was not active enough to prevent the maladies that sedentary habits bring on. It was by the advice of my excellent friend Dr McBride,[31] that I determined to put an end to them if possible, by this sort of relaxation and exercise. but altho' people laugh at my complaints because I look so healthy, I do not know whether I shall ever recover from ye shock I have given my constitution.

I hope, however, that no pains or afflictions will ever be a discouragement to me in the "race that is set before me." My hopes and pleasures all rest upon it & I should be forlorn were I not engaged in it—and besides, had I none of this enthusiasm for the sport itself, am I not selfish enough to aspire at the "noble palm" that has crowned your efforts?

I am very desirous of seeing you, that I may have a long conversation with you about your profession—the habits of mind it [so far?] induces, its relation to other sciences &c. &c. For I have some how or other a prejudice against it as a sort of Ishmael etc, with its hand raised against all sorts of knowledge, that are liberal & refined but happen not to fall immediately within its own dominion. Your opinion of this matter will be quite decisive with me—because it will not be, as those of the gentlemen of the gown usually are, ex parte—& as it is a case I am greatly interested in, I shall be much obliged to you for it. It is yet doubtful with me & will depend upon circumstances in a great measure accidental, whether I shall devote myself to literary or professional studies. My objection to ye one is the vulgar one of there being no market in this country, for that kind of attainments & to the other that the details of business; the quibbles of special pleading & the

30. Probably on the family plantation on John's Island, up the Ashley River, where he had been born.

31. Apparently James MacBride (1784–1817), who was graduated from Yale in 1815, and afterwards studied medicine. He practiced in Pineville and Charleston, S.C., and died of yellow fever at the age of thirty-three. He was a well-known early American botanist as well as a physician (see Howard A. Kelly, *Some American Medical Botanists* [Troy, N.Y., 1914]).

drudgery of an office, seem to be the farthest things in the world from the "immersum, infinitum &c"[32] that Tully talked of. There is, however, it must be confessed, one signal advantage that the practice of law gives above all other mental exercises—& that is, the greatest skill & dexterity in the management of the weapons of controversy. There is nobody more powerful in debate than a regularly disciplined lawyer. In that kind of warfare he is almost always an over-match even for men who are superior to him in every particular but the one I have just mentioned—He has a quickness of perception, a coup d'oeil, that the greatest men whose studies have been abstract & solitary have not—So far, ye aspect of the law is not so forbidding. But—the important question is, does he not buy this advantage at too great a price? For it is not impossible that he sacrifices to it, all the habits of a professional mind. He is so much accustomed to [torn] from the principle given, to the particular case, that he is no longer capable of those grand enquiries that are to develope principles by ye generalization of facts. Jurisprudence may be a science so complicated & extensive, that a competent knowledge of it is not to be expected by any body who is not almost exclusively devoted to it—at all events, this is the fact if he makes it a business. These & a number of other objections that do not occur to me, may be so weighty as to determine me to relinquish all ideas of ye Forum —Docte Trebati quid faciam doceas—.[33]

---

32. Legaré quotes from Cicero's *Second Oration vs. Verres,* II, iii, 149. The exact text (*The Verrine Orations,* trans. L. H. G. Greenwood [2 vols.; Cambridge, Mass., 1935]) runs *immensum atque infinitum lucrum esse factum.* The Loeb edition is used in all later Latin references in this paper. I am indebted to Professor Albert Rapp of the Department of Classical Languages of the University of Tennessee for his assistance in precisely locating many of the Latin quotations which appear below.

It is interesting to note that Legaré always quotes, or paraphrases, his Latin from memory, and that the "&c" he so often uses indicates that he takes for granted his reader's entire familiarity with the whole passage alluded to. In Gilmer, as he probably knew, he was not misplacing his confidence.

33. In this example of quoting from memory, or perhaps acting purposely, Legaré combines two passages from Horace: the first (*Serm.* 2. 1. 4.), "*Trebati, quid faciam? praescribe,*" the second (*Serm.* 2. 1. 78), "*. . . nisi quid tu, docte Trebati, dissentis.*"

I shall fix myself in a few days at Cambridge[34] where I shall spend some weeks reading French, & Latin, & continuing my study of Spanish. I shall be extremely glad to hear from you when ever you are at leisure. In the mean time

Accept the assurance of my most

Cordial esteem

Hugh S. Legaré

Philadelphia 1st Octr 1816.

I have the happiness, my dear Gilmer, of acknowledging your favour of ye 17th Ult. As it was some time since I wrote you, & I am at so great a distance from ye place I dated my last letter at, the pleasure I would at any time have derived from it was made more lively by a small portion of surprise that was mixed with it. I ought to have said "the pleasure I had in *receiving* it"—for in truth, I have read it so often that there is scarce a word on which novelty can rest & yet decies repetita &c—Nothing is wanting to my complete & perpetual happiness in the course of life I have undertaken to pursue, but that all the conversations I hold with those around me, should be full of so much wisdom, & set off with so much that is agreeable & interesting to me in the manner of communicating it, as your letter is.

I am very glad you have pursued the hint I gave you upon ye subject of professional life, so far. Your opinions with regard to the proper method of conducting the study of Law are precisely mine—such elevated & comprehensive views of ye whole field of Jurisprudence, are indispensably necessary to give the air of liberality to *your* ardor in pursuit of it, or to attach any importance to it as a branch of knowledge. It is, of course, in this light, that I have always considered its importance in the scale of human attainments—& I should be ashamed of my hesitancy in undertaking it as a business, if it proceeded from a more partial & limited acquaintance with its great, characteristic features.

Without considering myself as, by any means, the important being which your partiality has made me, I have been as deliber-

---

34. Rhea, *Legaré*, does not mention this early visit to Cambridge. Ticknor and Legaré could not have met at this time, for Ticknor was already in Europe.

ate, in embracing my pursuits in life, as if it were really a matter of consequence to the public. The last three or four years[35] of my life have been devoted to the most rigorous seclusion & study—& I have regulated my studying in such a way as to enable me to adopt any avocation I might see fit. During this short exile from society I have frequently had occasion to remark, the truth of your observation, "that a merely literary or scientific man, is an insulated being, without living cooperation," & almost without sympathy, in any of our American society. This is, indeed, a most serious disadvantage—not only because he is shut out from all pleasures but those which solitude affords him, but because where the life & vigour of competition is wanting, a solitude of this kind is able to become insufferably tedious. For my own part, I confess that I have often cast a longing & lingering look back upon those warm precincts of day which I abandoned by my seclusion—& it is only lately, that I can congratulate myself on such a singleness of view, such an exclusive & enthusiastic determination with respect to my intellectual pursuits as I have languished to experience. The sollicitations of certain prejudices that prevail in the world used to press upon me in my retirement, & even while engaged with unceasing assiduity & with what I flattered myself was a pure zeal, in the prosecution of my studies, I have felt many a violent & painful conflict of inclinations between ye desire of future eminence & that of present gratification. The hope of being one day among those "lights of ye world & demigods of fame"[36] who stamp their own characters upon that of the age & country in which they live—is to be sure, a most glorious & animating one, but how long is it to be realized? & what a faint impression does such a distant prospect make? Indeed, it requires an heroic self-command, a devotion something like that of martyrdom, for a young man in such a state of society as ours, without the spur of rivalship & competition, without any thing in the estimate generally formed of his pursuits, either to direct or to animate him, to abstain from the pleasures that are carrying away

35. This would cover some of his college years. As noticed above, he was graduated from the South Carolina College at the head of his class in 1814. He was then seventeen years of age.

36. Legaré quotes from Thomas Campbell, "The Pleasure of Hope," Pt. ii., line 316.

the hearts of all around him, to refuse the intoxicating charm of the eminence in society (however shortlived) which his talents can immediately command him, & to shut himself up in solitude for years—& all too, for the renown which it is *not impossible* he may acquire in his maturity or old age. For in the present state of the republic of Letters, no man who does not add something to ye stock of human knowledge by his researches—or finish his compositions in the highest style, can hope to be talked of at all: & the dreadful sentence 'mediocribus esse' relates nowadays as much to any other class of writers as to poets. So that it is not only the high price he has to give for literary distinction that shocks one's œconomy in this matter, but the uncertainty also of the article's being delivered after ye price is paid.

So far, I agree with you, that the probability of success in any literary or scientific pursuit in this country is, both from one's feelings—& from ye adventitious facilities that are as necessary to enthusiasm here, as a good system of tactics & ye use of military weapons are in the case of courage—is much less than at ye Bar, if you be content with what is usually called eminence at ye Bar. But if you are bent (as I am sure you are) upon filling up ye outlines of that character of a Lawyer & pleader that is omni cumulatis virtute, omnibus detractis vitiis,[37] as Cicero says of ye Orator, will you not have to encounter ye same difficulties of a solitary & unaided pursuit? All that is not merely technical & practical at ye Bar, is scientific—& in precisely as much as you approach ye character of Leibnitz, in precisely so much you leave the common pursuits of special pleaders & commit yourself—pennis non leguleio datis.[38] Here you as well as myself must struggle against ye iners pondus of our nature, that has fixed to ye ground "[So?] many a soul sublime," in motiveless apathy: & it is sure[ly] no objection that in achieving such a triumph we shall [rank?] with the pauci quibus &c &c. so far, as regards the influence which ye

37. Cicero, *De Oratore*, I, 118. The original reads: *detractis omnibus vitiis . . . atque onmi laude cumulatus.*

38. A curious reference, for *leguleius* ("shyster") seems to be used by Cicero only once (*De Oratore*, I, 236). As far as I was able to discover, only one other writer uses it, and he merely quotes it as a Ciceronian expression.

present state of society has upon the feelings of a man engaged in literary pursuits.

Your other consideration—viz—that ones usefulness is lessened is an equally important one; altho I think, that here too you over-rate active life. I see nothing to prevent a literary man from taking part in national affairs. Intellect is ripe enough by ye time we are thirty five or forty years of age, & that is the period that nature seems to have marked out for the management of the affairs alluded to. You remember what old Cato says in ye Golden treatise de Senectute about ye "juvenes Oratorculi."[39] At all events, in this republic we may revive the habits of the "old schools of Greece" —educate man, not as a technical or artificial being known only by one part of his divine nature, while he is as destitute of all the rest as tho they did not belong to him by birth—but educate him with a view to all the relations & duties of an intellectually social & active being, enlighten the mind thro' all her powers & capacities, bring him up in ye speculations of ye closet, in the details of office, in the dangers of ye camp, in the graces and ornaments of ye palaestra de cor—This is the "whole man"—this is the character which we should all aspire to maintain, & which I am afraid the *mere* scholar & ye *mere* man of business are equally distant from. What I mean by giving myself up to literature therefore, is to devote to more liberal & scientific studies the time, which in the practice of ye courts, you must give to the observance of artificial rules & the acquisition of technical knowledge. For I am far from being of those idolaters who blaspheme ye name of learning by imputing it to the pedants who feed upon the false quantities of old Greek Epigrams—& admire Homer for ye language he wrote in, instead of admiring the language because it contains the writings of Homer. This is one of those vanities that deserve a place in the Paradise of fools, in Milton.[40] Scholastic learning, like

---

39. Apparently coined by Legaré, using a perfectly permissible diminutive suffix in *oratorculi.* The words do not appear in *De Senectute,* nor has *oratorculi* been located in any Latin dictionary. Legaré may have had in mind the passage in *De Senectute,* VI, 20, in which Cato quotes a question from the poet Nacvius as to how a great state was overthrown and also the answer: *proveniebant oratores novi, stulti adolescenti* (Loeb trans.: "Through swarms of green, declaiming lads").

40. John Milton, *Paradise Lost* (London, 1897) III, 448 ff.

scholastic divinity is falling & ought to fall, more & more into neglect[.] The learning that I would aim at is that of Cicero—a learning that can be instrumental in promoting the purposes of active life, in elevating the man of business into ye sage, & the mere statement of wholesome truths, into sublime & touching eloquence—and in case there be no demand for our services in practical affairs, can embellish retirement & multiply before us the most refined & ele[va?]ted enjoyments.

But I have already indulged myself too far—particularly as I have some idea of visiting you according to your polite invitation, en passant as I go home. If I do travel by land, you may expect to *see me* in about 12 or 14 days—if I should not, I will expect to hear from you in Carolina when I get there. In ye mean time—

I remain your st &c
H. S. Legaré.

Washington 10th Oct. 1816.

Dear Gilmer

I am almost ashamed to *write* to you from Washington: & yet I think it quite superfluous to tell you that it is out of my *power* to visit Winchester. If I *could* make it convenient, [other hard?] inducements would conspire to bring me to you.

I dined yesterday at Col. Taylor's[41]—where I met a number of

41. Presumably Colonel John Taylor of Carolina (1753–1824), author of *Arator* (1813) and a Jeffersonian agrarian. I have been able to find little evidence that Taylor was living or staying in Washington at this time (he was U.S. senator in 1792–94, 1803, 1882). Colonel Taylor later (in 1817) offered Gilmer the headmastership of his cherished Rappahannock Academy (see R. B. Davis, *Gilmer*, 114). This statement may refer to another Virginian, Colonel John Tayloe of the Octagon House— see R. B. Davis, *Intellectual Life in Jefferson's Virginia 1790–1830* (Chapel Hill, 1964), 209. In January, 1817, Gilmer visited friends in Washington, and may have seen Legaré again there. The famous Washington hostess, Mrs. S. Harrison Smith, noted in her diary: "Governor Barbour (of Virginia) . . . and a daughter joined our party for the evening; Gen'l Harrison (our Western Hero) Col. Taylor, & a most agreeable man from So Carolina and several others. . . . But the one who most interested me, was *Mr. Gillmore,* a young Virginian, introduced to me by Miss Barbour. He is called the *future hope of Virginia*—its ornament!—its bright star!" in Mrs. S. Harrison Smith, *The First Forty Years of Washington Society,* ed. Gaillard Hunt (New York, 1906), 136–37.)

your countrymen. I of course, enquired after you—but none of them knew you as well as myself. They had all heard of Monsieur —but no one had talked with him—or ever seen him. One piece of information, however, I am indebted to them for—& that is, that you are the author of a pleasant little pamphlet I met in Philadelphia, entitled "Sketches of Orators."[42] Indeed, I was not surprised to hear that it was yours—for as soon as I read two pages of it, I told Ogilvie[43] (in whose hands I found it) that it bore your mark. He did not think so—but paid a tribute to the Anonymous gentleman, that you would not think the less of be-

42. *Sketches of American Orators* (Baltimore, 1816). The book is a series of vignettes about John Randolph, John Marshall, Thomas Addis Emmet, William Pinkney, Patrick Henry, Littleton W. Tazewell, William Wirt, and Henry Clay as public speakers, prefaced by a discussion of "eloquence." These incisive little studies have been recognized from the time of their appearance as among the best, if not the best, contemporary appraisals of these orators. They have been frequently quoted by such writers as W. C. Bruce, *John Randolph of Roanoke* (2 vols., New York, 1922), II, 67–97; and A. J. Beveridge, *Life of John Marshall* (4 vols.; Boston, 1916–19), II, Chap. 5). These *Sketches* were later incorporated into the posthumous volume of Gilmer's writings, *Sketches, Essays, and Translations* (Baltimore, 1828).

43. James Ogilvie (1775–1820), Scottish philosopher, orator, and friend and disciple of Godwin, had come to America in 1794. He had conducted schools in Albemarle County (where Gilmer and W. C. Rives, later minister to France while Legaré was *chargé d'affaires* in Belgium, were his pupils) and in Richmond, where he took his students to hear Burr's trial. In 1808–10 he toured the Atlantic coast, giving his "model" orations before large crowds of the curious and the cultured. In 1812–13 he had given sample orations before American troops in Kentucky and wrote Gilmer describing his phenomenal success. Early in 1815 he gave a three-month series of lectures and orations at the South Carolina College, from which Legaré had been graduated a few months before. Later, he conducted a class for girls in Legaré's city of Charleston under the sponsorship of Legaré's own law teacher Mitchell King. In 1816 he was again touring New York, Boston, Philadelphia, and Washington. It was while he was on this tour that Legaré conversed with him. His probable influence in shaping American spread-eagle oratory is an interesting problem. For a comment on Ogilvie see sketches in the *Dictionary of American Biography* and the *Dictionary of National Biography;* in R. B. Davis, *Gilmer,* 22–25; and in R. B. Davis, "James Ogilvie, an Early American Teacher of Rhetoric," *Quarterly Journal of Speech,* XXXVIII (1942), 289–97; and in "James Ogilvie and Washington Irving," *Americana,* XXXV (1941), 435–58.

cause it did not savour of personal flattery—I was a good deal taken with it—So much so, as to trespass upon my Lord Chesterfield, by reading it in company. The perusal, however, was hurried—& if it is yours, I should be glad to see it again.

I am on the eve of departure from this place—for—I believe—Richmond. The journey to Carolina is so long & tedious—the country uncultivated, roads bad, stage-coaches shattered & infirm drivers careless or drunk &c &c—that I sometimes think of returning to Baltimore & taking a packet there. However, I rather think, I shall go by land—& if I make up my mind to do so, undoubtedly the preponderating motive will be to see & know Richmond.—Now I should like to hear from you at Richmond—or if you can, why your presence would be more agreeable still. Segnius irritant per aurem demissa[44]—as Dr. Pangloss would quote from Horace.

If you think fit, you may be the means of introducing me to Mr. Wirt,[45] or any other gentleman who has your esteem & is therefore worthy of mine. Anything of this kind, however, must be dispatched quickly—as my stay there will not be over a week.

In case you should go to Baltimore—or should meet Maj: Stewart[46] any where else—I take this opportunity of mentioning

44. Presumably a conscious transposing in this case. The original (Horace, *Ars Poetica*, line 180) is *"segnius irritant animos demissa per aurem."* Dr. Pangloss was, of course, Candide's tutor in Voltaire's classic satire aimed at Leibnitz.

45. Gilmer's brother-in-law William Wirt (1772–1834) served as Attorney General of the United States from 1817–25. At this time, he was the leader of a group of Richmond *literati* who had contributed with him to *Letters of the British Spy* (1803), *The Rainbow* (1804), and *The Old Bachelor* (1814), all earlier appearing in serial form in Richmond newspapers. At this time Wirt was working on his *Sketches of the Life and Character of Patrick Henry*, which was printed in 1817. For sketches of Wirt see the *Dictionary of American Biography*; F. P. Cauble, "William Wirt and His Friends: A Study in Southern Culture, 1772–1834" (Ph.D. dissertation, University of North Carolina, 1934); J. P. Kennedy, *Memoirs of the Life and Character of William Wirt* (Philadelphia, 1849); and Jay B. Hubbell, "William Wirt and the Familiar Essay in Virginia," *William and Mary College Quarterly*, XXIII (April, 1943), 136–52.

46. Probably George Hume Steuart, listed in the Baltimore City Directory for 1816 as an attorney at law. No other Stewart or Steuart is listed as a lawyer in this issue. He was a militia officer and served as captain of the Washington Blues at the Battle of North Point. He was born

his name to you, with distinguished respect. He is a young lawyer
of that city—is very highly esteemed there—& I think deserves to
be so, both for his talents (which are considerable) & his goodness
of heart & polite manners. He knows you perfectly well by reputation—twill complete his happiness the first opportunity [by?] a
personal acquaintance with you.

Let me hear from you in Richmond—
& in th[e] mean time I have the
happiness to subscribe myself
your A'
H. S. Legaré—

P.S. I write you a postscript—This to let you know that I have
[arriv?]ed at Richmond—I shall [be here?] some days—perhaps
a week. If you write to me—as requested [go?] direct to Richmond—in care &c &c to be forwarded to Charleston, S.C.

H. S. L.

November 1, 1790 (within a month of F. W. Gilmer's birth), son of
Dr. James Steuart of Annapolis. For many years he commanded the First
Light Dragoons, Maryland Militia. In later life he was a member of the
city council and the state legislature. An ardent Confederate sympathizer,
Major General Steuart left his handsome home in the Baltimore suburbs
and settled in Charlottesville. He died in 1867, in Baltimore, though he
had gone to Europe immediately after the war. For this information I am
indebted to the late Mr. James W. Foster, director of the Maryland
Historical Society.

⟶(XV)⟵

The Jeffersonian Virginia Expatriate in the Building of the Nation

[This essay will demonstrate that by the 1830s the Virginians realized their great age was over, economically and politically. It implies that, had many of these expatriates remained at home, they might have been part of a flowering of Virginia intellect and literature on a great scale—a flowering that came by 1840 in New England but not until almost a century later in the South. Most of these expatriates actually remained in what is today called the South, but the regions to which they traveled were then primitive and unready for artistic creativity.

But other things are evident here also. The Virginians were a restless people, like many other Americans; younger sons, especially from 1800 to 1830 or 1840, found the combination of economic need and dreams of grandeur irresistible. A scansion of their record outside their home state reveals that they were aggressive, intelligent, and possessed of great political acumen. Though there is only one clue or guide to their preeminence, or to those who became prominent, the *Biographical Directory of the American Congress,* this assemblage of data shows that Virginia exported in our first national period more political leaders than any other state, and that through her sons in new territories she exercised an enormous influence on American political history. This survey implies much more: that Virginia's religious, intellectual, and social customs were in accord with her political persuasion; that her manners and codes of conduct furnished examples for count-less thousands if not millions; that through these men and the multitudes who were never members of Congress, Virginia has left her stamp upon the face of America.]

WHAT HAPPENED TO Virginia about the time of the death of Jefferson in 1826? Had her great age been entirely the result of the individual and concerted efforts of the glittering galaxy of Washington, Jefferson, Madison, Monroe, Marshall, George Wythe, John Taylor of Caroline, John Randolph of Roanoke, and two dozen others—a galaxy generation which literally failed to reproduce itself and thus brought on the decline in national power and prestige? No one who has read Hugh Blair Grigsby's account of the Virginia constitutional convention of 1829–1830 should believe this. For then as-sembled in Richmond, alongside the last of the Argonauts (Madison, Monroe, Marshall, and Randolph) were a group of young and middle-aged men of unquestioned ability. Among them, or nearby, were leaders who had from a decade to forty years of active life still before them, men such as Littleton Waller Tazewell, Chapman Johnson, William Cab-ell Rives, George Tucker, Henry St. George Tucker, John Tyler, Jr., Abel P. Upshur, Thomas Walker Gilmer, and Grigsby himself. Each of them had already given, or was soon to give, evidence of extraordinary talents comparable to those of the earlier generation. No, a complexity of other causes—including the relinquishment of Virginia's great west-ern territory; the growing northern antagonism to slavery and her own changing position on the question; and above all, her altered position in physical size, population, and geo-graphical location among the enlarged group of states—was more significant.

Yet the fact remains that Virginia, all during Jefferson's

long career, had lost manpower—individuals of remarkable ability as we now look back upon them—to other sections of the rapidly expanding nation. Joseph Glover Baldwin—himself an expatriate Virginian who left the state in 1836, lived in the Southwest, and died a prominent figure in California —put it this way in *The Flush Times of Alabama and Mississippi* (published in 1853): "from Cape May to Puget's Sound [Virginia] has colonized the other States and the territories with her surplus talent."[1] Baldwin was thinking especially of the Virginians who were already in the Southwest when he arrived, people who were his seniors and who therefore had grown to manhood before 1830.

A recent look at the *Biographical Directory of the American Congress, 1774–1949*[2] convinced me that Baldwin did not exaggerate at all if he meant "talent" in the realm of politics and even of the statesmanship for which the state had earlier been so famous. Particularly during the period beginning in 1774 and ending in 1829–1830 with her own constitutional convention, Virginia supplied to the rest of America, particularly to the South and Southwest, an extraordinary number of men who became distinguished. The names and birthplaces of these men, and their accomplishments outside their native state, add up to an impressive and perhaps significant commentary upon general American as well as upon Virginia history. In the course of this essay I will present rough statistics about Virginia's citizens, and make some comment upon them.[3]

1. Joseph Glover Baldwin, *The Flush Times of Alabama and Mississippi* (2nd ed.; New York, 1854), 78.
2. *Biographical Directory of the American Congress, 1774–1949* (Washington, D.C., 1950).
3. Under "Congressmen of, from, and to Virginia" an anonymous contributor to *A Hornbook of Virginia History* (Richmond, 1949), 65–66, gives interesting and useful figures concerning all Virginia-born and Virginia-representing Congressmen up to 1927. The study is evidently

Virginians born after 1809 will not be taken into account here. In other words, only persons who had attained their majority by the time of the constitutional convention of 1829–1830 (generally agreed upon as marking a turning point in Virginia's history) or, putting it another way, only those born by the year Jefferson went out of office, will be considered. Actually several of them had left Virginia about or just before the time of the Revolution. But the vast majority of those included in this appraisal left Virginia as *young men* after 1790, most of them after 1800.

Because the *Biographical Directory* is the only source available for comprehensive data, this survey of Virginia's manpower export must necessarily be confined to those who were members of the continental congress or the later United States House of Representatives or Senate at some time during their lives. Naturally there are other interesting ways by which to measure the number and calibre of expatriate Jeffersonian Virginians—for example, by their published writings—but these other ways are less exact, as data is fragmentary and hard to come by. In the *Biographical Directory* are concise statements of date and place of birth (when ascertainable), prominent offices held in state and federal government, and sometimes an indication of nonofficial occupation, intellectual interests, and education. The sketches are necessarily uneven, for much more information was obtainable regarding some persons than regarding others. Those considered as native Virginians were persons born in counties or cities of what is today Virginia and West Virginia, all of which was included in the state throughout this period. Persons born in Kentucky, which for a time was part of Virginia, are not included.

----

based on the *Biographical Directory of the American Congress, 1774–1927* (Washington, 1928). It shows twenty-five counties as *not* supplying Congressmen to other states and thirty-one other states as supplied with Virginia-born Congressmen through 1927.

Between 227 and 232 members of Congress representing other states were born in Virginia before 1810. In a few instances no date of birth, even year, is available, and one must judge by the date of the beginning of a public career or by the dates of attendance at college (the latter rarely given) as to whether a particular person falls within the time limit. Therefore the number cannot be determined exactly. These men came from fifty-one counties of what is today Virginia; nine counties of what is now West Virginia; and fourteen towns and cities, all in present-day Virginia. Seventeen are listed vaguely as simply born in the state, with no further details; and three are assigned only to regions, such as the Shenandoah Valley or the Panhandle (now in West Virginia). There is no evidence of any concentrated removal of a particular population, for the largest number from any one county is nine (Albemarle), with seven each from Brunswick, Culpeper, Fauquier, Frederick, and Prince Edward; six from Augusta, Caroline, Hanover, and Louisa; five from Berkeley, Goochland, and Stafford; four from Bedford, Halifax, Mecklenburg, Orange, and Prince William; three from Amherst, Botetourt, Charlotte, Fairfax, Lunenburg, Rockbridge, Spotsylvania, and Westmoreland. The remaining counties have one or two migrants each.

Among the fourteen towns and cities, Alexandria was the birthplace of seven men, Fredericksburg and Staunton six each, and Norfolk three. Perhaps the only thing worth pointing out here is that if one adds Staunton's six to Augusta's equal number, this Valley county emerges as the leading birthplace of congressmen which Virginia furnished to other states in this era.

Where did these restless future lawmakers go? Naturally the largest number went to Kentucky, once part of Virginia. Forty-two representatives and sixteen senators (sometimes of course the same men as the representatives here and in later listings) of Kentucky were born in old Virginia before 1810. And not unexpectedly one finds that twenty-two representatives and five senators of Tennessee were Virginia born. But really surprising to those not aware of the waves of migration southward will be the fact that nineteen representatives and ten senators from Georgia were born in Virginia. And perhaps equally surprising, that thirteen representatives and four senators from North Carolina first saw the light in the Old Dominion. South Carolina had ten representatives and three senators who were Virginia born. Alabama and Mississippi had a considerable Virginia contingent in Congress, in view of the fact that they came into the nation so much later than these above mentioned states. Alabama had nine representatives and five senators, Mississippi two representatives and eight senators, the latter an interesting and actually significant disproportion, for the senators were frequently men who had held some territorial office by national executive appointment before Mississippi became a state. Louisiana, bought during Jefferson's first term and administered like Alabama and Mississippi for some years as a territory, had later as a state ten representatives and six senators born in Virginia before 1810. Missouri had ten representatives and one senator, Indiana five representatives and two senators, Ohio (indicative of a migration we sometimes forget) seventeen representatives and four senators. Latecomer Arkansas had two representatives and a senator, Illinois a representative, Texas two senators, Florida one representative.

Interesting, but probably less significant, are the facts regarding Virginia expatriates in the states to her north and east. From among them, Maryland had six representatives and two senators, Pennsylvania two representatives and one senator, and New York two representatives. And again interesting, but perhaps not overly significant, are the four Virginia-born delegates from North Carolina to the continental congress (one, John Penn, was a signer), and one delegate each from Maryland and Georgia before the adoption of the Constitution. Another kind of delegate, to the United States Congress from the territories later to become states, is found too among the native Virginians, one each from Arkansas, Florida, Iowa, and "Northwest of the Ohio River," and three from Mississippi.

All these figures become more significant when one notes that while Virginia exported her 227-plus natives born before 1810 to become congressmen elsewhere, she imported only nineteen of her own congressmen born within the period. Not one of her senators was from outside the state. Of the nineteen congressmen, five were born outside the United States, one each in Bermuda and Scotland, and three in Ireland. Pennsylvania was the only state with which she had an unfavorable balance of trade: five Virginia congressmen were born within that state as compared with two Pennsylvania representatives and a senator born in Virginia. Perhaps more significant in comparing the export of the two states, however, are the figures of an overall export of congressmen within the period, of only 80 for Pennsylvania and the 227-plus for Virginia. As one might expect, almost all the Irish- and Pennsylvania-born Virginia representatives were Scotch-Irish who settled in the Shenandoah Valley or in what is now West Virginia.

Maryland was next after Pennsylvania in supplying Virginia representatives, for she gave four while Virginia repaid her with six representatives and two senators. Kentucky, New Jersey, New York, North Carolina, and Ohio each supplied Virginia with one member of the House.

Overall figures for states other than Pennsylvania offer

further basis for comparison of Virginia's export with that of her sister states. Massachusetts, smaller in size but denser in population, sent 147 future congressmen to other regions; the overwhelming majority of them went to the states that surrounded her: New Hampshire, Vermont, Maine, Rhode Island, and New York. South Carolina, potentially a feeder of the same region that Virginia fed, supplied to other states only twenty-three future congressmen born before 1809. A comparison based on a partial check of North Carolina indicates that Virginia supplied about four times as many future national legislators as her immediate southern neighbor did.[4]

The official positions other than membership in Congress held by the Virginia expatriates are varied and indicative. More often than not the expatriates rose to membership in the na-

4. The overall count for Pennsylvania, Massachusetts, and South Carolina will vary slightly according to the way one looks upon the uncertain dates and places, as we have suggested earlier for the Virginia count. The variation, however, would not in any case be greater than four or five individuals and would not affect percentages appreciably.

The North Carolina figure of proportion is based on a count of names under nineteen letters of the alphabet, which show thirty-three expatriates for North Carolina when the same alphabetical grouping shows 137 for Virginia.

Census figures for 1800 and 1810 prove nothing conclusively, for Virginia and Massachusetts areas were quite different, and many of the congressmen were born before 1800. But here they are for the reader who wishes to draw further conclusions of his own:

	POPULATION	
	In 1800	*In 1810*
Virginia	880,200 (807,557)	974,600 (877,683)
Massachusetts	574,564 (422,845)	700,745 (472,040)
North Carolina	478,103	555,500
Pennsylvania	602,365	810,091
South Carolina	345,591	415,115

The figures for Virgina include present West Virginia, and those for Massachusetts include Maine. Maine was separated in 1820, and West Virginia in 1863. The figures in parentheses for each of these states represent the population of the area included within the present state boundaries.

tional legislature through district attorneyships, judgeships, or seats in the state legislatures. These relatively minor offices (though this may not be properly descriptive of the several state chief justiceships held) because of their very number cannot be enumerated here, but governorships and national offices other than in Congress should be noted.

The expatriate who climbed highest was William Henry Harrison, whose family was more prominent than most to begin with. Son of a Virginia delegate to the continental congress who was also a signer, he was the father of an Ohio representative, brother of a Virginia representative, and grandfather of another president of the United States. Born at the famous "Berkeley" estate in Charles City County, he attended Hampden-Sydney College, served in the army, and became secretary of the Northwest Territory under President John Adams. He was territorial delegate to Congress 1799–1800; territorial governor of Indiana 1801–1813 and Indian Commissioner at the same time; distinguished in the War of 1812; congressman from Ohio 1816–1819; member of the state senate; then United States Senator 1825–1828; Minister to Colombia 1828–1829; unsuccessful Whig candidate for the presidency in 1836; and President of the United States for one brief month in 1841.

Fifteen United States cabinet posts were held by twelve of these expatriate Jeffersonians. Hanover-born Henry Clay of Kentucky served as secretary of state under John Quincy Adams; Fredericksburg-born John Forsyth of Georgia served in the same office under Jackson and Van Buren. Prince Edward-born William W. Bibb of Georgia was secretary of the treasury under Taylor; and Nelson-born William H. Crawford of Georgia (he was also an unsuccessful candidate for the presidency) held the same office under Madison and Monroe. Culpeper native Richard W. Thompson of Indiana came along late enough (born 1809) to become secretary of the navy under Hayes in 1877. William Taylor Barry of Kentucky (born in Lunenburg County) was postmaster general under Jackson; Aaron Venable Brown of Tennessee (born in Brunswick County) held that office under Buchanan; and Thomas Ewing of Ohio (born in Ohio County, Virginia) served in that position under William H. Harrison. John Breckinridge of Kentucky (born near Staunton, Augusta County) was attorney general under Jefferson, as were Edward Bates of Missouri (born in Goochland) under Lincoln, and Felix Grundy of Tennessee (born in Berkeley County) under Van Buren. Thomas Ewing was also secretary of war under Taylor. Charles M. Conrad of Louisiana (born in Winchester) was secretary of war under Fillmore, as was William H. Crawford under Madison.

Twelve of these Virginians were territorial governors, almost every one of them having lived and labored in other states before their appointments. William C. C. Claiborne of Tennessee (born in Sussex County; he was also governor of New Orleans), Cowles Mead of Georgia (born simply in "Virginia"), and Robert Williams of North Carolina (born in Prince Edward County) were governors or acting governors of the Mississippi Territory. George M. Bibb of Kentucky (born in Prince Edward County) served in a similar capacity in Alabama; Richard K. Call, a territorial delegate from Florida (born near Petersburg) and William P. Duval of Kentucky (born near Richmond City) were governors of the Florida Territory. Samuel Hammond of Georgia (born in Richmond County) and Thomas Bolling Robertson (born in Dinwiddie County; perhaps appointed to his territorial governorship straight from his Virginia home but later a representative from Louisiana) served as chief executives of Louisiana; William H. Harrison and Thomas Posey of Louisiana (born in Fairfax County) as governors of Indiana; David Meriwether of Georgia (born in Louisa County) as governor of New Mexico; and John Pope of Kentucky (born in Prince William County) as governor of Arkansas. One might add here that picturesque John Sevier of North Carolina and Tennessee (born in Rockingham County) was governor of "the proclaimed" State of Franklin for three years. Many other Virginians were secretaries of various territories.

Virginia supplied nine fully admitted states with governors born before 1810. She gave Kentucky six and Georgia five; Mississippi and North Carolina four each; Tennessee, three; Alabama and Louisiana two each; and Missouri and Ohio one each. Perhaps the three Virginia chief executives of Tennessee are the most renowned, or notorious: Samuel Houston (born near Lexington), John Sevier, and W. G. Brownlow (born in Wytheville). But men like Abner Nash (born in Prince Edward County) of North Carolina, W. C. C. Claiborne of Louisiana, Robert P. Letcher (born in Goochland County) and Thomas Metcalfe (born in Fauquier County) of Kentucky, John Forsyth and George Walton (born in Cumberland County) of Georgia, Henry S. Foote (born in Fauquier County) of Mississippi, and Thomas Worthington (born in Jefferson County) of Ohio, all have places in history for a variety of reasons.

Nine expatriates served in top diplomatic posts abroad. Curiously, most of them represented the United States in Latin America: Solon Borland of Arkansas (born in Nansemond County) was minister to Nicaragua and other Central American republics; James Butler Bowlin of Missouri (born in Fredericksburg) to New Granada (later Colombia); Beverly L. Clarke of Kentucky (born in Chesterfield County) to Guatemala; Powhatan Ellis of Mississippi (born in Amherst County) to Mexico; William H. Harrison to Colombia; Robert P. Letcher of Kentucky to Mexico; and Thomas P. Moore of Kentucky (born in Charlotte County) to New Granada. John Forsyth of Georgia was minister to Spain and James Brown of Louisiana (born near Staunton) to France.

Many lieutenant governors, military officers in the four major wars from the Revolution to the Civil (including several Confederate generals), and Confederate congressmen are among these native Virginians. Especially deserving of attention are the two signers of the Declaration of Independence, John Penn of North Carolina (born in Caroline County) and George Walton of Georgia. And occupying notable places in the history of the Republic of Texas are W. L. Underwood of Kentucky (born in Goochland County), a Texas cabinet officer; and Samuel Houston of Tennessee, first president of the Lone Star republic. Perhaps one should repeat that there are hundreds of other expatriate Virginians (Stephen F. Austin comes immediately to mind) who had offices in other states and territories but did not serve in the United States Congress, and therefore cannot be evaluated here.

The scantiness of information available to the compilers of the *Biographical Directory* makes any statistical conclusions about the education of these adventurous Virginians very tentative. In the late 1830s Joseph Glover Baldwin was impressed by the William and Mary-trained men he met in Alabama and Mississippi, but the record given in the *Biographical Directory* includes positive information that only fourteen of these expatriate Virginia members of Congress, from the whole nation, were alumni of the oldest southern college. Records also indicate that seven of the total group attended Princeton, six Washington College (now Washington and Lee University), three Hampden-Sydney College, and one each Harvard, Yale, Franklin (now the University of Georgia), Transylvania, North Carolina, Union (New York), Pennsylvania, and Virginia. Since the biographical sketches are frequently silent on the subject of education, except for some general statement about "good classical education" or "studied law" (both these seeming to indicate no formal higher education), one may surmise that there are several other college-educated men among them. In almost every case, it is evident that the member of Congress had at least studied at a classical academy or attended "private schools." The largest number of men, over half, studied law, usually in a lawyer's office; the next largest group, "engaged in agricultural pursuits," vary considerably in recorded formal training; but the large number of surveyors clearly had at least some technical training, even if primarily self given; and the several physicians certainly had extensive formal education. On the whole, the evidence indicates that the traditionally poor white family pushing west or southwest, without opportunity or urge to educate its children, rarely supplied the political leaders in the new region.

Actually most of these leaders of the frontier did not go there until they were in their teens or, even more often, their young manhood. In other words, they made their opportunity in the new region for themselves, deliberately. There are, of course, famous exceptions. But even Sam Houston, born near Lexington in 1793, did not move with his widowed mother to East Tennessee until 1806. He then attended Maryville Academy (now College), fought with distinction and rose from private to lieutenant in the War of 1812, studied law in Nashville, rose through various offices to be governor, moved to the Oklahoma Territory and subsequently to Texas. His is a fairly typical pattern for the Virginian who ended his days more than four or five hundred miles from his birthplace.

There are other patterns of movement and career. From one of the Piedmont counties, as far as we can tell from these records, sometimes families moved once and for all to particular spots in Kentucky or Tennessee. Equally often the career data indicate a progressive movement across one of these same two states. A familiar pattern too is the movement from Virginia to Alabama to Mississippi, sometimes continued to Louisiana or Arkansas, or along similar progressive lines west and northwest to Ohio and Indiana. Curiously little indication exists of progressive movement from Tidewater or Piedmont Virginia to what is now West Virginia for a few years before proceeding on to Ohio, Kentucky, or Indiana, though we know from other sources that families and individuals followed this pattern. Naturally the young man who completed his education before leaving home, and remained unmarried for some years thereafter, tended to move restlessly and progressively on. But the data given is insufficient to do more than suggest that at times this happened.

From what sorts of families, socially and racially, did these adventurers spring? The names of the 227-plus members of Congress are almost without exception still familiar ones in Virginia. But with a few exceptions it is naturally impossible to assign the individuals to large-planter, small-planter, yeoman-farmer, or poor-white status. As W. J. Cash in *The Mind of the South* (1941) has so convincingly indicated, the southern poor white with the same surname as his aristocratic or plutocratic neighbor is very likely to be a distant cousin of the more fortunate man, and both Virginia and southern society have *always* been reasonably fluid. Racial origins of the migrants remain equally vague. Only some two dozen of the 227-plus names are unmistakably Scottish or Scotch-Irish in origin. A few are French, a few perhaps anglicized German, but four-fifths are presumably English.

In several dozen instances one can tell something of family background. For one thing, a number of congressmen, men like John Breckinridge of Kentucky or William H. Harrison of Indiana and Ohio or Robert Carter Nicholas of Louisiana (born in Hanover County) were sons, brothers, or nephews of men of the same surname who represented Virginia in the national legislature. In other instances one can determine pretty conclusively (and frequently there are other data to support the determination) from combinations of place of birth and surname that men like W. C. C. Claiborne, Patrick G. Goode of Charlotte County (representative from Ohio), Bolling Hall of Dinwiddie County (representative from Georgia), Humphrey Marshall of Fauquier County (senator from Kentucky; cousin of the Chief Justice), James Monroe of Albemarle County (representative from New York; nephew of the President), or Thomas Bolling Robertson of Dinwiddie County (representative from Louisiana) were from the large-planter class in their native state. In all cases of known education at the College of William and Mary, Washington College, Hampden-Sydney College, Princeton, etc., one can be sure that the family in Virginia is quite substantial, though not necessarily always in the large-planter status. Incidentally, attendance at Washington College, Hampden-Sydney College, or Princeton probably (though certainly not always) indicates Scotch-Irish ancestry, or at least Presbyterian background on one side or the other of the family.

What impelled these Virginians to migrate? Some reasons have already been indicated. Going along with one's impoverished family is the traditional one, but, as we have indicated it does not appear to have been the usual situation for future congressmen. A more frequent motive among those moving west and south was an adult (albeit youthful) determination to grow up and prosper with the new country. Baldwin says that as a young lawyer he moved southwest "Urged by hunger and the request of friends" (p. 47). He doesn't say whether he means friends at home or friends already established in the new region. Aging President Madison in several instances urged his young friends and neighbors to settle in the territories. Then there were the young men appointed directly from their Virginia homes to official posts in the new territories of Florida, Louisiana, or the trans-Mississippi region (old letters exist by the score in historical repositories which show the young men's own efforts to secure these positions). Often they cast their lots permanently in the new places, even when they started at the top, as governors, and retired after their terms of office to "agricultural pursuits."

One may assume that the Virginians who became prominent in Maryland were impelled there by easy proximity, marriage ties, or other personal situations and opportunities; and those prominent in Pennsylvania and New York by accident or by individual design. And peculiar personal motives other than hunger and ambition clearly determined the movements of many of those who went west.

Particularly interesting among these expatriate Virginians are certain "originals," as the eighteenth century would have called them. There is the notorious "Parson" Brownlow of Tennessee; the archetypal frontiersman "Chucky Jack" Sevier of Tennessee; and the tavern keeper representative from Pennsylvania, William Anderson.[5] Among the notorious, one should point out Solomon P. Sharp of Kentucky (born in Abingdon), hero-villain-victim in "The Kentucky Tragedy," the seduction-murder-suicide-execution celebrated in literature

5. Sir Augustus John Foster, *Notes on the United States of America . . . 1804 . . . 1812* (San Marino, Calif., 1954).

by authors ranging from Edgar Allan Poe to Robert Penn Warren.

One should note, besides those already mentioned, the names of men whose fame is so thoroughly identified with their adopted regions that their connections with their native state are usually forgotten. Perhaps best-known among these are Joseph Calhoun and John Ewing Colhoun (both born in Staunton), respectively representative and senator of South Carolina; Wade Hampton (listed simply as born in "Virginia"), representative from South Carolina, as well as his better-known son and grandson; and Robert Goodloe Harper (born in Fredericksburg), representative from South Carolina and senator from Maryland, one of the ablest of the conservative orators and essayists in Congress.

The social, intellectual, and political results of the migrations of these Virginians would require whole volumes to delineate. Since the men here considered are primarily politicians, however, we may pause a moment and try to suggest some of the political implications and ramifications of their careers. For example, there may have been varied and far-reaching effects from the fact that a steady line of Georgia and Mississippi senators were native Virginians—effects on various measures passed in the United States Senate, from approval of cabinet officers and diplomats to the making of foreign treaties. Consider Georgia's situation merely in Jefferson's lifetime. From the first Congress in 1789 to 1801 one of her senators, James Gunn (born simply in "Virginia"), came from the Old Dominion. In 1795–1797 his colleague was another Virginian, George Walton. William H. Crawford became a United States Senator from the state in 1807 and remained in office until 1813. He was joined in 1809 by Charles Tait (born in Hanover County), who served until 1819. Crawford was succeeded by another Virginian, William W. Bibb, who resigned in 1816. John Forsyth represented Georgia in the Senate in 1818–1819. Freeman Walker (born in Charles City County) took a seat in 1819 and resigned in 1821. He was succeeded by Nicholas Ware (born in Caroline County), who remained in office until he died in 1824. Thus for twenty-three of Georgia's first thirty-five years one and often two Virginians represented her in the Senate. Most of these men had left close relatives and friends in their native state and visited it frequently on their way to and from Philadelphia and Washington. Potential influences, pressures, co-alitions, and understandings between the representatives of the mother state and the adopted state were, then, enormous. For a somewhat later period, a similar relationship existed between Virginia and Mississippi, and of course between Virginia and Kentucky.

This is not to say that expatriate Virginians remained true to their own or their families' political affiliations with Federalists or Republicans. Like men everywhere at all times, most of them were opportunists, in both the good and bad sense. They were affected by changing situations of time and place. One Virginian was the provisional Confederate governor of Kentucky during the same period another Virginian was that state's most prominent and uncompromising Unionist; both probably sprang from the same sort of liberal Republican (in the Jeffersonian sense) background. As we have seen, one native Virginian from Missouri served in Lincoln's cabinet. That Virginia was predominantly Republican in the two decades before 1810 may or may not account in part for the strongly democratic Republicanism displayed by the Southwest on most issues for some time thereafter.

Of necessity, I have devoted this survey almost entirely to Virginia as an exporter of political talent. She also exported a code of manners, a sense of honor, a special kind of love for family and land, a range of intellectual interests outside the realm of politics, and several peculiarly Virginia brands of religion and theology, particularly Virginia Presbyterian puritanism and low-church Anglicanism. All this is evident to anyone who reads the letters expatriates wrote home to their friends and relatives. Further evidence of exported Virginia traits and abilities can be seen in the writings printed in their adopted states by native Virginians. Presbyterian David Rice's theological tracts printed in Kentucky; physician and scientific researcher Nathaniel Chapman's medical treatises written in Philadelphia; and explorers Lewis and Clark's account of their great expedition—all bear some mark of Virginia. All this is another side of the story. From the present survey alone it is evident, I hope, that Virginia's "surplus" went to form the mold in which the character of other states, and to a considerable extent of the nation, would be cast.

Index